Miracle
in the
Making

The Adam Taliaferro Story

Miracle in the Making

The Adam Taliaferro Story

Scott Brown
and
Sam Carchidi

Foreword by Joe Paterno

TRIUMPH
B O O K S
CHICAGO

Library of Congress Cataloging-in-Publication Data

Brown, Scott, 1971–
    Miracle in the making : the Adam Taliaferro story / Scott Brown and Sam Carchidi.
        p. cm.
    ISBN 1-57243-422-8 (pbk.)
    1. Taliaferro, Adam, 1982—Health. 2. Quadriplegics—United States—Biography. 3. Football players—United States—Biography. I. Carchidi, Sam, 1955– II. Title.

RC406.Q33 .B765 2001
362.4'3'092—dc21
[B]
                                                                    2001041382

This book is available in quantity at special discounts for your group or organization. For further information, contact:

Triumph Books
601 South LaSalle Street
Suite 500
Chicago, Illinois 60605
(312) 939-3330
Fax (312) 663-3557

Printed in the United States of America

ISBN 1-57243-422-8

Interior design by Patricia Frey
Cover design by Concialdi Design

Front and back cover images courtesy of the Penn State Athletic Department

To my sisters Melissa and Ali. They helped me through a rough spot during the writing of this, and they have always been supportive of me. True, I always wanted a brother, but I couldn't have asked for better or more loving siblings.

—Scott Brown
June 2001

To my dear, sweet mom, who lost a courageous battle with leukemia during the early stages of this book, but whose inspiration, love, and compassion will be with me forever. You'll always be my hero, Mom.

—Sam Carchidi
June 2001

Contents

Foreword

The most terrifying moment of my 60-year association with the game of football unfolded on a gray, rainy afternoon at Ohio Stadium. It had been an unremarkable day until it suddenly got a lot worse than any of us could ever have imagined.

After coming up to make a tackle, our freshman cornerback, Adam Taliaferro, lay on the field completely immobile. When I reached him, I could see the look of fear in his eyes as the realization set in that he could not move. I will never forget that look as long as I live.

My wife and I were especially touched by Adam's tragedy because we have a son, David, who was gravely injured in a trampoline accident when he was 11 years old. David was in a coma for seven days. He recovered fully and lives today in State College with his wife and two children. That incident left me with great empathy for parents who spend sleepless nights in a hospital room not knowing what will happen to their child. When I saw Adam on the field, I flashed back to an image of David on the concrete floor after his fall.

Miracle in the Making

Adam Taliaferro's story since then is the most gallant, uplifting, and inspiring one I can imagine. It tested our faith to see Adam lying helpless on the turf. It restored our faith to see the remarkable recovery he has since achieved—with the compassionate care and courageous support of his physicians, nurses, therapists, teammates, friends, and most important of all, his extraordinary parents, Andre and Addie, and his brother, Alex.

Adam will never play football again. But he has had an impact on everyone associated with the game, an impact that transcends any accomplishments he might have achieved as an athlete. Adam is our miracle. From this day forward every time we see him or hear of him, we will contemplate the power of prayer, of a positive approach to adversity, of dogged determination, and of unconditional love.

Adam Taliaferro would have been a great athlete. But clearly, a higher power had another plan in mind for him. We have no doubt that he will be equal to whatever challenges the future holds. He is brave. He is strong. He is motivated and he is the beneficiary of the admiration and support of tens of thousands of college football fans, many of whom have no affiliation with Penn State University.

From the tragedy of a catastrophic accident, Adam Taliaferro has achieved a triumph that will forever be an inspiration to us all!

—Joe Paterno
June 2001

Acknowledgments

OK, now comes the hard part: remembering all of the countless people who helped us turn what was a murky vision last January into a book. With so many to thank we were concerned that we might miss somebody. We think we have listed everybody, *think* being the operative word, and we sincerely apologize to anyone who helped and whose name is not on this long list.

First and foremost we are incredibly grateful to the Taliaferro family. Andre, Addie, Adam, and Alex welcomed us into their lives and showed enormous patience with our constant phone calls and questions. Like everyone associated with this story, we came away inspired. The strength and courage they have shown in the face of adversity is a lesson to us all. And the happy ending to Adam's ordeal couldn't have happened to a more deserving family. Adam is one of the classiest people we have ever come across while covering sports, and his brother Alex is as genuinely sincere as Adam and similarly poised beyond his years. Suffice it to say, these two apples didn't fall far from the tree.

There are many people to thank at Eastern High School, Adam's alma mater. They include Dave Allen, Justin Barton, Jarid Brookins, Chaz Brown, Lance Evans, former Vikings coach Larry Ginsburg, Jen Greenberg, Fred Harris, Shirley Martinsek, Pat Milligan, Pat Montesano, Darryl Scott, Khary Sharpe, Patrick Smothers, Dan Spittal, and Jim Talarico.

A number of people associated with the Penn State football program provided invaluable assistance, especially Joe Paterno and Sue Paterno. Coach Paterno wrote a very moving Foreword while his wife, Sue, filled in a lot of blanks for us. Other Penn State players, coaches, and administrators who helped include James Boyd, Tom Bradley, Bruce Branch, Rashard Casey, Jordan Caruso, Tim Curley, Larry Johnson, Jeff Nelson, Joe Sarra, George Salvaterra, Dr. Wayne Sebastianelli, and L. Budd Thalman.

There are also many people to thank from Ohio State and the Ohio State University Medical Center. They are former Buckeyes coach John Cooper, David Crawford, Andy Geiger, Alice Herman, Dr. Jeff Laubenthal, Dr. John Lombardo, Kim McCulley, Dr. Gary Rea, Chris Schneider, Steve Snapp, and Jerry Westbrooks.

The staffs at Thomas Jefferson University Hospital and Magee Rehabilitation Hospital, both in Philadelphia, also proved to be more than helpful during our research of this story. In particular we wish to thank Jeffrey Baxt, Al Bernatavicius, Amy Bratta, Dr. Anthony Burns, Michael Criscuolo, Marygrace Mangine, Trish Power, Linda Rizzo, Ron Siggs, Dr. William Staas, Dr. Will Tally, Jamie Tomlinson, Dr. Alexander Vaccaro, and Geri Zelazny.

There was also a slew of others that helped us round out the story with interviews. They included Chuck Bednarik, Norm Brown, Duane Carlisle, Judy Caruso, Darren Drozdov, Ray Ellis, Jeff Fossen, Brad Gaines, Terry Geough, Michele Greenberg, Tim Gushue, Michael Kirschner, David Paterno, Robert Person, Bill Rider, Libby Rivera, Barbara Sarra, Jerry Segal, Tim Strachan, Brian Taylor, Mae Taliaferro (Adam's grandmother), Paul Tighe, and Herm Wood.

Also thanks to Christopher Reeve and Maggie Friedman, who allowed us to reprint a poignant letter the paralyzed actor sent to Adam; Renee DeChristie and Mark Nelson; the *Camden Courier-Post*; *The Philadelphia Inquirer; Florida Today*; and Penn State University.

Finally, many thanks to Triumph Books for believing in this project, particularly editorial director Tom Bast, who acted quickly to get this going. Finally, thank you to managing editor Blythe Smith both for working diligently and working with us on this project. We greatly appreciate it.

Miracle
in the
Making

The Adam Taliaferro Story

CHAPTER ONE

Death of a Dream

Get up, Adam Taliaferro kept repeating to himself. *Get up*!

The Penn State freshman cornerback had just made a helmet-first tackle and, as he pleaded for assistance and his arms flailed uncontrollably, his body felt glued to the ground by an unknown force.

Help was coming. Penn State's trainer ran onto the wet Ohio State football field and held Taliaferro's head. Wayne Sebastianelli, the Penn State doctor, was right behind him. Sebastianelli calmly started giving Taliaferro stern, lifesaving instructions. "Concentrate on me, Adam," Sebastianelli said. "Focus on my eyes."

"Help me up," Taliaferro said.

"Do not move," Sebastianelli cautioned. "Do not try to get up. Do not move your head from side to side."

This scene took place during the waning minutes of a one-sided Ohio State victory. No one cared about the score—or that it would become the most lopsided loss in Joe Paterno's 35 years as Penn State's coach. Players held hands. Most knelt and prayed. Some cried.

"Stop rolling your shoulders," Sebastianelli said firmly but gently as he tried to alleviate the fear in Taliaferro's chocolate-brown eyes. "We need to keep you still."

Ever since he was six years old, Adam had known that he would play in the NFL someday. That was before he became a New Jersey high school football sensation, before he earned a full scholarship to play for Penn State's highly distinguished football program. But now, as he lay on the ground, there were more important issues concerning the quiet and lovable 18-year-old. None concerned the NFL.

"I couldn't feel anything except my head and face," Taliaferro said later. "I didn't know what I had done to myself. It felt like my whole body was broken."

Taliaferro, a sleek and speedy 5'11", 183-pounder, had just tackled a 231-pound running back; the violent impact had caused his neck to snap backward. Though woozy, his first instinct told him to pop off the ground like he had done thousands of other times. Get up, he told himself as he stared at the sky while prone on his back. Mom is watching on TV, and you know how *she* gets. Get up and show her you're OK. Show Dad, Alex, and the millions of people watching across the nation, too. Show the 98,124 fans at Ohio Stadium that this is just a minor setback, that you can walk off the field and give a polite wave for their support.

Taliaferro didn't remember the hit. All he could remember was waking up on the ground. Waking up and asking for someone to take his hand and pull him up. Waking up and wondering why, for the first time in his life, he had no control over his body's movements. His arms were flapping back and forth in front of his face, and he couldn't stop them.

To those who were watching on national TV, seeing Adam's arms move seemed like a positive sign. What they didn't know was that it was involuntary movement, that Adam wasn't able to move his fingers, that he had no feeling in his hands or legs.

Back in Voorhees, New Jersey, an upscale suburb located 18 miles outside of Philadelphia, Taliaferro's parents and his 14-year-old brother, Alex, watched the scene on their big-screen, family-room television set.

Until that day, either one or both of his parents had attended every one of his football games since he was six years old. This was the first game they had ever missed. And now, when Adam seemed to need them most, they were helpless, 512 miles away. Watching from the comfort of their cozy, two-story home. Watching and answering frantic phone calls from friends and relatives. Watching and pleading and praying as Adam was given medical attention on the field—and a commercial, a damn commercial, interrupted their only connection with their soft-spoken, strikingly handsome son. "I wanted to jump through the TV set and be there with him," said Addie Taliaferro, Adam's mother.

When Adam played football in high school, Addie was so terrified that her son would be injured that, after watching the first quarter, she would retreat to the parking lot and sit in her car. It was her sanctuary, her way of coping. She would sit in the front seat, roll down the window, and listen to the public-address announcer give accounts of the game. "Fifty-five yard run! Touchdown, Adam Taliaferro!" The announcer's voice would echo around the stadium, around the parking lot.

It was a soothing sound for Addie. Not so much because her son had scored, not so much because he had broken off another long run, not so much because Eastern High was headed toward another victory. It was soothing because her son had not been injured on the play.

Addie could picture that oh-so-contagious smile as he crossed the goal line. She could picture him graciously hugging the linemen who had thrown the run-springing blocks. She didn't need to watch any of it. All she needed to know was that her son was safe, that he was in one piece. And if she could just sit in her car and think positive thoughts while opposing players were trying to snap her little boy in half, well, her Adam would be protected. "It was just so quiet and peaceful in there," Addie said.

There was no peace, no quiet, no comforting words from the PA announcer as the Taliaferros waited for the commercial to end and the camera to zoom in on their son on September 23, 2000. It was a day that changed Adam's life. A day that changed the whole family's life. A day that some frightening words, no matter how hard they tried to deny them, became a daily part of the family's vocabulary. Words like *quadriplegic* and *paralysis*.

At Ohio Stadium, those devastating words started to filter into some people's minds as Adam was given medical attention. In the meantime, four commercials that took a total of a minute and 30 seconds were shown to the rest of the country. When the commercials ended, Adam was still down; he was having problems breathing as he listened to the doctor's instructions in front of a packed, church-quiet stadium.

"Stay still and stay focused. Do not move." The words were especially difficult for Sebastianelli. He had developed a close relationship with Adam in the few months they had known each other. He had treated him for a dislocated thumb, which required surgery in the preseason, and they had developed a bond.

It was easy to develop a bond with Adam. He was so humble, so sincere, so polite. He wasn't the stereotypical football superstar. This is someone who worked as a nurse's aide as a high school senior, someone who had to be coaxed by his high school English teacher to miss a class so he could accept an award at a football banquet, someone who was an honor student and a model citizen, someone with "a fantastic smile and calmness and humility to him," Sebastianelli said. He fought back tears when he realized it was Adam who had been injured. This was the first on-the-field spine injury he had ever treated.

As Sebastianelli spoke, pads were placed behind Adam's neck and trainer George Salvaterra held his head so it wouldn't move. If the head doesn't remain still and in a neutral position, a fracture of the vertebra can sever and severely damage the spinal cord. That, in turn, can compromise breathing.

Adam didn't realize the severity of his injury. All he knew was that he had no feeling in his legs. And as he was lifted onto a stretcher, the other players knelt, held hands, and said silent prayers.

Joe Paterno, the legendary Penn State coach, took a look at Adam's condition and kicked the turf in disgust. It was the worst injury he had ever witnessed in his 60-year association with the sport. "Just looking in his eyes, he had so much fear there," Paterno said. When he went to Adam's side, he hoped it was a minor injury. "But then when I looked and saw the anxiety of the medical people and everybody else," he said, "I knew."

For Paterno, it was personal. In 1977, his then 11-year-old son, David, fell off a trampoline at his school and fractured his skull, slipping into a coma for seven days before making a full recovery. "As soon as I saw Adam on the field," Paterno said, "I remembered seeing my boy on the concrete floor at Our Lady of Victory."

Based on Adam's symptoms and the numbness he was describing, Sebastianelli knew immediately that the injury was serious. The rest of the nation drew a similar conclusion, mainly due to the fact that, from the time Taliaferro made the tackle, it took nine minutes and 51 seconds before he was placed into an ambulance. For the Taliaferro family, those minutes seemed like years.

The attending doctors and trainers were deliberate for a reason. They knew that if Adam was moved incorrectly, the injury could become even more catastrophic. There were indicators, including Adam's inability to move body parts in certain ways and the unnatural position of his legs (they were rolled up on each other), that this was a potentially life-threatening injury. "The motor control left behind indicated that his injury was at the cervical vertebrae," Sebastianelli said. From his examination on the field, it was pretty clear "that we were dealing with an injury of the fifth cervical level."

In layman's terms: a broken neck.

* * * * *

In central New Jersey, Adam's girlfriend and high school sweetheart, Rutgers University freshman Jen Greenberg, watched Adam make his life-altering tackle on her dorm TV—and celebrated.

Jen, blonde and attractive, outgoing and articulate, attended Adam's Eastern High football games to socialize and hang out with friends. It wasn't until her senior year, when Adam scored 28 touchdowns and was a two-way standout, that she actually became interested in the sport.

She couldn't believe what she had been missing.

And, now, as she watched Adam make a tackle on national TV, it seemed just like old times. Adam making a big hit. Adam in the spotlight. Adam on his way to becoming a collegiate star. She raced out of her Rutgers dorm to spread the good news—unaware that Adam was still on the ground and unable to get up.

Jen had been watching the game with two friends. They saw Adam make the tackle, made some small talk, and took their eyes off the TV for a few seconds. Jen ran next door to spread the good news: "Adam just made a great play," she said to her friend Matt.

When she returned to her dorm room a few minutes later, her friends were gone. She turned on the TV, but the network had switched to another game. "I just figured the Penn State game was over," she said.

She needed to talk with some people, needed to celebrate Adam's crunching tackle. She picked up the phone and called J. D. Benson, Adam's Penn State roommate.

"Were you watching the game? Wasn't it a good tackle?" Jen's cheeriness stunned J.D., who was still watching the on-field drama unfold on his TV.

"What?" he said.

"Did you see Adam's tackle?"

J.D. was dumbfounded by Jen's question. "What are you saying?" he said, the words coming out slowly, painfully.

"Did I wake you up or something?" Jen asked. "You sound like you were sleeping. You sound upset."

"Jen, what are you talking about? He's down, Jen, and he hasn't gotten up yet. Everybody's holding hands and crying and there's an ambulance there." She was unable to watch the developments because, at that time, her TV viewing area was given a different football game.

Jen began shaking and crying. Her exhilaration was replaced by shock, her euphoria replaced by depression. "I was scared because I couldn't see it. And I started panicking," she said. "I ran down the hallway to find someone to talk to and not many people were there because it was a weekend and they had gone home. I ran to a friend's room and told Matt and he tried to comfort me."

She quickly returned to her room and an all-night phone vigil began. First, it was her brother who called and told her to stay calm. Then her dad called. "He tried to tell me some football players get hit and they get a shock in the spine and get paralyzed for only a few seconds. He said they were probably only taking a precaution with the backboard and the stretcher; he was trying to comfort me and I was hysterical," Jen said. "I was shaking and in a state of shock. I got off the phone with my dad and called Adam's dad."

* * * * *

Andre Taliaferro had discovered that his son was naturally athletic when he saw him ride his bike without training wheels before he was four years old. Unlike his own dad, Andre took an interest in sports and knew firsthand about Adam's athletic exploits, having coached him in youth football and basketball leagues. His son was always the go-to player, the guy who took the big shot in basketball, who took the key carry in football.

When it came to athletics, Adam Taliaferro always seemed to be in control—until he tackled Ohio State running back Jerry Westbrooks with one minute, 39 seconds left in Penn State's eventual 45–6 loss. Taliaferro's head connected with Westbrooks' knee and thigh, fracturing the C5 vertebra located in the middle part of his neck. The collision was so powerful that Westbrooks sustained a deep thigh bruise and limped for the next week.

For four years, Westbrooks had rarely received much playing time and had clamored for the spotlight. Now, he was at center stage—for a terrible reason. "From the impact and the way he was laying on the ground," Westbrooks said, "I knew he was paralyzed."

Taliaferro was playing left cornerback for the first time in his Penn State career, having played right corner or on special teams in the first four games. And while his pursuit angle was slightly different than usual, there was nothing out of the ordinary about the play. It was a basic running play. Taliaferro read it and saw that Westbrooks was moving slowly. This would not be a difficult tackle, he thought. But at the last instant, two Penn State defenders came from behind and forced Westbrooks to speed up. Taliaferro was caught off-guard by the running back's acceleration. He lowered his shoulder to make the tackle and didn't have time to put his head up.

If he only could have had another split second. If he could have had time to pick his head up. Football players are warned that catastrophic injuries can occur if the head is down. The simple rule: tackle with your eyes looking straight ahead.

"I knew it was bad, but at first I thought it was a stinger and I'd be out the next day and then be fine," Adam said. But from the sideline, Penn State quarterback Rashard Casey said he heard Adam let out a piercing scream.

From the field, Penn State safety James Boyd tried to comfort Taliaferro. Boyd was on the same side of the field as Taliaferro when the tackle was made and he landed right beside him. "We were almost on top of each other," Boyd said. "Sometimes I wonder, 'If I would have made the tackle, if I could have got up there before he made the tackle, maybe it wouldn't have happened.'"

From his family's home in South Jersey, Andre Taliaferro had a different perspective as he watched the tackle on TV. "My first thought was that it was a good hit, a hit I've seen him make before," Andre said. "And when he fell down on the ground, I didn't think he was hurt because I saw him move his arm. And then he stayed down for a little while, and Addie said, 'He's not getting up. He's hurt.' I said, 'Addie, he's going to be fine. He's OK.' The commercial went off and the game came back on and by the somber tone of the announcers, I said, 'Something's wrong.' And then everybody starts. My wife is crying. My son is crying. Now I'm not sure what's really happening myself. I'm thinking, 'Maybe he is really hurt,' but never thinking he's hurt to that degree."

Barrel-chested Andre Taliaferro, a former semipro football player, was terrified. "I'm scared, but I'm trying to make sure no one panics and I'm trying to reassure everybody," he said. "But by this time, people are calling on the phone." He told Jen—and countless others—that he didn't know anything, that he was trying to get in touch with Penn State, that he would inform them when he heard some news.

Frantically, he phoned Penn State University, Ohio State University, and the Ohio police. Looking for answers. Looking to find out information about his son's condition.

* * * * *

As Adam was being whisked to the hospital—a four- or five-minute drive from the football field—he knew something was terribly wrong, knew this was worse than the broken collarbone or the broken ribs he suffered while playing football in high school.

Much worse.

"I can't be paralyzed," he said while being strapped down in the ambulance. "I just can't be paralyzed."

Those who sat in the ambulance, including Dr. Sebastianelli, wanted to tell Taliaferro that he was going to be all right, that he was going to be able to walk again. But they couldn't. All they could do was keep him calm and try to comfort him. One of the doctors kept touching Adam's lower legs and was encouraged that he had some feeling. Salvaterra told Adam there was a chance he was in spinal shock and that he might regain movement in a few hours.

That was the optimistic outlook. Too optimistic, as it turned out.

Once in the hospital, Salvaterra gently cut off Adam's uniform with scissors and the doctors catheterized him and gave him intravenous fluids (to control his blood pressure) and steroids (to reduce the swelling around his spinal cord). The steroids were administered about a half an hour after the injury occurred. The time frame was well within what doctors call the "Golden Hour" of trauma. "If you get someone stabilized and transported and have IV access within an hour of a major accident, you stand a real good chance of saving their life if it's a serious injury," said Sebastianelli.

When Adam was stabilized, taking off his helmet and shoulder pads—without moving his neck—became critical. First his facemask was removed. It wasn't until about 10 years ago that a facemask was developed that could clip off without causing a lot of movement. The need for this type of modern helmet was never recognized more fully than in this instance. Sebastianelli held Adam's head still. Salvaterra clipped off the straps that held the facemask in place, then removed the facemask. He removed the cheek pads with a tongue depressor and then ever so slowly scooped the helmet off. Next, the shoulder pads were removed and Adam was off for a magnetic resonance imaging test (MRI).

Adam became claustrophobic and passed out while having the MRI. When he woke up, the nightmare wasn't over. The MRI report was ominous. It seemed to confirm everyone's worst fears.

* * * * *

Back in the Taliaferro home, the phone rang. It was Dr. Sebastianelli. He did not tell Andre that his son, just three months after his high school graduation, had a broken neck—specifically, that his fifth cervical vertebra, just above the base of the neck, was shattered and his spinal cord was bruised and filled with blood. Adam had lost all motor function from below the point of the injury.

But the Penn State doctor would supply these details later. For now, he just needed Andre to know that his son was in danger, that he needed him to carefully get to Ohio.

"I'll never forget his words," Andre Taliaferro said.

"Andre, take a deep breath." Andre squeezed the phone tightly. "Adam has been seriously injured and you need to come out."

Andre did not like the tone of the doctor's voice. He threw some clothes into a travel bag and told Addie to stay behind. "I didn't want her to go because I know how she is," Andre said. "Emotionally, I didn't know if she could handle it. I didn't know if *I* could handle it. I knew I'd be stronger than she was, and I didn't want her to see her son like that. And then you have two people to deal with." Andre hopped into his black Ford Taurus, raced through red lights, and got to Philadelphia International Airport in 20 minutes, about half the time it normally takes.

The plane was delayed. When it took off, Andre spent the hour-long flight pondering his son's condition, praying that his child would survive, trying to avoid negative thoughts. "Lord, don't let it be bad," he said to himself. "Please don't let it be bad."

The plane flew through violent thunder and lightning. "It was surreal. It really was almost like it wasn't me . . . like it was happening to someone else," Andre said. It was the worst flight of his life, but not because of the storm. "I was scared, really scared. I just wanted to get there . . . and in a way, I didn't want to get there. But I knew I had to go. I was thinking, 'What am I going to see?' And you're just really fearful."

Fearful that his son might not live.

"I was thinking he could die. I knew it was serious, but I didn't know how serious. And even if someone said *paralysis*, it still wasn't registering. You know what I'm saying? It's my son and he's not going to be *that* hurt." Not the little boy who rode a bicycle without training wheels before he was four years old. Not the seemingly invincible young man who had been named the top high school player in the Philadelphia area after his senior season. "It was serious enough for them to call me out, and that's what scared me, because I didn't know what I was going to find when I got there."

When the plane landed in Columbus, Ohio, Andre was met at the airport by L. Budd Thalman (Penn State's associate athletic director for communications) and two Ohio State University police officers. It was pitch dark. The Ohio State University police drove Andre and Thalman to the Ohio State University Medical Center, located on the university's campus.

Andre started asking questions. "I wanted to know, but I didn't want to know," he said. "I didn't want to hear anything real bad."

At the hospital, he conferred with Dr. Sebastianelli. "It's serious, Andre," said the doctor.

Andre, an outgoing man with an engaging personality, tried to prepare himself as he walked into Adam's hospital room. "That," he said, "is still going to be the worst day of my life."

Andre gingerly walked into the room. Pitchfork-shaped tongs were attached to his son's head to take pressure off his spine. He was lying flat on his back. He couldn't move his head, neck, arms, or legs. "All he could do, and I'll never forget it, is move his eyes and his mouth," Andre said.

Adam looked up and his eyes filled with tears as he saw his father. "How you doing, Dad?"

"How you doing, son?"

"I guess my football career is over."

Andre nodded softly. "Yeah, I guess it is, but we aren't going to worry about that. Son, hey look, you're going to be all right, man. We're going to walk out of this. You're going to be all right. You're going to be all right." Andre repeated the words, as if he was trying to convince himself. A few minutes later, he snuck out of the room and broke down, crying loudly and uncontrollably.

After he regained control, he again met with Sebastianelli. "What's going to happen? What's the prognosis?"

"Well, Andre, it's not good. Most people are quadriplegics from this accident."

Again, Andre broke down. "No, no, no," he protested. "That might be most people, but no, no, no. Adam is going to make it."

A little later, after he again regained his composure, Andre wanted some specifics about the type of injury Adam had and how many people with those injuries make a full recovery. "Doc, tell me the truth. What are the odds?"

"Andre, maybe 3 out of 100 might recover from this."

Andre buried his head in his cupped hands, tears dripping down his fingers.

Sebastianelli had reason to support the odds: "A large loss of function. A very ominous-looking X ray, a more ominous-looking CAT scan, and an even more ominous-looking MRI scan," he said. "The X ray showed a burst fracture, which means there's a lot of pieces. It would be like taking two cinderblocks and hitting them together, and pieces go everywhere. As they shatter, they create pressure. They blow out the back of the spinal column, which puts pressure on the spinal cord. More importantly, now you're missing a whole segment of stability, so the head is just flopping everywhere."

Relaying Adam's condition to Andre was one of Sebastianelli's worst moments. And now Andre would have to call his wife to ask her to travel to Ohio, where spinal-fusion surgery would take place in a few days. "How is he?" Addie asked when Andre phoned their South Jersey home.

Andre hid the truth. "I couldn't tell her, 'Your boy is going to be paralyzed for the rest of his life—at least that's what they're telling us,'" he said. "So I told her, 'Well, they don't know yet.' I just accentuated the unknown. I told her, 'Addie, when you get out here, he's got tubes in him. He's not going to look good; he's in pretty bad shape. You're going to have to maintain your composure. You can't cry in front of him.'"

Adam cringed at the thought that his mother would have to see him like that, cringed at the pain it would cause her. "I'm worried about her," Adam, flat on his back, told the nurses. "I don't think she can handle it."

Back home, Addie was at ease. One of Adam's assistant high school coaches had reduced her concerns. So had Andre, who had been phoning her every two hours with updates. She expected Adam to be home in a few days. "He's a little sedated," Andre told her at one point, "but not in any pain." Adam and the family had gotten through a broken collarbone and broken ribs, she thought. They would get through this, too.

When Addie arrived in Ohio, she got off the plane and was greeted by her husband and Joe Sarra, a grandfatherly administrative assistant for Penn State's football program. She had no idea her son had been injured so severely, no idea that he would probably spend the rest of his life in a wheelchair. But she could see sadness in the eyes of the two men as they walked toward her. Andre put his arms around her and told her it was bad, told her that her Adam had broken his neck.

"You guys lie!" Addie screamed. She was angry at everyone for concealing the truth, angry that she had been told to stay at home the previous night. But, mostly, she was angry and frightened that her little boy had to go through this ordeal.

When she arrived at the hospital, she had stopped crying. She kissed Adam and told him things were going to be all right. Mom was here. It was time to stop worrying. And then Addie walked out of the room. The facade fell. Her knees buckled and she collapsed onto the floor in the hallway, out of Adam's sight.

Two days later, Adam would undergo spinal-fusion surgery; the bone fragments were removed and the missing vertebra was replaced by a bone graft that was supported by a metal plate. A day before being wheeled into surgery, Adam looked up at the slender, loving woman who was at his side. "Mom," he said, "I'm not going out like this. I'm not crawling around for the rest of my life."

Not everyone agreed with his assessment. Within a week of the injury, three doctors affiliated with different hospitals gave Adam's parents the same numbing news: Do not expect your son to walk. Ever.

Addie and Andre Taliaferro did not share the news with Adam.

CHAPTER TWO

The Star Without a Trace

His eyes popped open and Khary Sharpe found himself gasping for breath.

Disoriented from the darkness and his racing heart, Khary was comforted by the sound of his roommate, Darryl Scott, sleeping soundly in the bottom bunk.

Like Adam Taliaferro, their former Eastern High teammate, Khary and Darryl's football dreams had led them to a Division I-A school. They were at Duke University, a school known more for books and basketball, but still big-time football nonetheless. The two spoke regularly with Adam, often just to wish each other luck for their upcoming games.

Khary had awoke in a cold sweat after dreaming he had been hurt in a football game. He thought about waking Darryl. Instead, he called his girlfriend back in Voorhees, New Jersey.

"What are you doing?"

"Sleeping."

"Oh, I'm sorry. I had a bad dream. I was thinking about Adam."

"I saw him yesterday. Don't worry. He looks . . . OK." The tone of her voice suggested otherwise, and Khary's heart sank. He knew simply waking up would not make this nightmare go away.

It had all been so surreal for Khary—Cor or Keys to his close friends—ever since Darryl had pulled him aside at Nashville International Airport and said, "Cor, Adam got paralyzed." Those words jolted Khary more than any football hit ever had. Paralyzed? Adam had always been the most active person he had known, and the one Khary always figured would play in the NFL.

In the days following the injury, Khary's mind kept flashing back to a day in history class when he and Adam were juniors. The conversation had turned to Christopher Reeve, the actor who became a quadriplegic following a fall from a horse, and Adam had said, "I can't imagine not being able to move." Now that the worst had happened, those words haunted Khary.

When he thought about it, he still couldn't believe it had happened. He had watched the entire game except for those fateful final minutes. With the score so lopsided, he figured Ohio State would down the ball and run out the clock, so he had flipped over to *Rocky IV*.

Darryl had also watched much of the game, and he too had stopped watching as the final minutes of the meaningless fourth quarter ticked away. That is why the news about Adam had also stunned him.

After showering and dressing following Duke's 26–7 loss, he checked his cell phone for messages. There was one from his girl-friend. "Something's happened to Adam," she said. Darryl called her back but couldn't get in touch with her. He then called Justin Barton, the mammoth tackle who had known Adam since their kickball days, and asked him if he had heard anything. Barton, who was playing for North Carolina's football team, didn't know anything because he too had been at a game.

Since Darryl played defense (free safety) and Khary played offense (wide receiver), they had been on different buses to the airport. By the time those buses pulled in, Scott had received a grim phone call from

Chaz Brown. Chaz had lived two houses down from the Taliaferros in Voorhees and had lined up at the cornerback position opposite Adam during the previous year. He was attending a community college outside of Detroit and had planned to go to the Penn State–Ohio State game, since he had always rooted for the Buckeyes and, of course, wanted to see Adam play. His plans changed when his great grandmother died, and his life changed when he got a call from his dad about Adam, the kid who always knew how to make him laugh.

His father had reached him on his cell phone, and right after he told Chaz that Adam had been injured, the two were disconnected. Chaz drove home and watched the tape of the game. Because the game was so one-sided, ABC had cut away from it in the final minutes in most parts of the country, and Chaz's tape did not have the play.

He called the Taliaferros and got no answer.

Then Adam's girlfriend, Jen, called to see if he knew anything. When he said he didn't, she gave him Andre Taliaferro's cell phone number. He got in touch with Andre, who was already at Ohio State University Medical Center in Columbus.

"Say a prayer for him," Andre told Chaz. "My son's in a whole world of hurt."

* * * * *

Adam, Chaz, Khary, Darryl, and Justin were friends long before they got to Eastern High School. They as well as other players, such as Jarid Brookins and Pat Smothers, were traffic-jam tight by the time they were seniors.

They were also the foundation of a class that may have been the most talented in school history. Four would earn Division I-A football scholarships. A handful more would continue their college careers at Division I-AA schools, and a few would go to junior college in the hopes of landing at a Division I school.

But even in a class awash with size and breathtaking speed, Adam Taliaferro always stood out. When he arrived for the first day of football practice his sophomore year, he saw a jersey with the number *44* hanging in his locker and wondered why he had been given a linebacker's number. He turned out to be a linebacker's worst nightmare.

Although a broken collarbone cut short a promising season just three games into his varsity career, Adam rushed for 1,228 yards and 27 touchdowns as a junior and led South Jersey in scoring with 162 points. He possessed the instincts that had him zigging when defenders zagged, but his ability to accelerate is what really set him apart and allowed him to live up to enormous expectations during his senior season.

Adam averaged 9.3 yards a carry against defenses that were always geared to shut him down, and as a cornerback he essentially closed down one half of the field on passing downs since many teams refused to throw to his side. He piled up obscene numbers (1,584 yards rushing and 28 touchdowns as a senior) despite playing in a Delaware wing-T offense, which doesn't feature any one back.

Perhaps the best measure of Adam's greatness as a running back is this: ask his coaches and teammates about the most amazing play they ever saw him make, and all will invariably cite a different one.

Dan Spittal, Eastern's offensive coordinator during Taliaferro's varsity years, will recall the time he and the coaches watched a game film in disbelief: Adam gained 12 yards without ever taking a stride upfield. Bouncing off numerous defenders like a pinball, he shuffled sideways, like a basketball player does on defense, for a first down.

Pat Smothers will recount the time two defenders had perfect tackling angles on Adam as he raced down the sidelines, before he somehow managed to split them and score a touchdown.

Perhaps no rival coach saw more of Adam's highlight-reel runs than Shawnee High School's Tim Gushue. "I'll never forget one play," said Gushue, who had coached Penn State offensive lineman Jordan Caruso. "He's literally within inches of [Shawnee's] sidelines and he hadn't turned his shoulder upfield yet. Our kids have great angles and I'm thinking, 'He might gain a couple, but we've got a fence around him.' He comes right to the sidelines, plants his right foot, and then it was like he was shot out of a cannon and our kids were grabbing air. I can still see the play. In my career, he is the single most outstanding player I've ever seen. . . . Adam did so much damage to us over the years. When you're one of 22 players and can still single-handedly win a game . . ."

Adam did just that in a playoff game against Shawnee, a team whose uniforms were replicas of the ones Adam would don the following season at Penn State. He rushed for a school-record 265 yards and scored four second-half touchdowns, including three in the fourth quarter, as Eastern rallied from a 13–6 halftime deficit.

Near the end of Eastern's 34–19 victory, Gushue, long an admirer of Taliaferro because of his graciousness as well as his grace, grabbed him after he had been tackled on Shawnee's sidelines. "Now that you're going to be wearing blue and white, I can root for you full-time," Gushue said.

"Thanks, coach," Adam said, grinning.

Dan Spittal felt like he had seen a ghost after watching that same game.

When he had been an assistant at nearby Pemberton High School, Spittal had coached a running back by the name of Octavious Gould. No one could stop him in high school, and he had been good enough to start at tailback for the University of Florida as a true freshman.

Gould called Spittal after the season to tell him he was transferring. It seemed some hotshot recruit had signed with Florida and Gould worried that he would be nudged out of a starting job, so he transferred to the University of Minnesota. But his career was cut short when he hurt his neck in a car accident, while the player who succeeded him at Florida, a guy by the name of Emmitt Smith, went on to have a pretty nice career.

In spite of Gould's unfulfilled college career, Spittal had sworn that he would never coach a back like that again. He just didn't think he'd see another kid that good. But after watching Adam single-handedly destroy Shawnee, Spittal said, "He's better than Octavious."

If the Shawnee win showcased Adam's ability to take over a game, the South Jersey Group 4 championship a couple of weeks later showed a toughness that was often overlooked amidst his breathtaking runs. In the second quarter, Adam threw a block for fullback Ed Carter, and Carter, who had his head down, ran right into Adam. He stayed in the game, but as the players walked to the locker room for halftime, Adam turned to mammoth tackle Justin Barton and said, "I can't breathe."

"What's wrong?" Justin asked.

"My ribs hurt," Adam said.

Spittal noticed that Adam didn't look right in the locker room, but Adam himself never said a word to any of the coaches about it. This was, after all, a championship game. He continued playing both ways the entire second half, and in the third quarter he caught a long touchdown pass from Darryl Scott on a play in which he had to extend his arms and expose his throbbing ribs.

Ultimately, Eastern's dream season met a heartbreaking end when Atlantic City drove down the field at the end of the game and kicked a last-second field goal for a stunning 31–29 upset.

After the game, the stabbing sensation in Adam's right side became too much to bear, and his parents took him to the hospital. His teammates were as surprised as anyone when they learned he had played through two broken ribs. "There's nothing even to describe it," Barton said. "It amazed me because I've bruised my ribs before and I know how bad that hurts."

With basketball season already in swing, Adam got fitted for a flak jacket so he wouldn't miss any additional time. He was told to wear it for at least two weeks.

He wore it for two days.

* * * * *

Fred Harris, the vice principal at Eastern High School, never attended Penn State, but his allegiance to the school runs deep.

He has over 5,000 trading cards of past Penn State players, over 500 autographs, and even belongs to an Internet group that trades and collects Penn State memorabilia. "The sickness," as Harris jokingly called it, was so pronounced that he named his son after Shane Conlan, the two-time All-American linebacker who led Penn State to a national championship in 1986.

Harris often remarked about how neat it would be to have someone he knew play football for Penn State, which is why he was so excited when Adam signed with the Nittany Lions. Adam visited the room that Harris proudly calls his "Penn State shrine" before leaving for school—Harris had installed another bookcase that he was planning to devote solely to Adam's Penn State career—and Harris visited him at school that summer. He could barely contain his excitement when Adam introduced him to Joe Paterno.

Harris had acquired tickets for Penn State's September 30 game against visiting Purdue, and he and his son had made plans to meet with Adam after the game. Harris marveled that Adam had e-mailed 10-year-old Shane and told him how much he was looking forward to seeing him. Imagine that, Harris thought: even with football and classes, he still has time for my son. Their visit was supposed to happen exactly one week after Harris settled into the couch in his recreation room for the Penn State–Ohio State game.

He watched in dismay as the Buckeyes sent the team that had been upset by Toledo and shut out by Pitt to another ignominious loss. However the real nightmare started after Adam tackled Ohio State tailback Jerry Westbrooks with less than two minutes to play. Harris dropped to his knees shortly after the hit. He had coached football before becoming a school administrator and he could tell by the unnatural way Adam was lying on the field—his right hip twisted toward the sky with his right leg hanging over his left leg—that he was badly hurt.

That night he tried several times to get in touch with the Taliaferros but didn't have any luck. Desperate to find out anything about Adam's condition, he emailed Kenny Jackson, the Penn State wide receiver coach who had recruited Adam and who had met Harris several times during his visits to Eastern High School. When Jackson called the next day, he said, "Fred, things aren't looking good."

"What do you mean things aren't looking good?" Harris replied.

Jackson paused. "We don't know if he'll ever move again, except for his hands."

As Harris and Jackson cried on the phone, Harris' wife and kids burst into the room thinking there had been a death in the family. It was in fact very close to a death in the family for Harris. He had always joked to the Taliaferros that if they ever put Adam up for adoption, he got first dibs. He had grown to love Adam like a son. The depth of the despair that Harris felt at that moment spoke volumes about what Adam meant to him.

If all of the kids had been like Adam, Harris' job would have been country-club easy. The only time he had ever summoned Adam to his office was when he had a new kid at school and he wanted some of the seniors to help that student make a smooth transition. "In 22 years, I've met a lot of different kids, coached a lot of different kids, and I'll say a few have been up to his level, but not *at* his level," Harris said. "I guess the best compliment I can give him is when my children grow up, I want them to be like Adam."

There were a lot of people who wanted to be like Adam, and not just the peewee football players who asked him for his autograph. Pat Montesano, an English teacher at Eastern, remembered one of her students writing a paper about how Adam was his hero. This was not some starry-eyed freshman who was thrilled just to walk the same hallway as the great Adam Taliaferro, but rather a junior who played on the football team with Adam.

Montesano smiled when she saw the paper, but it didn't surprise her. She too had been quite taken with Adam, a student who carried a 3.45 GPA, never disrupted her class, and always apologized when he had to miss it because of some football awards banquet. That had happened frequently during his senior season, since he had class right around the time awards luncheons were held.

Near the end of the season, Adam was to receive a prestigious award from the Brooks-Irvine Club on the day he had an English test. When he told his coach, Larry Ginsburg, that he couldn't attend the luncheon, Ginsburg all but did a double take. He pleaded with Adam to go to the banquet and when that didn't work, he explained the significance of the award to Montesano. She agreed to intervene. And so the petite English teacher had to get tough with the star football player because he had insisted on attending her class.

"If you took all of the qualities he has and instituted them in all of us, it would be one world," Montesano said. "He has no clue how special he is."

Andre Taliaferro had always preached the value of humility to his son, and that virtue seemed to fit Adam, who was quiet by nature and preferred to blend in with his teammates and classmates. Of course, that was nearly impossible by the time he reached his senior year, since Adam was routinely asked for his autograph and had already had volumes written about him by the local newspapers. Yet he was always so accommodating—to the little kids who thrust paper and pens in his face, to reporters who were as captivated by his engaging smile as they were his electrifying runs, and even to teachers who wanted to make good use of his exalted status.

One day during Adam's senior year, a teacher in the English department approached Dave Allen, the young basketball coach with whom Adam was very close. The teacher explained to Allen that a freshman in her class had shown improved behavior. She wanted to reward him, and she figured that eating lunch one day with Adam Taliaferro would be quite a thrill for the kid. "Adam would do it," he told her.

Sure enough, one day Adam had lunch with the boy, who liked football but was too small to play it. Allen saw the kid about a month later and asked him how the lunch had gone. "Adam is my friend now," the kid told Allen. "I'm going to follow him at Penn State."

Adam had a knack for making everyone feel important.

There was a special-needs student who attended Eastern and was on the football team but rarely played. He idolized the Eastern players, especially Adam, and they took a liking to him. "Big Killer," as he was known to the players, was also a huge Deion Sanders fan.

Adam had received an authentic Sanders jersey for Christmas a couple of years earlier, but "Prime Time" had seen little time outside of Adam's closet. From what he knew of Big Killer, Adam figured he probably didn't find much under the tree for Christmas or get many presents for his birthday. So one day before football practice, Adam went to his locker, pulled out the Sanders jersey, and walked over to Big Killer. He handed him the jersey. When Big Killer realized what Adam had done, tears welled up in his eyes. None of the other players watching said anything.

"I was just sitting there with a big smile," Pat Smothers recalled. "I bet Big Killer still thinks about that every day. I could tell by the look on his face that that meant the world to him."

* * * * *

The cutup Adam Taliaferro often replaced the quiet, kind Adam Taliaferro when he was around his close friends. As serious as he could be on the football field, he was also the guy who would try to make your pants fall down in the huddle by grabbing your belt and yanking it. Or the guy who would moonwalk into a restaurant or imitate the dance of the brainy character, Carlton, from the TV sitcom *The Fresh Prince of Bel-Air*.

"Don't get Adam wrong," said Chaz Brown, who has known him since fourth grade. "He has more of a sense of humor than he lets people believe. He's a real nice guy, but he's definitely one of the funniest guys I know."

Adam always knew how to push Chaz's buttons. One day Chaz told Adam that he wanted to quit the football team because he was upset about his lack of playing time. Adam looked at him with a straight face and said, "Yeah, you do stink, don't you?"

"Shut up!" Chaz said.

Then he cracked up.

Adam rarely missed an opportunity to ham it up around his good friends. One of his better pranks came when he showed up at Jarid Brookins' house one night and told Jarid and Justin Barton how he had gotten sick and had a, uh, little accident. He then revealed his hands, which were covered with chocolate pudding, and chased the two around Jarid's house. They finally stopped when Adam licked one of his hands.

This was the football star who was as beloved for his humility off the field as his heroics on it? The honors student who was conscientious enough about his grades that he carried around a small book in which he kept track of all of his test scores?

Gotcha!

* * * * *

Adam gave Joe Paterno a verbal commitment during an unofficial visit to Penn State in August of 1999. But that didn't stop recruiters from calling the Taliaferros with the frequency of telemarketers, and their persistence could be attributed to more than Adam's transcendent talent. Adam couldn't make his commitment to Penn State binding until the first Wednesday in February, and Adam and Andre had said he would take advantage of NCAA rules that allow high school seniors to make official visits to five I-A schools.

If that left folks wondering how solid his commitment to Penn State was, more than a few wondered if Happy Valley was even the right place for Adam. When he recruited Adam, Paterno had made it clear that he saw Taliaferro's future as a cornerback or wideout (if he preferred playing offense), not as a tailback. But because Adam turned in one of the best seasons for a tailback ever in an area that had produced such greats as Franco Harris, Lydell Mitchell, Ron Dayne, and Mike Rozier, a handful of Big East schools recruited him as a tailback.

Meanwhile, a columnist from *The Philadelphia Inquirer* wrote an open letter to Joe Paterno, titled "Born to Run." Paterno claims that he never reads newspapers during football season, but the column that implored the coach to give Taliaferro a serious look at tailback found its way to his desk, and he called the Taliaferros. "Look, Adam can play 10 years in the NFL," Paterno told Andre. "Running back? He's going to take a beating. He can get hurt."

Truth be told, Paterno and the Penn State fans, who follow recruiting as rabidly as they do the regular season, never had anything to worry about.

Adam's high school coach, Larry Ginsburg, who encouraged him to take visits to other schools, agreed with Paterno that Adam was better suited for the defensive backfield because of his size. Ginsburg had coached Chris Canty at Eastern, and Canty had gone on to be an All-American cornerback at Kansas State and a first-round draft pick of the New England Patriots. And Ginsburg felt Adam had a chance to be better than Canty.

While schools such as West Virginia, Syracuse, Boston College, and Rutgers wanted Adam as a tailback, most of the others that continued recruiting Adam saw him as a cornerback. Perhaps Stanford assistant Mose Rison (the cousin of NFL wide receiver Andre Rison) put it best when he told Adam's dad: "We believe he can be a 1,000-yard rusher, but we think he can be a first-round draft pick as a cornerback."

Addie was thrilled with the idea of Adam playing cornerback, and not because it might yield a big payday down the road. She never really liked football and hated watching Adam get beat up. That is why she always retreated to her car long before halftime at Eastern's games. She would take one look at Adam's battered and bruised body after games and shake her head. "Is this really fun for you?" she would ask.

"Don't start, Mom," Adam would say. "Don't start."

If playing cornerback would keep her son from getting beat up, she was all for it.

So was Adam. His thoughts of playing tailback in college turned out to be as fleeting as he was on the football field. By the end of the senior season, all of the aches and pains that came with the glory of playing running back started to make him think. If I feel this way playing in high school, he thought, imagine how I would feel after running against a team in the Big Ten Conference. Plus, he knew Penn State had a logjam at tailback, and he wanted to play where he'd have the best chance to get on the field early. That would be cornerback, where Penn State would lose starters David Macklin and Anthony King following the 1999 season, the year before Adam became a freshman.

However, Adam did take Ginsburg's advice and made several visits. One of those was to Tennessee, and he loved Knoxville. But he also knew deep down that it was too far from home. That left Penn State, which at one point would have been an unlikely frontrunner.

When Adam first attended summer camp there, he hadn't been too enthralled with the idea of spending four years on the remote campus nestled into the mountains of central Pennsylvania. But when he returned to camp during his senior year, he really warmed to the coaches, who remembered his name and made no secret of the fact that they wanted to see him in a Penn State uniform.

In early February of 2000, Adam became one of 29 players to sign a letter of intent with Penn State. The class was widely hailed as one of the most talented in the country. Curiously enough, Adam was not readily mentioned when the names of the top recruits of the class were rattled off. However, it didn't take long for Adam to establish himself as one of the most promising prospects of the entire class.

The ascent toward the top of his recruiting class started soon after Eastern High School's basketball season ended in March. Adam decided not to go out for the track team—a decision met with some chagrin by the track coaches, since he had set a school record by high-jumping 6'6½" as a junior—and opted to get ready for Penn State. Kenny Jackson, who had recruited Adam, sent him a thick packet detailing the weight-lifting regimen Penn State's players followed during the off-season. There was also a section on nutrition. Adam, who had eaten Wendy's before every high school football game, cut fast food out of his diet. He also stopped drinking soda. He worked out five days a week that spring and part of the summer under the watchful eye of Duane Carlisle, a former Penn State assistant track coach who had carved out a nice living as a speed enhancement coach and athletic trainer.

The drive to push himself harder than ever at a time when he could have been enjoying what was left of his senior year stemmed from the healthy sliver of doubt that Adam had always carried with him. When he arrived at Eastern as a sophomore, he had looked at the seniors and wondered if he could compete with them. When he attended Penn State's summer camp before his junior season at Eastern, he had regarded the thickly muscled and fleet-footed Lions cornerback David Macklin with a sense of awe. Could he ever be as good as him? (Never mind that, during the following year, Adam led drills with Macklin during camp.)

When he signed with Penn State, Adam was well aware that his class was stocked with Parade All-Americans and players who had been every bit as decorated as he had been in high school. If he wanted to compete, he would have to work.

That work paid off big when he played in the Governor's Bowl (an annual all-star game between New York and New Jersey) at the end of July. He had bulked up considerably since his senior year, and he couldn't help but notice that some of the players on his team looked a bit skinny to him.

Nobody played bigger than Adam in New Jersey's 48–7 rout of New York. He somehow managed to dominate the game from his corner spot, intercepting a pair of passes and returning one for a touchdown while causing one fumble and recovering two.

He returned to Penn State with more than an MVP trophy. He brought back the confidence that he could make an immediate impact for the Nittany Lions.

* * * * *

The most memorable of Adam's initiation rites to Penn State football came during a practice prior to the Nittany Lions' home opener against Toledo.

Adam had been covering wideout Rod Perry; when Perry broke into a sprint on an out-and-up pattern, Adam took off after him. He tripped over Perry's feet and went sprawling to the turf. He had had been on the ground for only a second when he heard the piercing, high-pitched shout that belonged to none other than Joseph Vincent Paterno.

"Taliaferro, get up! This isn't high school anymore! You want to lay down, you'll be laying down on the scout team!" The scout team is where most freshmen find themselves toiling in their first season at Penn State.

However, according to first-year defensive coordinator Tom Bradley, it took Adam about "30 seconds" to show that he was ready to play right away. "He's a coach's dream: good student, great kid, great character, great work ethic, wants to be great, is willing to work." That scouting report vaulted Adam to second on the depth chart behind senior Bhawoh Jue at right cornerback, though his impressive preseason nearly came to a halt during one Saturday scrimmage.

Adam had blitzed on a running play and slammed into starting tailback Eric McCoo. Three plays later, Adam said, "I can't move my thumb." Dr. Sebastianelli, who was at the scrimmage, needed only one look at his right thumb to know that it was dislocated.

Damn. The last thing Adam wanted to do was redshirt, and he knew an injury now could mean just that. That is why he tried to stay on the field even as Sebastianelli waved him off it.

Fortunately for Adam, the injury was similar to one sustained by defensive end Courtney Brown a couple of years earlier, and Brown had played with it. Sebastianelli performed minor surgery on it the next day and Adam, with his thumb protected by a cast, was back practicing with the team by Wednesday.

Sebastianelli took Adam to lunch following the surgery and helped him eat, since Adam had the use of only one hand. Over the next couple of weeks, Sebastianelli would change the cast every 48 hours to ward off infections. He grew very fond of Adam, and not just because he saw him frequently.

"I'm not saying this to be negative about anybody, but there are some people that you just become more attached to," Sebastianelli said. "I could just tell that he was a very, very genuine, very, very down-to-earth young man. The fact that someone could be so good and so intense on the field and yet be so modest and humble off the field means . . . he's very sure of himself and very confident. He knows deep in his heart he doesn't have to blow smoke or ring his own bell. There's not many people like that."

Even with only one good arm, Adam made the traveling squad, though he couldn't claim the jersey number (44) that he had worn at Eastern. When Adam had made his official recruiting visit to Penn State during the previous year, he had stayed with Bryant Johnson, Yaacov Yisrael, Deryck Toles, and Ricky Upton. Upton, who wore No. 44, took one look at the 44 medallion hanging from Adam's neck and said, "You know you're not getting that number next year." Adam settled for 43, the number worn by All-American linebacker Brandon Short during the previous four years.

Adam played primarily on the kickoff and punt coverage teams as Penn State started with humbling losses to Southern Cal and Toledo and also got shut out by Pitt. The loss to Pitt in the final game between the once-bitter rivals dropped Penn State to 1–3 with a tough game at Ohio State looming next on the schedule. At about this time, Bradley felt it was time to play the precocious freshman more frequently at cornerback.

Bradley, who had previously coached the secondary, preferred to err on the side of caution when it came to young defensive backs. He'd rather play them a week later than a week too soon. No other position was as fraught with the potential for embarrassment as cornerback, and

Bradley knew that getting beat a few times might do irreparable harm to a young corner's confidence. But he had seen Adam enough to know that he could be a special player, one who would play in the NFL one day. With Penn State about to embark on its Big Ten schedule, Bradley felt the kid was ready for more than special-teams duty.

"Taliaferro," Bradley told him, "I'm going to get you in there early this week."

Bradley's words thrilled Adam. He had recently shed the cumbersome cast and felt he was getting back to the level at which he had been prior to his injury.

He proved as much on the last play in what would be his final practice in a Penn State uniform. The first-string offense had been running a two-minute drill against the second-team defense, and Adam again found himself matched up with Rod Perry. When Perry ran an out pattern, Adam made a textbook break on the ball and intercepted Rashard Casey's pass. Had it been a game, Adam would have scored easily.

He was ready.

The day of the Ohio State game brought rain showers as well as flashes of lightning, which were threatening enough that the officials delayed the game for nearly half an hour. Unfortunately for Penn State, Mother Nature didn't wipe out its Big Ten opener altogether.

The same bugaboos that had doomed Penn State to its worst start since 1983 followed the Nittany Lions to Columbus. Putting together consecutive first downs turned out to be a colossal chore for the offense, and the defense again had trouble stopping the run. As a result, Ohio State's 17–0 lead at halftime had swelled to 38–6 by the start of the fourth quarter. Midway through the fourth quarter, Bradley went over to Adam, who had played a little bit in the third quarter, and said, "Now get in there, because I'm not taking you back out."

Fifteen minutes later, the excitement in Adam's eyes had been replaced with a look of helplessness and fear, a look Bradley could not describe but would never forget.

CHAPTER THREE

Trying to Stay Positive

Flat on his back in the Ohio hospital with tubes pumping nutrition and medicine into his body, Adam bravely tried to smile as Joe Paterno visited with him. This was Sunday, the day after he had sustained the injury, and doctors were planning spinal-fusion surgery the next day. They had informed Paterno that Adam's prognosis was not promising.

Adam seemed weak and thin, nothing like the well-sculpted football player who had worked so hard over the summer to prepare for his first season at Penn State. He was still unable to move his fingers and legs.

When Paterno looked at Adam, he again flashed back to 1977, when his son David fractured his skull and went into a coma after falling off a trampoline in his school's all-purpose room. It was a memory he didn't want to revisit. He could still recall the doctor telling him the same thing that Adam's parents were being told: that his son might never fully recover.

Paterno had been an emotional wreck ever since Adam was injured. He broke down crying when he returned to his modest home, only a brisk walk away from Penn State's campus, on Saturday night. The next morning, he returned to Columbus to be with Adam. Sue Paterno had given her husband a religious medal—the Infant of Prague, a replica of the Christ child that some believe to be miraculous—along with some prayers to St. Jude, the patron saint of hopeless causes and miraculous cures. She asked her husband to recite the prayers; they were the same prayers she had said when David had been seriously injured. She also asked Joe to give the Taliaferro family a message: "Tell them they're going to win. Tell them they're going to lead the team on the field next fall."

Paterno gave Andre the medal. The two men did a lot of crying together. Paterno talked to Andre about his son's trampoline accident and how the doctors had said he might never recover—but did. He told Andre they needed to pray for some divine intervention.

"The worst thing was that everybody was so sad, and that's not what you want," Andre said. "I understood why, but I kept saying, 'Adam is going to be all right.'"

Andre spent a lot of time sitting in the waiting room of the intensive care unit. He talked to one man whose son had become a paraplegic due to a motorcycle accident. They talked during the day and prayed together at night. He talked with members of another family whose mother had lung cancer and was taken off of a breathing machine before dying. "Everybody kind of became your family," Andre said.

Joe Sarra, 63, the Penn State football administrator who had served as a Nittany Lions assistant coach for 16 years, was also a part of the Taliaferros' fast-growing extended family. He was always at Andre's side, always offering comforting words, always there if Andre needed someone to lean on.

John Cooper, the Ohio State head coach, visited Adam. So did several of his football players. Jerry Westbrooks, the player Adam had been tackling when he suffered the spinal-cord injury, went to the hospital but was too upset to visit Adam's room. He left Adam a card with a heartfelt note inside.

Paterno wiped the tears out of his eyes and went into Adam's hospital room. The visit wasn't pleasant. The 73-year-old coach's heart ached for Adam and his family. After leaving the hospital and returning to Penn State, he glumly updated his players and the media on his visit with Adam. "I have trouble even talking about it," he said.

Doctors had decided not to operate on Taliaferro immediately after his injury. When Dr. Gary Rea looked at Adam's MRI, he saw a huge bruise on his spinal cord that extended over several segments. Upon examining the MRI and conferring with Penn State's doctor, Rea did not believe that there was sufficient pressure on the spinal cord to make surgery immediately necessary in order to alleviate a possible buildup.

If there had been abnormal pressure and stretch on the spinal cord, it would have been like crimping down a garden hose and expecting water to shoot out, said Sebastianelli, the Penn State doctor. The water wouldn't get through. In this case, if the blood had not been getting through and the tissue tension from the top part of the neck to the bottom part was so great, surgery would have been needed immediately.

Sebastianelli thought the surgery could wait until Monday. So did the highly respected Rea, a decision he called an educated guess. He felt there were advantages to delaying the surgery. When you operate quickly after this type of injury, he believed, there would be more bleeding, more swelling, and a messier surgery. By waiting a few days, Adam's blood pressure would become more stable and everything would run smoother. It would also give Rea time to get his usual operating team there. It would enable him to have a cleaner, more organized approach. "I felt pretty good that we could wait after I saw all the scans," Rea said.

Rea, a down-to-earth man who liked to wear cowboy boots and jeans, had been watching the football game at home when Adam was injured. He sometimes attended Ohio State's home games, but on this day had given his tickets away. He watched Adam go down and waited for him to pull up his knees. They didn't move. Still, like most people who watched, Rea was encouraged to see some movement in Adam's upper arms. But nothing else moved, and it wasn't until an hour later, when he received a phone call from Chris Kaeding, a surgeon for the Ohio State football team, that he learned the extent of the injury.

Rea went to the hospital. Adam seemed alert and could feel Rea touching him in different spots but couldn't squeeze his hands. Rea touched and squeezed for about 45 seconds, and then Adam went to have an MRI.

Adam seemed concerned, but not frightened or frantic. "Nobody believes that this is going to happen to them, and nobody believes that they're not going to walk again," Rea said. "At this point and time, that is not part of their thought process." It takes time for the brain to assimilate these conditions. Adam's brain wouldn't allow the news to penetrate.

Somehow, Adam never felt sorry for himself or asked "Why me?" The day before the surgery, though, he felt he needed to talk to someone from his high school days. He asked his mom to phone Dave Allen, his basketball coach at Eastern High. "He always has the words of wisdom," Adam said. "He really does."

Allen, 29, had a great rapport with his players. He was young, passionate about basketball, a good rapper—in high school, his classmates called him the "Lyrical Technician"—and cared deeply for his players. Allen had been watching TV accounts of Adam's injury and had been getting updates through Adam's 14-year-old brother, Alex.

Addie dialed the number (Adam, despite being heavily sedated, had remembered it) at about 2:30 in the afternoon. "Adam wants to talk to you, Coach Allen," she said. She held the phone so Adam could talk and listen.

Allen was shocked to receive the call. He tried to comfort Adam, tried to remain upbeat. He was stunned by Adam's good mood. Adam seemed to be more positive than *he* was. "Adam, we're pulling for you. We're praying for you," Allen said.

"I'm going to be all right," replied Adam. Adam was being his old optimistic self—even if he couldn't move most of his body.

When Allen hung up the phone, tears trickled down his cheeks.

Everybody seemed to be crying. Everybody accept Adam.

The next day, a few hours before the surgery, Addie was shaking outside Adam's hospital room. She didn't know if she could go into the room, didn't know if she'd be too emotional.

Herm Wood, a family friend who was Adam's first youth football coach, gave her a pep talk. Wood had traveled from New Jersey to try to comfort the Taliaferros. He told Addie she had the right to feel scared, but that she had to compose herself for Adam's sake. "Addie, you have to be strong. He's already nervous and he's going to get his strength through you and Andre," said Wood, who years earlier had coached with Andre and had become one of his closest friends. "Adam is going to get through this and you'll get through it."

Addie, Andre, Wood, and Sarra went into the intensive care room and visited with Adam. Wood took a black band that had four white letters on it—WWJD, which stands for "What Would Jesus Do?"—and placed it on Adam's arm. He told Adam he wanted him to have unrelenting faith, that everything would be all right. A few minutes later, Adam was wheeled into surgery.

About 500 miles away, Allen's head was pounding as he tried to teach his special-education class at Adam's old high school in New Jersey. He couldn't keep his mind off Adam. Students would stop by between classes to ask Allen if he had received any news. He had a difficult time concentrating, especially as the day grew late and no one had heard any surgery reports. All he could think about was the day former NFL linebacker Derrick Thomas, a few weeks after sustaining a paralyzing spinal-cord injury in an auto accident, died while being transferred from his hospital bed to a wheelchair on February 8, 2000. Adam had been the first person to tell Allen about Thomas. Allen couldn't get the thought out of his mind. And with no word on Adam's condition, those thoughts started to haunt him.

* * * * *

Andre conferred with Dr. Rea before the surgery and asked him the same question he had asked Dr. Sebastianelli: will my son ever walk again?

Rea said he didn't think so.

"Well, hold up, doc. He feels everything," Andre protested.

"Well, I know, but I've done this a lot of times, and . . ." Rea's southern drawl was screeching into Andre's brain. "Mr. Tal-i-a-fer-ro," he said in that slow Texas-bred voice of his, "I wish I could tell you something better, but he sustained a lot of bleeding in his cord."

After the surgery, doctors assured Andre and Addie that everything had gone well. Their son would be asleep for several hours in the recovery room. They told the Taliaferros to get away from the hospital for a few hours.

Reluctantly, they decided to drive to a restaurant a few miles away. Addie didn't want to be there, didn't want to think about ordering food or making small talk with Andre, Herm, or Sarra, a man they fondly called "Coach." All she wanted was to be next to her 18-year-old baby. At the restaurant, people were gabbing, laughing, enjoying each others' company. Addie was agitated. How could they be laughing? How could they not have a care in the world? How could they be smiling at a time like this?

She looked around at the crowded room and realized she had no right to be angry at the patrons. They didn't know her, didn't know her family, didn't know her son's precarious situation. Still, it hurt her to see other people enjoying themselves.

Herm and Sarra ordered steaks. Andre didn't feel like eating but, at the urging of Herm, ordered a salad. Addie told the waiter, "No thank you." Her stomach was in knots. She ate a piece of bread and sipped some water. She wanted to get back to the hospital, back to Adam's side.

Doctors had removed the broken pieces from Adam's fifth vertebra (C5), which left no structural support. The gap was filled with a piece of leg bone from a donor. And, in order to support the neck so that Adam could move without further injury, a plate and screws were inserted to hold several vertebrae together. The plate spanned the fourth through sixth vertebrae.

The spinal cord had been bruised, not cut. That was a positive. If it had been cut, there would be no chance that Adam would ever walk again. Now there seemed to be some slight hope. And even if it was only a 3 percent chance, the Taliaferros would cling to their hope, cling to their prayers, cling to their belief.

Back at a news conference at Penn State, Dr. Sebastianelli said he was hopeful but realistic. The whole process, he said, could take a year. Asked about the normal recovery rate for this type of injury, Sebastianelli was blunt. "Most of them do not recover much," he said. "The majority would not."

The goal of the surgery, Rea said, was not to make the spinal cord better. The goal was to stabilize the spine so Adam could begin to sit up and not reinjure his spinal cord.

The surgery did not give Rea an indication of whether Adam would walk again. The fact that Adam never had a complete loss of all sensation was good, Rea thought. On the other hand, the fact that he had sensation but no movement was a negative sign. "Statistically, that's bad," Rea said. So was the fact that he had a big contusion on the middle of his spinal cord.

Two days after the spinal-fusion surgery, a news conference was held at Ohio State to update Adam's condition. At one point, a reporter asked Andre what he thought about Ohio State Coach Cooper running up the score and throwing the ball in the game's final minutes, after the injury. "I have no comment on it," Andre said.

Maybe it wasn't the classy thing to do, but Cooper's desire to score more points in a blowout victory had nothing to do with the injury, Andre thought. Cooper had visited Adam three times in the hospital and had taken the Taliaferros and Sarra out to breakfast. He seemed like a good man to Andre.

Andre was almost offended by the question about Cooper running up the score. It seemed so trivial. Andre had more important things on his mind.

"My boy is strong; that's why I'm telling you my boy is going to come back," said Andre, with conviction, at the news conference. "My boy will walk again."

Andre was shown on CNN, saying those words on a sports highlight show: "My boy will walk again." The camera went back to Fred Hickman, the show's anchor. "I believe him," Hickman said.

On September 27, four days after the injury and two days after the spinal-fusion surgery, Adam was transported from Ohio to Philadelphia International Airport in a tiny Lear jet, a vehicle that didn't have much more space than a van. Andre was told to sit in the back. Three attendants from Thomas Jefferson University Hospital in Philadelphia were also aboard, along with two pilots. Adam was lying down on a stretcher and heavily medicated. Months later, he still would not remember anything about the flight. Two of the attendants continuously monitored his vital signs and checked his medication levels. The other attendant worked the hand-operated ventilating device, pumping oxygen into Adam's lungs with each squeeze.

Even though Adam was sedated and not comprehending much, one of the attendants still gave him instructions. "Don't move your head. Don't fight the ventilation." For the entire flight, which took about an hour, the device made an annoying, whining sound—like a dog crying by a door as it begs to go outside—that would forever be etched in Andre's mind.

Upon arriving at Philadelphia International Airport, an ambulance transported Adam to Jefferson Hospital. Andre was right by his side.

"Hang in there, son. Hang in there."

* * * * *

When he arrived at Jefferson, located a half-hour drive from the Taliaferros' South Jersey home, Adam was still in critical condition. He had developed a slight case of pneumonia and, due to an overflow of secretions, wasn't passing air in one lung. His lungs were working, but just minimally. A respirator was helping him breathe. And his father and the nurses were helping him cough up mucus that was blocking his passageways.

Adam's diaphragm was weakened, so he couldn't cough effectively. Trish Power, one of his Jefferson nurses, had a sore arm from making a fist and pushing at his diaphragm, which forced him to cough and bring up the mucus. Trish was getting exhausted. Andre took over and pushed at Adam's diaphragm, continuing a procedure called a "quad cough." Adam never complained.

The Taliaferros wanted Adam to have as much privacy as possible. Trying to get through this ordeal was the most uphill climb of their lives. They needed to keep their focus and help Adam to keep *his*. They had Adam admitted into the hospital under the alias "Scott Jones" to ward off the media. They also didn't bring their mature-beyond-his-years son, Alex, 14, to visit with his brother during his first night in the Philadelphia hospital. Alex arrived the next day.

He was not prepared for what he saw.

Alex and Adam had a typical relationship for two brothers who were four years apart. Alex, who wears glasses and is quite studious-looking, admired his brother and wanted to be with him and his friends. Adam, like most teenagers, wanted something else: his privacy. Adam and his friends would be playing Ping-Pong in the family's finished basement when Alex would try to become part of the gang.

"I'm sleeping down here tonight," he would tell Adam. Adam would offer Alex one of his football figurines. Or perhaps a CD. They were bribes to entice his little brother to go back upstairs.

But now, as Alex walked into his brother's hospital room, there was no feeling of brotherly competitiveness. No brotherly bickering. No brotherly jealousy.

Addie had warned Alex that his brother didn't look good. "Be strong for him," she said. "Don't let him see you cry." Yet crying was the first thing Alex wanted to do as he took a step toward Adam's bed. It was the worst day of Alex's life.

Adam had tubes in his nose to help him breathe, tubes in his arms giving him nutrition, and a rigid cervical collar around his neck to stabilize that area of the body.

Alex held his brother's hand and gently wiped his forehead with a wash rag. And then he excused himself. He walked out to the hallway and waited until he turned the corner before crying. Sarra, the gruff-looking but teddy bear–like former Penn State coach, put his beefy arms around Alex and told him everything would be all right.

After he composed himself, Alex went back into the room. Adam could sense that his little brother was terrified. "Come here," Adam said. "Come over here and give me a kiss." Alex kissed him on the cheek. It was the first time he could ever remember kissing his brother. He squeezed Adam's hands and then touched his brother's arms.

"Can you feel that?" Alex asked.

"Yeah."

Alex gently stroked Adam's leg. "Feel that?"

"Yeah."

Adam could feel, but he couldn't move his legs or fingers. And he still could not distinguish between a light touch and a pinprick—a critical distinction.

A few days later, some positive signs emerged. Working hard to bring up the mucus had helped Adam to clear his lungs. He was able to breathe more easily and was taken off the ventilator. He started taking fluids by mouth and was transferred from the neuro intensive care unit to the intermediate intensive care unit.

"Adam was tireless," said Trish, the Jefferson nurse. "He really was one of the most determined people I've ever met."

Penn State, meanwhile, was rallying behind Adam. Six days after his injury, a prayer vigil was held on campus. The bells from venerable Old Main, a majestic, stone administration building that overlooks a sprawling expanse of lawn on campus, chimed at noon as thousands of people, including Penn State students, athletes, and coaches, gathered to show their support. The football players, clad in the blue home jerseys they would wear the next day against Purdue, stood along Old Main's massive pillars with solemn expressions.

Defensive line coach Larry Johnson, with Paterno and athletic director Tim Curley seated to his right, began the afternoon proceeding by reading religious passages that seemed to elevate the crowd's spirits. "We're having faith here," Johnson said. "He's going to return here."

Quarterback Rashard Casey, a soft-spoken senior who usually does not like talking in front of huge crowds, read an emotional poem entitled "Don't Quit," which was given to him by a fellow student in his ballroom dance class.

Johnson urged those in attendance to continue praying for Taliaferro so that he could someday return to Penn State and complete his education.

Two days after that prayer vigil, another one was held in South Jersey. This was at the Solid Rock Worship Center, a nondenominational Christian church that the Taliaferros often attended. On this Sunday, their friends filled the pews. The church was so packed that people stood outside and watched the vigil on big-screen TVs that had been set up. Several of Taliaferro's former Eastern High teammates spoke at the service. So did some of his former coaches, along with township and school officials.

"Give up the 4s for him," Amir Khan, the church's pastor, said at the service. And a sea of perhaps 800 people held up their hands, each displaying four fingers—thus making a 44, the number Adam wore in high school.

That night, as Sunday turned into Monday morning, Trish sat by Adam's side and watched him fall in and out of sleep in the Philadelphia hospital. Suddenly, she saw Adam's left foot jerk. Maybe it was an involuntary twitch, she thought. Or maybe his nerves were regenerating and a signal was trying to get through. She didn't hesitate. She woke Adam.

"Adam, can you move your foot for me?" Adam was groggy. Still, he managed to flex his left foot up, lifting it about three inches off of his white bedsheet, and down.

"Adam, you moved your foot!" Trish said.

"No, but I dreamed that I just did," Adam said in a deep, almost monotone voice.

"You're not dreaming, Adam. You did it!"

Adam's expressive eyes widened. Trish shouted toward the hallway. Kate Mansfield, another nurse, ran into the room.

"Do it again, Adam," Trish said.

He did. And his eyes filled with tears. By the excitement in the nurses' voices, Adam sensed that this was a significant development. "Can you call my dad?" he asked.

Trish nodded. Before she phoned Andre, however, she asked Adam to move his foot again. She wanted to make sure; she didn't want to give anyone false hope if the movement was just a spasm.

Just then, Will Tally, a doctor not connected with Adam's case, happened to walk down the hallway. Kate flagged him into the room. Tally asked Adam to move his foot. When he did, the doctor said the movement was voluntary because he had done it on command.

Trish had enough evidence. She walked quickly out of the room and went to the nurse's station to phone Andre.

* * * * *

Andre had spent that entire day and night at Jefferson Hospital with his son, and when he went home that night, he was exhausted—physically, mentally, emotionally.

Mostly emotionally.

Earlier that day, a prayer service was held in Adam's room. The Rev. Khan, who had also coached Adam's midget football teams with Andre, led the service. Andre, Addie, and Alex were there, and so was Khan's wife, Aughtney. Andre wasn't a very religious man. Until now. Now he was constantly praying, constantly asking for help.

As the day ended, Andre was praying again. He prayed in his family room, then went upstairs, knelt by his bed in his gray gym shorts and white T-shirt at 1:00 A.M., and asked for some guidance. "God, give me a sign. Please give me a sign," he prayed.

He felt a shiver and a calmness pass over him. It was a feeling he had never experienced, a feeling that seemed almost spooky to him.

Andre was jolted out of his tranquility by the ringing of the telephone in his bedroom. It was Trish.

Andre recognized the voice and, for a split second, his heart raced. "What happened to Adam?" he thought. "Why is she calling at 1:00 A.M.? Why did I leave the hospital?"

"Andre, this is Trish. Don't worry. Nothing is wrong."

Andre took a deep breath. There was excitement in Trish's voice.

"You wouldn't believe it, Andre. Adam moved his foot!"

Andre was momentarily stunned.

"Andre, Adam just moved his ankles! *He's moving his ankles! He's moving his toes!*"

Tears poured out of Andre's eyes. "You know what, Trish? I'm coming back. I'm coming back to the hospital!" He had to be there to share this momentous occasion with his son. Adam may have scored 62 touchdowns in high school and may have had hundreds of highlight-film runs in his career, but nothing, absolutely nothing, could ever compare with these four sweet words: Adam moved his toes!

Andre excitedly woke up Addie, told her about the developments, and gave her a long hug. He splashed some water on his face and prepared to drive back to the hospital. The phone rang again. It was Trish. "Andre, this is something! Adam is moving his leg!"

Again, tears streaked down Andre's cheeks. He got into his Taurus, picked up the Rev. Khan, and headed to the hospital. His heart hadn't felt this much joy in ages.

At the hospital, Adam smiled softly, proudly, at the sight of his dad.

"Move your ankle," Andre said, excitedly.

Gently, Adam complied.

"Move your leg."

Adam focused hard. Nothing happened. After about 30 seconds and a lot of concentration, he again was able to get movement. Only his left leg and left foot moved.

Adam, Andre, Trish, and the Rev. Khan clutched hands and formed a circle over the bed. The pastor led them in prayer. "Dear Jesus, thank you for giving us this chance, for giving us this hope. . . ."

Andre kissed Adam, walked quickly to the nurses' station, and phoned Dr. Sebastianelli and Paterno to share the joyous news. So what if it was after 2:00 A.M.? So what that he would wake them out of a deep sleep? This wasn't time to sleep. This was time to celebrate.

When her shift ended near 8:00 A.M. and she drove home from the hospital, Trish was also in a triumphant mood, even if she did feel emotionally spent. She had been a nurse for 16 years, and she had never felt so exhilarated by one of her patient's experiences. Working in a neuro intensive care unit is a depressing job, but this, this had been so uplifting. This made her realize why she was in the medical field. This made her feel as if she wanted to go to church. This young man, who could barely breathe but never failed to say, "Thanks a lot" after Trish would assist him, had made her feel special. On the drive home, she phoned her husband and her mom. She needed to share this moment.

Adam had moved!

Before the next sunset, however, the feel-good atmosphere—and some of the hope—had started to fade. In the next three days, Adam tried his hardest but couldn't move his leg or toes.

* * * * *

Anthony Burns, a young, good-looking doctor who resembled Denzel Washington, had been working at Jefferson for a month when Adam was admitted to the hospital. Prior to arriving at Jefferson, he had been doing a spinal-cord-injury fellowship at the University of Alabama.

Burns, 32, looked at Adam's films and did not like the bleeding he observed in his spinal cord. It was an ominous sign. "Usually if there's blood in the spinal cord," Burns said, "those patients don't walk." Like Dr. Rea, Burns was in an uncomfortable position: being the person who had to explain Adam's still-developing case to his parents.

The publicity surrounding the injury made this a highly unusual case. The publicity had caused lots of well-meaning people to deluge the Taliaferros with information on experimental treatments or stories about recoveries. Burns was concerned that the Taliaferros might be getting incorrect data. "So because of that, I wanted to provide the most accurate information available that was based on scientific research to the family," Burns said. "I wanted to help them sort through all the noise they were hearing."

Under other circumstances, Burns said, he probably wouldn't have given the family as much medical information so early in the case. "It's tough sometimes for people to know how to interpret information like this," he said. "But I thought, in this particular circumstance, that it was really an obligation to make sure they had the most accurate and best information that we had available. Information that wasn't based on opinion or hearsay."

The information provided by Dr. Burns was painful for the Taliaferros to digest.

The American Spinal Injury Association (ASIA) has published guidelines to classify the severity of spinal-cord injuries. Patients are classified ASIA-A (no sensory or motor function) through ASIA-E (normal function). Adam was classified as an ASIA-B, which meant he had sensation, although it was impaired below the level of injury, but no motor function. In other words, he couldn't move.

The most important variable in determining a patient's ability to recover, Burns said, is whether a person has pinprick sensation below the level of injury. Strange but true: millions of dollars are spent each year on spinal-cord research, equipment, and technology, but in Adam's case, the key factor was simply how he felt a pin—the kind he got for free with the prom shirt he had rented a few months earlier—that pierced his skin.

When he arrived at Jefferson, Adam could not reliably distinguish between light touch and pinprick. Dr. Burns took that into consideration when he met with Andre and Addie and discussed their son's situation. He also took into consideration that Adam was in the hard-to-predict ASIA-B category. Dr. Burns didn't want to give the Taliaferros false hope. He lowered his head and dejectedly told the Taliaferros that, based on statistics, they shouldn't expect their son to walk.

Andre was incensed. "You're not God," he said. "You don't know."

Addie was so upset she walked out of the room. Later, she told Burns he was too negative. "I know you see this every day and I know this is your job, but I don't see this every day and that is the love of my life laying there," she said. "Can't you have a little bit of compassion?"

Addie felt she wasn't being given any hope—until Adam slightly moved his leg and foot for two nurses and a doctor in the early hours of October 2. Later that day, Dr. Burns came into the room to verify the movement. But once again, Adam couldn't move.

Dr. Burns said Adam still had to be classified in the ASIA-B category. That, coupled with the fact that he still could not differentiate between light touch and pinprick, stacked the odds against Adam ever walking. The case was still evolving, but Dr. Burns knew that, based on one study, if Adam remained at this level after one month, he would have about an 11 percent chance of walking.

Again, Andre was furious. To him and his wife, a conflict was building with Dr. Burns. "But your nurse saw him move!" Andre said.

Burns was concerned that the movement could have been involuntary, could have been a spasm. This was a murky area because in the early stages, when nerve fibers are sort of rewiring and trying to repair, they don't work consistently.

Even Sue Paterno, the coach's wife and a person who, like Andre, is an eternal optimist, wondered if it had been an involuntary movement when Andre phoned her near 2:00 that morning and explained that Adam had moved his left foot and left leg.

She had remembered a similar instance when her son, David, moved his finger while in the intensive care unit in 1977. She excitedly told the doctors, but they told her it was just involuntary. That thought drifted through her mind as she heard Andre's excited voice. Her excitement about Andre's news was tempered by her own experience.

Joe Paterno was also cautious. Less than 24 hours after hearing Adam had moved his foot and leg, Paterno addressed reporters and did not tell them what had transpired at the hospital. "Maybe there will be a miracle," he said. "Sometimes, you don't know what courage is until you are around some people who have to look forward to what Adam's parents have to look forward to, as far as a whole different lifestyle with their young son." The implication: life in a wheelchair was not going to be easy.

Andre didn't want to hear it, didn't want anyone putting any negative thoughts in his son's head. "My boy will walk again," he kept repeating, even though, for the next three days after Adam's seemingly break-through moment, he could not repeat the movement in his leg or foot.

Andre knew the odds were against his son. He also knew his son was a lifelong achiever. Nothing had ever stopped him. Whether it was athletics or academics. Whether it was running around a 250-pound defensive lineman or acing a world history test. And nothing would get in his way now, either. These doctors didn't know Adam, didn't know the type of person he is, didn't know the type of focus he possesses. These doctors will see. These doctors, Andre said to himself, will learn that they underestimated his son.

Andre Taliaferro was in denial.

And he cringed when Paterno, who had good intentions, tried to arrange for Adam to talk with one of his former recruits, Tim Strachan, who had broken his neck in a 1993 swimming accident and was a quadriplegic. Paterno thought Strachan, a motivational speaker and football broadcaster for the University of Maryland, could show Adam that he could still live a productive life in a wheelchair.

"Why would I want Adam to talk with him?" Andre thought. "Give me someone who was injured and got out of a chair." Andre Taliaferro wanted hope; for a while, no one seemed to give it to him.

No one except Adam.

CHAPTER FOUR

Roots of Strength

"Hey Taliaferro, you suck!"

Those words had been the catalyst for one of the greatest postseason performances in South Jersey prep football history. Almost a year later they cast an illuminating light on the competitive spirit that Adam Taliaferro would take into the fight of his life.

The kid whose own mother sometimes worried that people would take advantage of him because he was too nice had proved that he ached to win even before he went to kindergarten. When Adam was four years old his father set up a miniature basketball hoop in the laundry room and the two would often retire to the makeshift court after dinner. It didn't matter to Adam that he barely came up to his father's waist. The more Andre won, the more he fumed and cried.

By the time he got to high school, there were both subtle and not-so-subtle signs of this competitive streak.

Subtle: Adam's report cards were always filled with As and Bs because he simply hated to get Cs.

Not so subtle: One day at basketball practice during his junior year, Adam, the team's point guard, committed a careless turnover against the press. "I can't believe Penn State's recruiting you!" Eastern basketball coach Dave Allen yelled. Adam subsequently missed a dunk and Allen continued to ride him. He told Adam he couldn't dunk. On the next play, Adam, who stands only 5'11", soared high above the rim and threw one down. He turned to Allen and glared at him.

That side of Adam was often overshadowed by the quiet, easygoing manner that most people saw. Even during football games, Adam rarely returned the trash talk that he heard on a regular basis. As players untangled themselves from the piles of testosterone, Adam would hear how he was overrated and how Penn State had made a mistake recruiting him.

Yeah, yeah, yeah. Adam usually laughed off the bluster.

On the night of November 12, 1999, however, Adam was already simmering by the time Eastern got to the locker room for halftime. And it was more than just the usual talk that had him so upset. His mother, who was sitting in her car in the Eastern parking lot, could see what she called Adam's "pout walk." The agitated strut made her wonder if Adam had been in an argument with one of his teammates.

Actually, he was perturbed at what had transpired during the game's first two quarters. The Vikings were ranked No. 1 in South Jersey by *The Philadelphia Inquirer*, but they were in danger of getting knocked out of the playoffs for the second year in a row by archrival Shawnee. And if there was one team Adam did not like losing to, it was Shawnee.

Located in a neighboring affluent town, Shawnee had a reputation for being a tad arrogant due to the sustained success many of its athletic programs enjoyed. Nowhere was this more evident than in basketball. Shawnee was a perennial powerhouse, and its raucous students were South Jersey's equivalent of Duke's "Cameron Crazies." They could be brutal on opposing players; during Adam's junior year they had waved Dunkin' Donuts boxes at his good friend Justin Barton, the 6'6", over 300-pound center.

Shawnee usually got the better of Eastern in basketball, but football belonged to Eastern. At least this year it did: Eastern had won a 61–41 shootout earlier in the season. Now Adam was determined to bring the Vikings back from a 13–6 halftime deficit.

The game actually turned before the second half started. As the players were making their way back to the field, a voice belonging to a pint-sized Shawnee fan pierced the dark, brisk night. "Hey Taliaferro, you suck!"

Starting quarterback Darryl Scott looked through his facemask at the offending fan. "You just messed up, buddy," Darryl said.

Big time.

Adam returned the second-half kickoff for a touchdown, and the rest is school history. In addition to finishing with 265 yards rushing and his momentum-turning kickoff return, Adam scored a trio of fourth-quarter touchdowns to send Shawnee packing, 34–19.

"I would like to thank that kid, wherever he is," said Eastern's then–offensive coordinator Dan Spittal.

The competitive fire that could crackle like a five-alarm blaze wasn't the only thing Adam had going for him by the time his broken body had been delivered to Thomas Jefferson University Hospital in Philadelphia. Adam possessed a work ethic that had reached mythic proportions by the time he graduated from Eastern.

This characteristic, too, had manifested itself at an early age. When Adam played midget football he never missed a practice. Even on days when it rained so hard that Addie was sure practice would be canceled, Adam insisted she drive him to the field.

Not that this came as any surprise to Addie. Once, when Adam was six years old, he had been upstairs getting ready to go play football. It didn't matter to him that it was pouring outside. Addie's mother, who was visiting from New York at the time, said, "I can't believe you're going to let that boy play in the rain."

That's when they heard a high-pitched but earnest voice: "Nana, when you're in the NFL, you've got to play in the rain," said little Adam.

Addie had laughed then, but sometimes Adam's insistence on attending practice drove her nuts. Once it had been raining so hard that she and another mother decided they would instead take the boys to Pizza Hut. It took a phone call from the coach, who assured Adam that it was all right to miss practice that day, for Addie to get him to Pizza Hut.

That devotion coupled with his natural talent paid off later for Adam. He started as a sophomore in high school—a heady feat in itself at a large-enrollment school like Eastern—and he scored three touchdowns in his varsity debut.

The defining moment in Adam's career came two games later; it also happened to be one of his lowest moments. He made a diving touchdown catch but came down on his shoulder. The defensive back who had been covering him landed on top of him, and Adam's collarbone was broken. He spent the rest of the season pedaling away on a stationary bike while his teammates practiced. The only time he got on the field was when he fetched his older teammates water. From star running back to water boy.

Adam hated it, and he counted the days until basketball season. He also vowed that he would return to the field next season bigger and stronger so that he wouldn't have to go through this again. "I really wasn't into lifting weights. I did it, but I didn't go all out," Adam said. "Getting hurt made me realize that I wasn't strong enough. I always thought if I had more muscle around my shoulder area, [my collarbone] wouldn't have gotten broken."

The profound effect the injury had on Adam would soon be seen by his coaches and teammates. Even though he had basketball practice almost every day during the summer, Adam never missed the so-called "optional" morning workouts for football players. He became so maniacal about working out that after games, he would retire to his bedroom and do sit-ups and other abdominal exercises—never mind the bruises and scrapes that covered his body. Addie would walk by his room and just shake her head.

Even after a senior season in which he earned *Philadelphia Inquirer* all-area player of the year honors as well as the full scholarship to Penn

State, Adam didn't let up. In fact, he pushed even harder. A week after basketball season ended, he started working out five days a week with Duane Carlisle.

Carlisle looked forward to Adam's workouts even though he constantly had to tell Adam to drop the "sir" stuff. He found that Adam challenged him as much as he challenged Adam.

One broiling summer day, Carlisle had been putting a group of football players that included Adam through an exhausting workout. After a series of sprints on the track at Voorhees Middle School, the players dropped in a heap on the grassy infield and started taking off their shoes.

"You guys aren't done," Carlisle said flatly.

Their scattered shoes and sweat-streaked faces said otherwise, but there was Adam slowly rising and telling the others to get up. They followed him back to the track and proceeded to run their best times of the day.

"Adam Taliaferro in my opinion probably has the best work ethic I've ever encountered from the pro level to high school level," said Carlisle, who is now a speed consultant for the Philadelphia Eagles. "Nothing was too much in terms of what you put on his plate as far as training. He would run through a brick wall for you."

Carlisle was at a wedding in New Orleans the weekend Adam got hurt at Ohio State. He returned home and found the light on his answering machine blinking furiously. When he learned the devastating news he was heartbroken.

Carlisle had been coaching Adam for three years and had grown quite attached to him. His eight-year-old son Amir idolized Adam, in part because Adam always took time to talk to him.

Carlisle called Andre to see if there was anything he could do. Said Andre: "Just put him in your prayers because my boy is going to walk again."

Of course he would walk again, Carlisle thought. He had seen Adam push himself to the brink both physically and mentally on a daily basis.

He knew the grueling rehabilitation that lay ahead would not break Adam's spirit.

Yet the conviction he heard in Andre's voice that day soothed Carlisle more than anything.

As it turned out, nothing would loom larger in the recovery of Adam Taliaferro than the conviction and care of his parents.

* * * * *

Addie Garrett grew up the youngest of three daughters in Troy, New York, a small industrial town along the Hudson River about eight miles north of Albany. Her father died of cancer before she was born, and her mother worked and raised the three girls on her own.

Still, Addie never found herself wanting for anything as she grew up. She had never known her father so how could she miss what she didn't have? Plus, she had an uncle who spent a lot of time with the girls. A baker, he lavished the girls with donuts and other goodies as well as attention.

Addie played volleyball in middle school but that was the extent of her athletic career. She preferred attending sporting events to playing sports.

After graduating from high school in 1975, Addie got a job as a payroll clerk for a company that manufactured microscopes and telescopes. That is what most people did in Troy: they went to work right out of high school and eventually got married and started a family. They never left. Addie was no different. She bought a car and found her own apartment when she started working and figured life was good. She never gave any thought to what else was out there.

One day while Addie was crossing the main street on her lunch break, a yellow Camaro pulled over and its horn blared. The young man behind the wheel had thick shoulders, an easy smile, and a gift for gab. He had gotten lost trying to find a bank. Addie pointed him in the right direction, and he asked her if she wanted to go have a Coke.

Addie declined. She had a serious boyfriend at the time. Besides, she wasn't about to get in a car with a man she had just met. But he *was* driving her favorite car and she didn't have a ring on her finger, so she did oblige his request for a phone number. She actually gave him her mother's number and didn't think much more about the encounter.

About three weeks later she got a call from her mother at work. "Addie, this guy Andre has been calling the house looking for you."

"Andre who? Mom, I don't know anybody named Andre."

"Well, he knows you!"

Addie called Andre back, and they made plans to go on a date. They went out a few times but the romance hardly blossomed.

He sure talked an awful lot, Addie thought. Besides she had been dating the same guy for five years, and she decided to go back to him. She and Andre parted ways after only a couple of dates. By the time Addie showed up at one of Andre's semipro football games—she had gone with her sister, whose boyfriend was on Andre's team—Andre already had a new girlfriend. She was in the stands that day, which is why he barely talked to Addie.

One morning, Addie's sister dropped by her apartment and told her she had bumped into Andre the previous night. So what, Addie said. But later that day, Andre called her and they talked. He came over and took her out for dinner.

They have been together ever since.

When Andre found out he was being transferred to Pittsburgh, he asked Addie to go with him. They decided to get married. Two days after they exchanged vows—November 17, 1979—Addie left the cocoon of Troy for Pittsburgh and a whole new life. She had Adam on January 1, 1982.

Almost two years after that, Andre took a job that allowed him to move his family to the Philadelphia area. They decided to live on the other side of the Delaware River in South Jersey, and that's how they ended up in Voorhees. A growing bedroom community, Voorhees met two important criteria: it had a well-regarded school system and the Taliaferros wouldn't be the first black family there.

They bought a house in a development that was a picture of suburbia. The nights were so quiet and the grass so green that sometimes Andre would have to laugh. How did the kid who had been raised on the mean streets of north Philly, the kid who had been shot at several times, end up in Beaver Cleaver country?

* * * * *

Andre grew up in a rough neighborhood not far from Connie Mack Stadium, where the Phillies played. His father never finished high school and never made more than $5,000 a year working as a night watchman and elevator operator.

Money was always tight around the Taliaferro household, but it never dawned on Andre that he was poor. There was always food on the table and his mother kept the three-bedroom row house clean. She also seemed to find money for camping and trips with the Boy Scouts.

Boy Scouts? That's right, the kid who had learned early that fighting was a matter of survival in his world had also been an enthusiastic Boy Scout. Other kids in the neighborhood teased him about it, but the experience gave Andre a more panoramic view of the world. Through the Boy Scouts he rode on an airplane for the first time and experienced spectacular mountain scenery during a camping trip to Wyoming. He met white kids from the suburbs and learned they really weren't that different from him.

Unfortunately, while those camping trips and other activities may have given Andre a different vantage point, they were only a brief respite from his reality. He came of age in the crucible of the civil rights movement, and north Philadelphia was not immune to the unrest that was happening in inner cities across the country. Violence and drugs were taking over. "Do a good turn daily"—the Boy Scouts' slogan—rarely prevailed in the streets.

Andre, who graduated from Dobbins High School in 1971, did make it out of north Philadelphia, even though he had to come home after a year at Virginia State University because money from a federal program for inner-city kids had dried up. He attended Temple University at night while working as a lab technician at a chemical company during the day.

Shortly before he received his degree in marketing, he was accepted to the police academy. But, deciding he had seen too many shootings on the street, Andre instead took a job as a marketing specialist with General Electric and relocated to rural upstate New York.

One day in 1978, Andre received a stark reminder of what he had left behind in north Philly—in the last place in the world he ever expected to dodge gunfire. He was getting dressed for football practice when he heard a gunshot. He kicked out a window in the back of his apartment and walked around to the front of the building, where one of his neighbors told him that he had seen someone shooting at his apartment. Andre ran back upstairs and called the police.

Police and a SWAT team raced to the scene. TV cameras arrived shortly thereafter. The gunman had been the tenant who lived directly above Andre in the two-story apartment. The two had exchanged words one day because Andre had been playing his music loudly. The disgruntled neighbor retaliated by firing six shots from a .30-06, a high-powered rifle, into Andre's apartment.

One of the officers had been blunt about what would have happened if one of the bullets had found their intended targets. "We would have been putting a tag on your toe," he told Andre.

To this day Andre is thankful he and Addie were broken up at the time. If they had been together, she might have been sitting on the sofa that was shredded by bullets.

* * * * *

If Andre's experiences in north Philly taught him that he didn't want his children to grow up in that environment, his upbringing also shaped his beliefs on how he wanted to raise his kids.

Miracle in the Making

Andre played on the junior varsity football team as a sophomore at Dobbins High, but he quit football after that season so he could work and earn spending money. He later played during his year at Virginia State, but he summed up his football career in two words: "frustrated athlete."

Sometimes he wondered if things might have been different had his own father been into sports. His father liked to fish but never showed any interest in football or baseball, even though the Phillies played five blocks from where the Taliaferros lived. While Andre loved his father, his relationship with his kids would be different simply because he was a sports enthusiast.

The strong influence he would have in his sons' lives could be seen not long after Adam started walking. If Andre wasn't pushing Adam's Big Wheel to the top of one of Pittsburgh's hilly streets, he was pitching Wiffleballs to Adam outside of the family townhouse after work. When the Taliaferros moved to New Jersey, Andre would often take Adam with him when he played pick-up basketball or strap him into a seat on the back of his bicycle and take him for a long ride. By the time they got back to the house, Adam was often fast asleep.

With Andre enthusiastically exposing his kids to sports at an early age, Addie naturally had some suspicion when Adam announced at the age of five that he wanted to play football. But any thoughts she had that Andre had steered him toward the sport vanished the day Adam came home from midget league registration in tears because he had been told he was too young to play.

Addie didn't show it in front of her crestfallen little boy, but she was thrilled; she didn't want Adam to play football. The situation looked ripe for an ice cream cone. But Andre knew what would really dry those tears; he took Adam to shoot some hoops.

Even though he traveled frequently because of his job, Andre was always a central figure in his sons' lives. He would arrange his schedule around parents' nights and school plays. Even when he was on the road, he would call home as many as five times a day.

Addie frequently reminded Adam and his younger brother Alex about the things their father did for them. The nice clothes and vacations to Disney World are made possible by all of the traveling your father does, Addie would tell them. When she and Andre were growing up, such vacations were unthinkable.

Like Andre, Addie also had strong ideas about how she wanted to raise her kids; most of the things she demanded from her sons stemmed from her sense of common decency. For instance, she insisted that if Adam and Alex saw someone they knew, they had to go over and say hello. And her No. 1 rule: the boys always had to call and let her know where they were. Even if it meant calling at 1:00 A.M. and waking her—Addie, an avowed early riser, often went to bed long before the 11:00 P.M. news—that was OK. As long as she knew where they were and that they were safe. That was not too much to ask, considering all that she had done for her boys.

Addie was a stay-at-home mom and never missed a basketball game or a football game, and even came up with a good compromise for the latter. Since she didn't like watching Adam get tackled, she would work the snack bar during his midget league games. Even after Addie took a job at a local daycare center, she still drove Alex to school and picked him up afterward every day. On days that Adam had a basketball game, she would stop and get Alex a personal pan pizza from Pizza Hut.

Addie truly enjoyed her kids. Years later she would tell parents with young children to treasure them now because they would be teenagers soon enough.

She can recall only one day—one day!—when she and Andre didn't talk to the boys. They were taking a cruise to the Caribbean and phone calls from the ship cost $15 a minute. They briefly considered calling home but decided they could wait. When the boat docked the next day, Andre and Addie ran to the nearest phone.

Even after Adam went to Penn State, his parents continued to call him every day. Andre would talk football. Addie would make sure he was eating right and that the other players were treating him OK. "Mom, stop!" Adam would say when she pressed about the latter.

Addie was very excited when Adam called her at work a few hours before the team plane left for Ohio State. She and Andre were not making the trip to Columbus. Addie had been so worn out from traveling to the other games that she had wrangled a promise out of Andre that they would stay home for this one. They could watch it on TV and order in some Chinese, Addie had said.

"Mom, I'm getting a lot of playing time tomorrow, so make sure you're watching," Adam said.

"Adam, you know I'll be glued to the TV set."

* * * * *

The Taliaferros were no stranger to tragedy.

Andre's father had died at the age of 65 from an emphysema-related illness, and he had also lost a sister to sickle-cell anemia at the age of 30. The family had also watched their house burn down in 1989, a few days after Christmas. Andre, Addie, and the kids got out safely, but they lost everything, including the family dog, in the fire, which was caused by a leaky kerosene heater.

But even that traumatic experience didn't come close to preparing Addie for what she saw when she first walked into Adam's room at Ohio State University Medical Center.

His head was fastened to giant tongs, tubes snaked out of his body, and his bed rotated back and forth so he wouldn't get bedsores.

"Hi, Adam," Addie said softly.

"Hi, Mom," he said in a voice that was barely audible. "I'm not looking too good, am I, Mom?"

She got up and told Adam she was going to the bathroom. The tears she had been holding back streamed down her face when she got behind a closed door. She washed her face and returned to Adam's side. She gently held his hand while Andre poked his legs to see if he had feeling. He did.

Another positive sign: even though he was heavily sedated, Adam showed the same resolve that had left those Shawnee tacklers coughing on his fumes almost a year earlier. He told his mother not to worry, that he wasn't going to be crawling around for the rest of his life.

"Adam, I have no doubt. This is going to be the fight of your life. You fight like you've never fought before."

Addie would also make it the fight of her life.

Her husband may have needed to use his fists to make it out of north Philly, but Addie was also a fighter—even if she didn't look the part. A petite woman with a button nose who often wore her hair in a bun, Addie looked more like 33 than 43. She looked more like a young aunt than Adam's mother.

However, she could be a bulldog, especially when it came to her kids.

Joe Paterno and assistant coach Kenny Jackson found that out when the Taliaferros dropped Adam off at Penn State. "Kenny, you guys better treat my son fairly because your [office] is right in the woods, that window backs up right in the woods. I'll be right there with my BB gun."

Jackson laughed. "Addie, I believe that." She was half kidding, of course.

Addie got her strong will from her mother, who had worked and raised three daughters with a no-nonsense approach. Once Addie and her older sister deliberately blew off curfew to stay at a party. Their mother marched over to the party with rollers in her hair, collected her mortified daughters, and took them home.

Addie would show a similar single-mindedness when it came to Adam's recovery.

She and Andre had agreed that Adam should not be told about the long odds doctors had given for his walking again. Addie all but threatened to strangle the doctors with their stethoscopes if they told her boy he might not walk again. She also bluntly told friends not to visit if they were going to cry in front of Adam.

Not that grim news or puffy faces ever had a chance to get past Addie and Andre. From the time Adam returned to Philadelphia, at least one of them was with him all of the time except when he was sleeping.

If Addie emerged as the mother hen who fiercely guarded her son, her 47-year-old husband was seen as the eternal optimist, always exuding a confidence that Adam would walk away from this. Together, they would get Adam back on his feet.

Allen, the Eastern basketball coach, visited Adam one night at Jefferson Hospital in Philadelphia and witnessed a sobering scene. The kid who had once taken his breath away during a scrimmage—Adam had leaped high into the air to intercept a pass that had been thrown by the player he was guarding, with one hand, no less—could hardly breathe. Fluids had built up in Adam's lungs. Since he didn't have use of the muscles that are needed to cough, Andre had to frequently perform the quad-cough that doctors had showed him.

Andre patiently did this for two straight hours. The whole time he coaxed and encouraged Adam, telling him all the while that he was going to be all right.

Allen, a student of basketball, had studied coaches like John Chaney and Bobby Knight. When he left Jefferson that night he wondered if he had ever seen a finer job of coaching than what Andre was doing with Adam.

CHAPTER FIVE

Unhappy Valley

He had turned in another uninspiring performance at Ohio State, and what had been touted as a breakthrough year for Rashard Casey, the fifth-year quarterback with breathtaking physical ability, was playing out as some Edgar-Allan-Poe-meets-Stephen-King script.

Things started unraveling for the soft-spoken Casey long before Southern Cal buried Penn State, 29–5, or Toledo stunned the Nittany Lions, 24–6, the following week in Happy Valley.

The previous May, Casey had been arrested in his hometown of Hoboken, New Jersey, in connection with the beating of an off-duty cop. Allegations emerged that the altercation had been racially motivated since the police officer, who was white, had been with a black woman. It was a particularly ugly story for a football program that had long been considered one of the cleanest in college sports. Those who knew him best, including Joe Paterno, rallied to his defense as Casey maintained his innocence.

There were questions about how much the distraction of a possible felony charge would affect Casey's play, and his awful start seemed to provide a pretty good answer. He struggled so badly at times that he was pulled for at least a series in four of Penn State's first five games. Casey looked like anything but the quarterback who had Nittany Lions fans rejoicing when he signed with Penn State in 1996.

The Nittany Lions had never had a quarterback with Casey's athletic ability, and the hype that surrounded his arrival was one reason why fans were so harsh on Kevin Thompson, whom Casey shared time with but could never unseat in 1998 and 1999.

Even with the position all to himself in 2000, Casey still looked unsure of himself. At times the quarterback known for his improvisational skills looked altogether lost in Penn State's no-frills offense. Meanwhile, his flair for the spectacular play was nowhere to be found.

The latest hook had come early in the fourth quarter of the 45–6 loss at Ohio State, and the next day Casey felt as low as he ever had during his football career.

"Why am I playing this game?" Casey asked himself that repeatedly the day after the loss that dropped Penn State to 1–4. He dearly wished that his soul-searching had been caused by his on-field struggles. Unfortunately, he kept thinking back to the scream he was sure he had heard coming from Adam Taliaferro after a headfirst tackle had left the freshman cornerback unable to move at Ohio Stadium.

Like a lot of the upperclassmen, Rashard had taken an instant liking to Adam because of his infectious smile and quiet, understated ways. He had also been so impressed by what he saw from Adam during informal workouts held in the summer that he had touted him as a future star to senior safety James Boyd.

Casey had seen Adam's head snap down after tackling Jerry Westbrooks, and when Adam didn't get up, Casey figured Adam had a concussion or was just dizzy from the collision. But it didn't take much time for him and the rest of his teammates to grasp the seriousness of the situation. Before long many were kneeling and holding hands on the sidelines as they watched medical personnel work on their fallen teammate. The concern that creased Paterno's face and the stretcher and neck brace that were wheeled onto the field told them that this was like no other injury any of them had ever seen.

Boyd, a fearless hitter who had nearly tackled Westbrooks before the 231-pound Ohio State tailback crashed into Adam, had been so shaken that he all but refused to go back in the game when play resumed. "Take me out of the game," Boyd told Penn State defensive coordinator Tom Bradley. "I don't want to play anymore. Not today." Boyd was on the field in body only when Ohio State tacked on a late—and controversial—touchdown in the final minute of the game.

When the players got back to the locker room, there was no mention of their offensive woes—which had again included dropped passes and a nonexistent running game—or of the Swiss cheese run defense that had led to the most lopsided loss of the Joe Paterno era.

"Adam is hurt pretty bad," Paterno quietly told the players. "We don't know how serious it is yet."

By the time the players arrived at the airport in Columbus, they had learned the harrowing news: Adam might never walk again.

Bruce Branch, who hadn't even seen the hit, may have been the player most shaken by the news. Adam had replaced him at left cornerback. It could have been him on the wrong end of that tackle.

Casey, meanwhile, thought about the young son he had back in New Jersey. Who would take care of him if something happened to Rashard? He also thought about Adam's mother and couldn't imagine what she must be going through right now. As the team boarded the plane that would take them back to State College, Casey pulled out a cell phone and called home. He talked to his son and his mother, and told each of them that he loved them.

The next night Wayne Sebastianelli took the loneliest ride of his life. The Penn State team's doctor, with his salt-and-pepper hair, easy smile, and handsome, Italian looks, was in the plane that was taking Paterno and athletic director Tim Curley back to State College. Like them, he was trapped in his own private hell.

Adam may have been an anonymous freshman to the legions of Penn State fans who were watching the game at home and the ABC announcers who initially were not able to identify him, but Sebastianelli knew him. He had been on the opposite end of the field when the injury happened. When he realized Adam was the player lying in the unnatural position with his arms flapping in an alarming manner, Sebastianelli wanted to cry.

He rode with Adam in the ambulance to Ohio State University Medical Center. There, he made one of the hardest phone calls of his life.

When Andre Taliaferro got to Columbus that night, Sebastianelli was the one who had to break the news to him. Said Andre: "I understand what you're telling me, doc, but I know my boy. My boy is going to walk again." Sebastianelli told him to hold on to those positive thoughts. Meanwhile he did everything he could to give Adam that chance.

Shortly after Adam's arrival at the hospital, Sebastianelli had huddled with Dr. John Lombardo, Ohio State's team physician, asking, "John, if this was your son, who would you want taking care of him?"

Replied the doctor: "Gary Rea, no question." Sebastianelli quickly ceded to the Texas neurosurgeon with the long drawl. He hated leaving Adam and the Taliaferros, but he figured the last thing Rea needed was someone looking over his shoulder.

He met with Rea one last time before leaving with Paterno and Curley, asking, "Are you happy with your team? You're absolutely sure you don't need me to provide anything else?"

When the doctor assured him he had everything he needed, Sebastianelli got out of his way.

Sebastianelli had become an orthopedic surgeon because he was drawn to the idea of fixing people and making them better. As he flew back to State College with a heavy heart, he now found himself on the other end—hoping that someone else could fix the young man who had touched him like few others.

He, too, had been reduced to praying like he had never prayed before.

* * * * *

L. Budd Thalman, Penn State's associate athletic director for communications and Paterno's longtime right-hand man, helped write the first press release following Adam's injury.

The words that had been used in that release—*incomplete paralysis*—were still fresh in Thalman's mind as he drove back to State College on Sunday night. So was the other word he had heard at the hospital the previous night: *quadriplegic*. The tragic and dizzying events of the previous day had him thinking about his own children and how their lives could be dramatically altered, like Adam's had, in an instant.

Thalman met Andre Taliaferro for the first time under the worst possible circumstances. He was the one who went to the airport to pick up the father whose injured son he knew virtually nothing about.

Penn State does not include freshmen in its media guide and first-year players are off-limits to the reporters who cover Nittany Lions football. Thalman didn't even know if Adam was white or black prior to the Ohio State game, and he didn't know Adam had been hurt until after the game. With about five minutes to go in the fourth quarter, he went to the media room to get ready for Penn State's postgame press conference. He wondered why in the heck those final few minutes took so long to play.

He soon found out.

Since he had driven out to Columbus (instead of flying with the rest of the staff) because of a previous speaking engagement, Thalman volunteered to stay behind. It was decided that he would wait for Andre at the airport.

By the time Andre got to Columbus, he desperately wanted information on his son. Thalman, not wanting to speculate, gently told him to wait and talk to the doctors.

It was a helpless feeling, which is why Thalman started to feel a little bit better Monday morning as he talked to his counterpart at the University of Mississippi, Langston Rogers. In 1989, Ole Miss had also endured a tragic football injury. Chucky Mullins, a reserve defensive back, shattered his third, fourth, fifth, and sixth vertebrae while making a tackle, and he never regained feeling below his neck. Mullins eventually returned to school, but died of complications from the injury less than two years after it happened.

With calls pouring in from fans inquiring about Adam's condition and wanting to know if there was anything they could do, Thalman asked Rogers for advice. Rogers told him about the fund they had set up at Ole Miss, which had raised over $1 million for Mullins.

The Adam Taliaferro Fund, which emerged from that conversation, would help with medical costs not covered by the NCAA's catastrophic insurance, Penn State's insurance, and/or the Taliaferros' insurance. Within days of its inception, donations became as voluminous as the autumn leaves that cover State College in October.

Scores of former Penn State players, including Lenny Moore, who had starred at tailback in the fifties and then went on to have a Hall of Fame career with the Baltimore Colts, also called to see if they could help.

While the phones were ringing continuously in the sports administration offices at Penn State, the coaches were groping through that Monday. Practice had been canceled but they stayed busy fielding phone calls about Adam. More than a few callers offered advice on how to handle the current situation, including an interesting suggestion received by defensive coordinator Tom Bradley. It came from a friend of a friend; the caller told Bradley that he had been in the military and had dealt with what is called "battle fatigue." Essentially, the caller said, soldiers who were taken off the front lines of battle were put back there as soon as possible. If they stayed away too long, it would give them time to think about what they had witnessed and they might lose their nerve. There was a correlation to Penn State's situation, since the players couldn't have seen anything worse than what happened to Adam at Ohio State.

From a practical standpoint, the Nittany Lions had to get back to practice as soon as possible. They were playing nationally ranked Purdue and their Heisman Trophy candidate Drew Brees that Saturday, and Brees badly wanted to beat the Nittany Lions. For all he had done to turn around a Purdue program that had bottomed out prior to his arrival, Brees had never beaten Penn State, Ohio State, or Michigan. He would have little sympathy for the 1–4 Nittany Lions, grief-stricken or not.

With the challenge of Brees and Purdue's pass-happy offense looming just ahead and the need to get the players back to the field as soon as possible, Bradley decided he had to be strong. The phone call he had taken had convinced him of that. The players would take their lead from the coaches, Bradley thought, and he had to approach the coming days as if they were just like any other.

If only that were true.

Bradley, who answered to "Scraps"—he was given the nickname because of his hard-nosed play as a defensive back and special teams terror at Penn State in the late seventies—had called his girlfriend in tears shortly after the team returned to State College on Saturday night. Long one of Penn State's best recruiters because of his outgoing personality and ability to connect with players, Bradley may have carried around more guilt than anyone in the days following the injury. Adam usually played right cornerback behind Bhawoh Jue; but Bradley, wanting to get Adam some experience, had him play for Bruce Branch on the left side.

The responsibilities were no different at left corner than they were at right corner. Still, Bradley wondered if the change had contributed to the injury—just as Joe Paterno would second-guess himself for playing Adam on defense instead of offense. Andre Taliaferro assured Bradley that the change had not caused this tragedy: "Tom, he made that tackle a thousand times. It didn't matter where he was."

Bradley watched a replay of the tackle only once, when he was breaking down film of the Ohio State game. He vowed never to watch the hit again, and would later have the play spliced out of the tape.

When he looked around the defensive backs' meetings that week, Bradley couldn't help but notice how empty the room felt. The upperclassmen had always provided their share of laughs at those meetings. Titcus Pettigrew would tell James Boyd he wasn't allowed to talk on Thursday because he talked so much on the other days, and Bhawoh would start in on Titcus. Adam would sit in the back of the room cracking up. What Bradley would have given to see that megawatt smile now.

Somehow he kept it together that week, and with the help of seniors such as Boyd and Jue and tight end Tony Stewart, the Nittany Lions made it through that first practice on Tuesday, the day notoriously known as "Bloody Tuesdays" because of the full-scale hitting.

With Paterno's consent, Bradley crafted a risky game plan. Instead of sitting back in a zone, Penn State would go after Brees. That meant leaving its defensive backs in a lot of one-on-one coverage situations against the Big Ten's most feared passing attack.

The secondary, led by the brash Boyd, loved it.

* * * * *

While playing TV video games in his and Jue's off-campus apartment, Boyd decided he wanted to do more for Adam than just win Saturday's game. "I'm going to wear Adam's number," he announced to the gathering, which included Branch, Casey, and linebacker Eric Sturdifen. Joe will never let you do it, they told him.

In a meeting, Paterno told Boyd he'd have to wear his usual No. 6 for the game, since it wouldn't be fair to the rest of the team if he let one player wear Adam's number. "Well, get us something to put 43 on," Boyd said. So it was decided that small numerical stickers would be affixed to the back of each player's helmet.

Boyd also tried to inject some much-needed attitude into a team that had stumbled to a 1–4 start. In a story that ran in the *Centre Daily Times*—and one that surely found its way to West Lafayette, Indiana—

Boyd upped the ante for the upcoming game, talking about how he and his secondary mates looked forward to knocking Brees "off the Heisman ballot."

His words conveyed a succinct message to Brees and anyone else who doubted that the Lions could regroup in time to win one for Adam: bring it on.

* * * * *

There is a giant *S* in the middle of the floor in the Penn State locker room at Beaver Stadium, and the players have an unwritten rule that no one walks on it. When the team got back from Ohio State, players and coaches huddled around that *S* while assistant coach Larry Johnson and linebacker Shamar Finney led a prayer for Adam. One of Adam's closest friends on the team was Johnson's son Tony, a freshman wideout.

Adam's injury had added another chapter to what had been an already trying season for the elder Johnson. As if Penn State's worst start since 1964 wasn't bad enough, Johnson, whose soft voice didn't match his burly body, had been placed in a most awkward situation by another of his sons following the stunning loss to Toledo on September 2. Following that 24–6 embarrassment, tailback Larry Johnson Jr. lashed out at the coaching staff. He questioned its play calling and groused that the offense was too predictable. The beat reporters, who are usually fed a steady diet of vanilla quotes by the Nittany Lions coaches and players, lapped up Johnson's "postgame analysis." The resulting headlines and stories that his son's words generated couldn't have made reporting to work on Monday any easier for Johnson.

Of course, the team's slow start and the controversy sparked by Johnson's son hardly seemed to matter now when juxtaposed against the uncertain future that Adam and his family were facing. As with others connected with what had happened at Ohio State, Adam's injury triggered such powerful emotions for Johnson that memories of a past tragedy came spilling back into his consciousness. Back in his office, he pulled out an emotional letter he keeps in his desk. As he read it, tears rolled down his face. The letter was written to Johnson by one of his players while he was the head coach at McDonough High School in suburban Washington, D.C. The player thanked Johnson for his guidance and support. He thanked Johnson for turning him into a man. Less than a month after Johnson received that letter, the player was killed in a car accident. He was 18 years old.

The same age as Adam.

Feeling the need to do something for Adam, Johnson, who concludes his message on his answering service at work with "God bless," organized a public prayer rally. The day before Penn State's game against Purdue, thousands of students and faculty members crowded onto the plush lawn framed by trees whose leaves were just starting to change color. Players and coaches sat or stood on the granite steps of Old Main, an administration building that is the symbolic center of Penn State's sprawling campus. The scene on this sun-dappled day confirmed what Tim Curley would say during the half-hour prayer rally: "We have assured Adam that he will not walk this journey alone."

To understand the profound effect Adam's injury had on the Penn State community one need look no further than the person who sat front and center that day: Joe Paterno.

The coach was closing in on Paul "Bear" Bryant's record for all-time wins, had raised millions of dollars for the Penn State library, and commanded top dollar as a public speaker. His fame and influence were so far-reaching that in 1988 he was asked to second George Bush's nomination for president at the Republican National Convention (an honor he gladly accepted).

On this day, however, one of the most powerful and influential men in college sports hardly cut the figure of a legend. Wearing a gray suit and a somber expression, Paterno looked like a man who had been very humbled by what had happened at Ohio State. "What happens to Adam is out of our hands," Paterno said, his voice heavy with emotion. "It's in the hands of a God who is still creating miracles, a God we believe in, and a God we pray to."

Paterno's chin started quivering. "So thank you for coming."

The next day brought more gorgeous weather to State College, as well as fans who had more than just tailgating and that afternoon's game on their mind.

The normally bustling College Avenue was filled with fans wearing *43* buttons. At the Student Book Store, people lined up to sign a giant scroll of paper that SBS co-owner Norm Brown planned to send to Adam. Brown, a Penn State graduate and rabid Nittany Lions fan, was also in the process of printing stickers with Adam's *43* on them. Over the next two home games, he would distribute 13,000 and still not meet the demand.

Fred Harris, the vice principal of Adam's high school, had brought his son (Shane Conlan's namesake) up for the game; their plans to meet Adam following the game had obviously changed. Fred and Shane, wanting to show their support, went downtown to buy *43* jerseys. Fred also collected a bunch of "We Believe" signs that were being passed out in front of the Student Book Store to take back to Eastern High School.

When Fred and Shane passed a man holding an 8" x 10" photo of Adam in his Penn State uniform, Fred approached him and explained his connection to Adam. Fred wanted to incorporate a picture of Adam and the "We Believe" mantra (which was taking over State College) onto a magnet, and he asked the man if he could have one of the pictures. Sorry, the man told Harris, but it was his only one. However, after Fred and Shane bought their jerseys, they passed the man again. He called Shane over and gave him the picture.

* * * * *

On evenings before home games, Penn State sequesters its players at Toftrees Resort, a couple of miles away from campus and galaxies from the festive atmosphere that takes over sleepy State College on game weekends.

On Saturday morning at Toftrees, cornerback Bruce Branch was getting his ankles taped and watching ESPN's *Gameday*. This was usually a time of quiet reflection for the players. That changed, however, when ESPN's Kirk Herbstreit offered his analysis on the Purdue–Penn State game: he made it sound like Brees' right arm would resemble a carving knife by the time he got through with the Nittany Lions. Branch's fellow defensive backs bounded into the room shouting, "You hear that?!"

The Nittany Lions had already dedicated the game to Adam, who would watch from his bed at Thomas Jefferson University Hospital in Philadelphia. They had been galvanized by what he had said to his mother—"I'm not going out like that"—prior to surgery.

Now, the secondary had found another rallying point.

As the first quarter played out on a resplendent autumn day, no one's play was more inspired than safety James Boyd's. He planted his facemask in Brees' sternum after one safety blitz and knocked the All-American quarterback down on another blitz up the middle. He stuffed a Boilermakers running back a yard behind the line of scrimmage and seemed to be around every pass in the secondary.

Boyd's ball hawking set the tone for a defense that harassed Brees into a slow start. Brees connected on just 4 of his first 14 passes; by halftime the Boilermakers' fun-and-gun offense had only matched the two field goals that Penn State had produced in the first half.

The Boilermakers wasted little time in getting into the end zone in the third quarter. Casey, coming off his best half of the season, was intercepted near midfield on Penn State's first possession of the second half. Two Brees completions and a trick play led to a touchdown and a 13–6 Purdue lead.

Inspired as Penn State had been by the constant reminders that they were playing for Adam—including the *43* buttons, which were so pervasive that even ABC announcer Brad Nessler wore one, and the signs hanging like curtains in Beaver Stadium—this was precisely the point where the air could have started leaking out of a team that had endured a disastrous start to the season. That's when the embattled Casey turned in a few of those highlight-reel plays that had been mysteriously absent from his repertoire. He scrambled for a key first down and then sandwiched another long run around a pass-interference call on Purdue.

With the Lions just outside of Purdue's 30-yard line, Casey faked a handoff to the fullback and made a quick pitch to tailback Eric McCoo. McCoo scooted down the right sidelines; at the 10-yard line he jolted a Boilermakers defensive back after lowering his shoulder. He was finally forced out at the 2-yard line.

Penn State had to settle for a short Ryan Primanti field goal, but the team had answered Purdue and set the stage for the two plays that would turn the game. They had also bolstered the idea that the Nittany Lions were somehow meant to win this game for Adam.

Before his injury, Adam had been a regular on the kick coverage team, lining up next to fellow freshman Derek Wake. Adam and Derek (D Wake to his classmates) had emerged on defense as the most promising newcomers. They raced to the top of their class, which was fitting since they always raced each other down the field on kickoffs. Oh, how Adam used to laugh while watching D Wake get leveled by an enemy blocker.

Now it was D Wake's turn—to level Brees' goal of beating the Nittany Lions. Coming straight up the middle on a Purdue punt midway through the third quarter, Wake reached Travis Dorsch so quickly that the Purdue punter had time only to tuck the ball in and assume the fetal position. He was smothered at Purdue's 11-yard line. A couple of plays later, another of Adam's classmates, Paul Jefferson, had a one-yard touchdown run that gave Penn State a 15–13 lead.

Wake and Penn State's special teams weren't finished yet. After Brees and Purdue went three-and-out, Wake came barging up the middle. This time Dorsch was swarmed under at his own 6-yard line. Casey scored on a two-yard run on the final play of the quarter to give the Nittany Lions a 22–13 lead.

As the shadows lengthened over Beaver Stadium, Brees stayed calm and cool. Vinny Sutherland turned what looked like a harmless flat pass into a 40-yard catch-and-run touchdown with 11 minutes, 30 seconds to play, and Penn State would spend the rest of the game hanging on for dear life. The offense couldn't do much, and the Boilermakers, facing a 22–20 deficit, mounted a late drive that reached Penn State's 29. After the offense stalled, Purdue called on Dorsch to give them the lead with a 46-yard field goal. His afternoon of misery continued as his kick hooked just to the left of the goal posts.

Penn State took over with 2:25 to play, got a quick first down, and forced Purdue to use all three remaining timeouts. The Nittany Lions ultimately had to punt; they pinned Purdue at its own 5-yard line with 1:23 left in the game.

Brees kept the Boilermakers alive with a clutch fourth-down completion; then he nearly killed the drive on the very next play. His pass sailed over the head of its intended target and landed right in the lap of Titcus Pettigrew. But Pettigrew, who had arrived at Penn State as one of the most heralded wide receiver recruits in the county, couldn't hang on to the ball. On the Penn State sidelines, Joe Paterno bent over, looking like he might lose the hot dog that he always eats at halftime.

Brees took advantage of the reprieve and moved the Boilermakers into Penn State territory. A pass that would have put Purdue in field-goal range was defended by Boyd, and with less than five seconds to play Brees would have to try a "Hail Mary." Normally, these passes don't inspire much fear. The previous year, however, Minnesota had completed a fourth-down desperation throw in the same stadium. That led to a last-second field goal that knocked the Nittany Lions from their No. 1 ranking and sent them into a tailspin from which they had yet to recover.

This will not be another Minnesota, Boyd told himself in the huddle. Sure enough, as Brees' final pass descended on the sea of bodies in the right corner of the end zone, Boyd leapt high and batted it to the turf.

Given the circumstances, the win was one of the greatest in Penn State history. It was easily its most cathartic victory.

Lynn Swann, an ABC sideline reporter, grabbed Paterno for a postgame interview. The coach struggled to keep his composure: "Adam, if you're out there, we're still praying, kid. We're praying for you."

Following the emotional win, Casey dedicated the game ball he had been awarded to Adam, and the exhausted members of the secondary sounded off about the "field day" Herbstreit had predicted Brees would have with them. Boyd, who had the strongest pregame comments, made some strong postgame ones as well, saying he'd tell Herbstreit what he thought of his prognostication skills if he ever saw him.

That evidently got back to Herbstreit, who called defensive coordinator Tom Bradley a few days later. "Coach, they took that the wrong way," Herbstreit said. "You know I wasn't being critical after all you have been through." Bradley, who hadn't been aware of Herbstreit's comments, liked the former Ohio State quarterback and believed him. Bradley assured Herbstreit he hadn't taken any offense at the comments. After hanging up the phone, Bradley wondered if he should have asked Herbstreit if he could do that every week.

* * * * *

If the scene taking place after the Penn State–Purdue game inside of Coasters, a sports bar in the coastal Florida city of Melbourne, was any indication, Penn Staters everywhere were thinking of Adam.

Prior to the game, a raffle had been held with all proceeds going to the Adam Taliaferro Fund. Members of the Space Coast chapter of the Penn State Alumni Association also signed a large card that would be sent to Adam.

After Brees' final pass fell harmlessly to the turf, Penn State fans exhaled, exchanged high fives, and raised their glasses. That's when the chant started: "Adam! Adam! Adam!"

It didn't seem to matter one bit that Adam Taliaferro had never even heard of Melbourne, Florida.

* * * * *

A little more than a week later, Bradley visited Adam for the first time at Magee Rehabilitation Hospital in Philadelphia. He gave Adam the hat he had worn for the Purdue game. He had taped *AT 43* over the *PS* that was on the front of the hat.

After looking it over, Adam said he knew it was the hat Bradley had worn during the game because there was some dirt on it. Bradley looked at him quizzically. "I know this is the real one," Adam said, "because I know you must have thrown this at Titcus about 10 times after he dropped that interception."

CHAPTER SIX

Doctors' Dilemma: Hope or False Hope

Jen Greenberg considered traveling to Ohio to be with Adam after he was injured, but decided to stay in New Jersey because she didn't want to be in the way. Besides, she didn't know if she could be strong enough to put on a "happy face" for her boyfriend.

She was constantly on the phone with Adam's parents. The day after the injury, Addie called from the hospital and said Adam wanted to speak with her. Addie did some coaching. "You have to be calm, Jen. And don't cry. He needs to hear your voice and you have to be strong."

When she talked with Adam, Jen tried to be stoic. But it was more difficult than she had imagined.

"Adam, I'm really sorry it happened to you."

"Why are you sorry?" said Adam, who was heavily medicated.

"I'm sorry I can't be there with you," she said. "I love you." Jen started crying. So did Adam.

Addie, agitated that her coaching had failed, got on the phone. "Jen, you're both crying and it's not a good idea to talk right now."

Jen continued to sob loudly. "Tell him I love him," she told Addie. "Tell him I love him."

Four days later, on the second day after Adam was transported to Thomas Jefferson University Hospital in Philadelphia, Jen met with Adam for the first time in two months. She didn't have a car at Rutgers, so her dad picked her up and made the 58-mile trip from the central Jersey campus to the Philadelphia hospital.

Jen could feel her body shaking nervously during the entire ride. She brought a huge teddy bear to the hospital as a get-well present for Adam. At the information desk she said, "I'm here to see Scott Jones," using Adam's alias.

The woman behind the counter seemed surprised. "How did you get that name?" she asked.

"I'm his girlfriend. I talked to his dad and he gave it to me."

The woman gave Jen the room number. Jen and her dad took the elevator. They waited nearly 10 minutes before going into the room. It took Jen that long to compose herself and feel ready. Addie had told Jen that she needed to be stronger than she was on the phone. "He can see by the look in your eyes how bad he is," Addie had told her. "Let him see on your face how good he looks."

Adam had been having an exhausting day. Earlier that morning, as a nurse was using a suction catheter to remove secretions from his mouth and a physician was changing one of his IV access lines to his chest, Adam needed comfort. He looked up with those big doe eyes and asked one of the nurses for a favor: "Please hold my hand," he said.

Geri Zelazny complied.

"Adam, can you squeeze my hand?" she asked. He couldn't.

"Can you feel my hand?" He could.

"Do you feel it the same way that you used to?"

"No."

A few hours later, Jen took a deep breath and walked into Adam's hospital room with the dark brown teddy bear. Her dad was close behind.

Jen was so happy to see Adam that she forgot about being scared. She was overjoyed that Adam, the young man she had been dating for the past 13 months, was finally in front of her. "Hi!" she said sweetly.

Adam, still heavily medicated, flashed a wide grin.

"I got this for you," she said, displaying the teddy bear.

Adam, unable to move, looked like he had been through combat. He was wearing an oxygen mask that was helping him breathe. He had a tube in his nose and a brace around his neck. He looked glassy-eyed and tired.

"Hey, baby," Jen said.

"Hey, Jen. What's going on?" Adam's body was full of drugs, but he still had that unmistakable charm, Jen thought. His body may have changed, but his personality hasn't.

Jen and Adam had been dating since the month before their senior year in high school. They were a stunning couple. He was a star athlete with a gracious personality, strikingly handsome looks, and a superior grade point average. She was a head-turning blonde who had brains to match her beauty. She had been a member of her high school student council and was such an achiever that she was embarrassed by what she thought was a horrible SAT score, even though she had scored an impressive 1,100.

Adam was different from most guys, Jen said. It wasn't just his great athletic ability. It was his quiet sense of humor. It was the way he frequently broke into rap songs (some that he made up to make her laugh, some that he copied) when he phoned her. It was the way they could talk for hours and not get bored with each other.

Several of her family members, including her dad and her brother, had attended Penn State and were big Nittany Lion football fans. So, yes, Penn State was a central topic of their conversations.

"We just connected," Jen said.

As Jen walked gingerly into Adam's hospital room that day, she wanted to hug him. She resisted. She was afraid to touch him, afraid to hurt him. She gently rubbed his arm and glanced at his legs, hoping they would move. He was wearing a gown and socks and was lying flat.

Addie and Andre were in the room, making sure Jen didn't break down. They didn't want any negatives to filter into their son's mind, didn't want him to see anyone crying. Jen returned to her South Jersey home that night and, the next morning, her dad dropped her back at the hospital.

This time, when she walked into the room, Adam was by himself. Jen clutched his hand and talked to Adam. He was in a deep sleep and didn't hear her soothing words. She stroked his forehead. "I love you, baby."

She held his hand gently and began crying. Just then, Addie and Andre walked into the room. Addie tried to console Jen and took her into the hallway as Adam continued sleeping. "We have to be strong for him, Jen," Addie said. But in a few seconds, Addie was crying, too. Addie and Jen needed to share this moment together, needed to cry together.

They walked back into the room, where Adam was groggy but starting to wake up. He was still pretty much out of it, and Jen was in a daze.

Jen saw Adam's left leg appear to twitch later that day. A few hours later, it happened again, this time with Andre in the room. "Did you see that?" Andre asked Jen.

The twitch may have been an involuntary movement, doctors said. No one knew. All anyone knew was that Adam still did not have any controlled movements, and his parents were being told that he would spend his life in a wheelchair.

* * * * *

Dr. Alexander Vaccaro, professor of spine surgery at Jefferson Hospital, had been a two-way football player at his north Jersey high school in the late seventies. In the fourth game of his senior year, however, he tore the anterior-cruciate ligament in his right knee and needed surgery. Until then, he had hoped to play football in college. He turned to baseball at Boston College, but his knee was too unstable and didn't hold up. Vaccaro shifted his focus to medicine.

Some at the hospital refer to the 39-year-old Vaccaro as a George Clooney look-alike. He has dark hair with a hint of salt-and-pepper coloring, and a likeable, confident but not stuffy air about him. He deeply cares for his patients and goes out of his way to make them feel at ease. To him, a doctor's bedside manner is just as important as his or her expertise. You can teach somebody how to operate, teach medical facts. But Vaccaro wants doctors who are sensitive, empathetic, and caring as well—especially in his specialized field, in which they deal with so many people who may be spending the rest of their lives as quadriplegics. These are devastated families whose lives were changed in a split second. Vaccaro takes pride in easing these families' concerns, in letting them know that he has dealt with similar injuries and that, even though their loved one may not be moving his or her legs, they could still be OK.

When Vaccaro examined Adam early on September 27, the day after he arrived at Jefferson Hospital, he administered a pinprick test: he took a pin and touched different parts of Adam's body. A blanket was used to shield Adam from what the doctor was doing. This enabled Vaccaro to "fake out" Adam on occasion, pretending that he had stuck him and asking how it felt.

"Feel that?" asked Vaccaro as the pin pricked Adam's ankle.

"Yes."

"And that?"

"Yes," said Adam as the doctor pierced his thigh.

"And that?"

"No. I don't feel it."

That was the answer Vaccaro wanted. He had faked that last pinprick. He had not stuck him, but wanted to see how Adam would respond.

What happens, Vaccaro said, is that the patients want to say "yes" to everything, and they'll say "yes" even if you don't stick them. "And they fail the test because you realize they don't have the sensation," he said. Adam passed this test and, to Vaccaro, this meant he had a good chance to walk.

He did not share the news with Adam, however. He wanted to wait until he did another test. Two days later, Vaccaro again did a pinprick exam. Again, Adam passed. Vaccaro, sensing that Adam was dejected, explained what it meant.

Vaccaro told Taliaferro, whose grandmother was in the room at the time, that he thought he had between a 75 and 85 percent chance to walk. He was the first doctor to make such a projection.

Andre cried joyously when he heard the news later that day. "I told you son! I knew you were going to make it!"

Later that afternoon, Dr. Anthony Burns came into the room and did a similar test on Adam. This time, just like when Burns had administered tests earlier in the week, Adam did *not* get the pinprick sensation that he had demonstrated in the morning. Maybe it was a function of neurological fatigue that prevented him from having the sensation again. Maybe he had the sensation in the morning because it was early and he had more energy at that time and was more perceptive. Or maybe he wouldn't ever feel the sensation again. There was no way of knowing.

But before Vaccaro learned about Burns' negative finding, he received a phone call from Dr. Sebastianelli at Penn State. Vaccaro was driving home from the hospital when he received the call on his cell phone. Sebastianelli was preparing for his medical duties at that afternoon's Penn State–Purdue game. "I think he's going to walk again," Vaccaro told him. The Penn State doctor was stunned . . . and joy-struck.

Vaccaro was thrilled to share the news, but his happiness was short-lived. He got home, went out to his patio, and was working on a research paper when he received a phone call from Dr. Burns, his associate at Jefferson. "I really think your exam was incorrect," Burns said. "I don't think he had pinprick."

It's not unusual for doctors to disagree, but Vaccaro did think that Burns' next response was unusual: "I think I'm going to have to call the Penn State doctor and tell him you were wrong," he said. Embarrassed, Vaccaro rolled his eyes. He told Burns he didn't think that was necessary, that he stood by his examination.

Burns disagreed and said he would call Sebastianelli.

"Whatever," Vaccaro said. "Whatever you want to do."

Vaccaro was a professor and codirector of the Delaware Valley Regional Spinal-Cord Injury Center. He was sort of the "captain" of Adam's ship at Jefferson, he said, and ranked above Burns. But Burns was Adam's rehab doctor and felt a sense of obligation to call Sebastianelli. This was a high-profile case and he wanted to make sure accurate information was being released.

Vaccaro, though frustrated, seemed more amused than annoyed by Burns' reaction. He turned to his wife and explained the situation: "I have a doctor calling another doctor, saying my exam is wrong," he said. He shook his head and smiled softly. "What are you going to do?"

Meanwhile, Sebastianelli had already shared Vaccaro's positive findings with Joe Paterno before the team's Adam-inspired upset of Purdue that afternoon. "Nothing is guaranteed," he told the veteran coach, "but this puts it into a whole new prognostication category."

A few hours later, just before the start of the game, ABC's Lynn Swann did a live on-the-field interview with Sebastianelli and asked him about Adam's progress. Sebastianelli told him that he had received great news from Dr. Vaccaro and Dr. Burns in the morning and that the outlook was better but that they still wouldn't know for about a year. Little did Sebastianelli know that, at about the same time he was sharing this positive news on national TV, Burns was telling Vaccaro that he did not think Adam had pinprick sensation.

After Penn State's emotional 22–20 victory that afternoon, Sebastianelli was finishing his work in the team's new on-campus football building when his beeper went off. It was Dr. Burns. Once Sebastianelli reached him, Burns explained that he disagreed with Vaccaro's pinprick assessment.

The Penn State physician was now in an uncomfortable position: he was in the middle of a disagreement between two other doctors. He tried not to pick sides. He told Burns he didn't plan to retract the statement he had made on national TV. "I respect both of your opinions," he said, "but you know as much as I do that his exam can change from one hour to the next. There are too many ups and downs. Let's just see how this thing pans out."

Being an orthopedic surgeon like Vaccaro, Sebastianelli knew which assessment he thought was accurate—or at least which assessment he *wanted* to believe. But he didn't tell Burns. He really didn't want to add fuel to the conflict. All he wanted, like everyone else involved, was for Adam to get better.

Vaccaro stood by his findings but, at the same time, realized it had been a mistake to share the information with Adam and his family. In this case, it was his job to handle any surgery if it was needed and to confer with Burns on Adam's case. It was Burns' job, as the rehab doctor, to work on the neurological prognostication and the counseling and rehabilitation of the patient. "So it's really the rehab doctor's role to counsel the patient as to the prognosis," Vaccaro said. "And the surgeons stay out of it . . . but I got caught up in the moment."

He also got caught up in Adam's charm. "He's got a special smile that looks like he's enjoying everybody and he makes you feel good," Vaccaro said. "He's the one who's paralyzed, he's lying in bed, but you actually feel good when you talk to him. He never became the victim of this thing. He became the guy who was always saying, 'Thank you,' and had a 'how-can-I-make-you-feel-better?' attitude."

On that day, Vaccaro wanted to make *Adam* feel better. "The kid was definitely bummed. He's paralyzed and can't move his legs. And that was a very positive finding in my examination and I shared it with him. I said, 'Listen, there's hope.'"

But Burns thought it might be false hope.

* * * * *

There is a thin line between hope and false hope. Burns wanted Adam and his family to believe that recovery was possible but, at the same time, he didn't want to give them any unrealistic expectations. It was a difficult juggling act.

"If you paint an overly optimistic picture," he said, "then people often times will have some resentment if it doesn't occur." In diagnosing cases, Burns tries to deal strictly with facts based on similar patients and what has been reported in medical literature, and not with emotions.

Burns was reporting that Adam's pinprick test was "not definitive." For whatever reason (perhaps the medication or the fatigue factor), Adam did not demonstrate the same sensation for Burns that he had for Vaccaro. That made it difficult to assess his chances.

It also made it difficult for Adam's parents to feel a bond with Burns. A conflict was developing and it would escalate in the upcoming days.

Meanwhile, though his condition was filled with uncertainties, Adam still kept his perpetual smile for relatives, friends, and the medical staff. Mae Taliaferro, Adam's grandmother, sat by his hospital bed almost every day and marveled at his optimism. He reminded her of her daughter, Phyllis, who died of sickle-cell anemia in 1978. Adam and Phyllis were from the same mold: strong, courageous, and determined. Phyllis might be in a crisis, needing a blood transfusion, but she would bounce back and, while lying in her hospital bed, would ask her mom to get her a newspaper. She would scan the want ads to look for a job, determined to make a contribution to society when she left the hospital. No matter what health problems she was enduring, Phyllis never complained. Neither did Adam. "Even if he had a bad day, he would always say, 'I'm doing all right, Grandmom,'" Mae said. "He never seemed depressed. He always took it in stride. I never saw him cry."

Adam was putting up a brave front for his grandmother. For everyone, really. He still couldn't move and his days seemed to be interminably long. But during the rare times when his spirits started to sag, there was always a friend or a relative to lift them.

Sometimes even strangers could be comforting. One such person was Paul Tighe. Tighe had learned to walk again after sustaining a broken neck while diving into a swimming pool in 1996. He was just the type of person Andre wanted Adam to meet. He was someone who had gotten out of a wheelchair, although the doctors had initially told his wife that he would be a paraplegic for the rest of his life.

Dan Spittal, one of Adam's assistant football coaches at Eastern High, had put the Taliaferros in contact with Tighe. Spittal's son played Little League baseball for a team coached by Tighe's brother-in-law.

Tighe was in a wheelchair for the first five months after his injury; then he was able to use elbow crutches and, finally, a cane. About six months after his injury, he was walking and back to work. Now he was running his own hardwood flooring business, playing in a men's ice hockey league, and helping his wife raise their two young daughters.

Tighe and Andre talked on the phone, and then Tighe visited Adam at Jefferson Hospital. Coincidentally, he visited the same day Adam had demonstrated his breakthrough movement. When Tighe was there, Adam briefly moved his left leg. And even though he couldn't always move the leg on command, Tighe wasn't concerned.

"Relax. It takes time," Tighe told him. "You're way ahead of where I was. It's trying to come back, trying to get the signals from the brain to the leg. It's probably just fatigued." Tighe explained that it took six weeks before he had any movement after his injury. Adam had movement within eight days of his ill-fated tackle at Ohio State.

In private, the 33-year-old Tighe told Andre not to listen to some of the doctors' negativity. He explained to Andre that doctors had painted a bleak picture in his case, too. "Don't listen to anything the doctors say, because they wrote me off from day one," he told Andre.

Andre was a captive listener. "They don't want to give you false hope because if you don't walk, they can come back and say 'You told me I was going to walk.' They stay neutral so no one gets misled." Andre nodded.

"The doctors don't know," Tighe said. "Everybody is different. The spinal cord is so complex that no one can figure out what I can do. No disrespect to the doctors, but if I went by what they said, who knows where I'd be. Stay positive and let time work things out."

That same day, Tighe took Andre down the street to the Magee Rehabilitation Hospital, which combines with Jefferson Hospital to form the Regional Spinal-Cord Injury Center of the Delaware Valley. Tighe had spent three months in Magee during his rehabilitation. He showed Andre around Magee's gym and introduced him to his doctor, William Staas, and some of the other staff members. He recommended his two therapists, Marygrace Mangine and Amy Bratta.

Andre was still undecided about where to send Adam to do his rehabilitation work, but he was leaning toward Magee. Tighe, who had spent the first 17 days after his injury at a Camden, New Jersey, hospital, was making Andre's decision easier. He told Andre that, before he went to Magee, he had done lots of research. He told Andre that Magee "did wonders for me" and that Adam shouldn't waste his time anywhere else. "It's not a miracle hospital," he explained to Andre, "but it gives you every opportunity to adapt." And if you get any movement or feeling back, he said, "they work you to the fullest to get it out of you."

Andre, aware that his son was close to being moved to a rehab center, was sold on the idea.

* * * * *

Toward the end of Adam's nine-day stay at Jefferson Hospital, Andre and Addie felt that they were in their *second* conflict with Dr. Burns. This conflict centered around whether Adam could move his toes or leg. Burns still had not observed it. Trish, the nurse, had. So had another nurse and a doctor, along with Andre and the Rev. Khan. But, after having moved again later that day, Adam couldn't generate any movement for the next three days.

Andre was starting to doubt what he had witnessed. "Tell me the truth" he asked the Rev. Khan. "Did Adam really move or was I seeing things? Tell me what you saw."

"He moved, Andre," the pastor said. "He definitely moved."

Some doctors were telling Andre that Adam's quest for movement was like a battery-operated toy with old batteries in it. The toy moves a bit, then stops. When the battery recharges, the toy moves again. The hope was that Adam would regain function, that the nerve impulses from his brain would transmit to the rest of his body.

That was the hope, anyway.

Adam had moved a little for Tighe when he had visited, but that seemed like years ago. Actually, only three days had passed. During that time, Adam was unable to get any movement from his leg or toes. Addie would spend all day staring at Adam's big left toe, the one that had moved a few days earlier but was now dormant. She was trying to "will" it to move.

Adam got excited; he felt the toe flicker. "It's moving, Mom," he said. "Look at it."

Addie stared intently at the toe. As much as she wanted it to move, she hadn't seen it. But she didn't want to crush her son's spirits, didn't want to tell him she hadn't seen a movement, or even a flicker. "That's great," she said. "You're doing great, son."

Early in the morning on October 6, Adam's last day at Jefferson before being transferred to Magee, Geri Zelazny observed him slowly wiggle his left big toe. He had also done it the previous day, for the first time in three days. But this was the first time Zelazny, one of the many nurses who had grown fond of Adam, had ever seen it move and, knowing that Dr. Burns had not observed the movement yet, she excitedly gave her patient some instructions: "I don't care who tells you to move it. Don't do it," she said. "Tell them you have to wait for Dr. Burns." She didn't want him to get fatigued and not be able to move it for a while. "Save it for Dr. Burns."

Burns entered the room later that morning and, finally, four days after his initial movement, Adam was able to barely wiggle his left big toe. Andre's deep, distinctive voice grew louder and louder as he questioned the doctor. "Do you see it, Dr. Burns?! Do you see it?! He's moving his toe!"

Dr. Burns smiled. "He's moving his toe," the doctor agreed.

Andre threw his arms around the doctor. He had seen it! He had seen Adam move his toe!

Because he had observed the movement, Dr. Burns would place Adam into a new spinal-injury classification and his prognosis would be upgraded. What this did, said Zelazny, who besides being a registered nurse was the clinical coordinator for the Regional Spinal-Cord Injury Center of the Delaware Valley, was give Adam a chance to walk. Nothing more.

At about the same time that Adam was able to wiggle one of his toes, Burns observed some pinprick sensation. In his October 6 hospital notes, Burns wrote that Adam had shown "spectacular improvement." The odds that Adam would ever walk again, which Dr. Sebastianelli had originally placed at 3-in-100, were starting to be adjusted. Adam was transferred from Jefferson to Magee, two hospitals that form one of the 16 regional spinal-cord injury centers in the nation.

"Now," Sebastianelli said, "is when his real work begins."

Magee would be Adam's home for the next three months. Magee would be where he would have a Christmas tree in his room, where people from around the world would send thousands of get-well cards and letters. Magee was where Adam would try to get out of a hospital bed, out of a wheelchair. "You need all the strength you've got, because when you get to Magee," Tighe told Adam, "the fun and games are over."

Fun and games? He was lying in a hospital bed, virtually paralyzed, and using a catheter to urinate. Someone had to wash him. Someone had to feed him. Someone had to lift him into a bedpan when he had a bowel movement. When he was in bed, he stared at the ceiling, bored out of his mind. Adam wondered how this could be considered "fun and games," wondered what was ahead.

He was still facing the fight of his life.

CHAPTER SEVEN

Hellfires of 2000

In Joe Paterno's autobiography, *Paterno: By the Book*, there is a chapter titled "The Hellfires of '88," in which he writes in detail about his only losing season as a head coach.

The season had actually taken a disastrous turn long before Penn State's opener. Tailback Blair Thomas blew out his knee during a December 1987 practice for Penn State's Citrus Bowl game against Clemson. Thomas, who Paterno believed would have been the Heisman Trophy frontrunner in 1988, didn't return until 1989.

After a 2–0 start, Penn State absorbed another devastating blow when starting quarterback Tom Bill dislocated his kneecap against Rutgers. With his second- and third-string quarterbacks out with injuries, Paterno turned to true freshman Tony Sacca. Sacca, not ready for the pressure of college football, would take most of the snaps the rest of the season, and the Nittany Lions would lose five out of their last six games.

There was much hand-wringing during that 5–6 season, and much soul-searching done by Paterno after it. "The Hellfires of '88" infringed on his sleep many a night as Paterno reevaluated every aspect of the program and conducted a meticulous audit on his own job performance.

As Penn State's 2000 season lurched toward the midway point, "the Hellfires of '88" now seemed like a small brushfire by comparison. The Nittany Lions had lost four of their first five games, and what seemed like a foregone conclusion heading into the season—Paterno getting the seven victories he needed to break Paul "Bear" Bryant's record for all-time wins—was looking more like a long shot. He had been criticized for his play calling by one of his own players (along with the fans, who grumble annually that Paterno calls plays with the same conservative bent in which he votes), and his integrity had been called into question.

As in 1988, an ominous harbinger arrived before the season in the form of quarterback Rashard Casey's arrest in May. After meeting with Casey, Paterno declared that his status as the starting quarterback had not changed. "*Et tu?*" screamed newspaper columnists and college football fans alike. Paterno, long hailed as a coach who won the right way in the all-too-Machiavellian world of college football, had seemingly compromised his principles for victories. To those who roasted Paterno, it seemed too much of a coincidence that the player he firmly backed held the key to Penn State's season.

Of course, Adam's injury turned the controversy over Casey and the worst start of the Paterno era into mere footnotes.

Sue Paterno, the coach's wife, was watching the Ohio State game back in Pennsylvania when Adam was injured. She got a bad feeling when she saw the unnatural way in which Adam's body was contorted on the field. The look on her husband's face confirmed for her that something had gone terribly wrong in the same stadium where 25 years earlier she herself had taken a life-altering spill. In the hours following the game, she was an emotional wreck. Even the presence of her grandchildren, on whom she doted, failed to soothe her.

Joe does not carry a cell phone, so Sue couldn't call him in Ohio to find out about Adam's condition. He didn't return home until long after darkness had fallen—about a half an hour after a nearly frantic Sue had called nearby University Park Airport to see if the plane had landed. When Joe entered the house from the garage, Sue's anxious eyes locked onto his ashen face.

"How . . . " she said.

Tears streamed down his cheeks. "I don't think he's going to walk."

* * * * *

In 1975, Sue Paterno was accidentally knocked down by a fan during a Penn State–Ohio State game at Ohio Stadium. The fall would leave her with two blown out disks and back problems that would last for the rest of her life. But her mind had been such a blank in the aftermath of Adam's injury that it wasn't until a few days later that it registered with her that Ohio Stadium had been the site of her injury, too. "I was wondering when you were going to connect," Joe said.

The overwhelming guilt that consumed the Paternos over the next couple of days always led Sue back to one haunting thought: the Taliaferros had given Penn State their healthy young son and Penn State had returned his broken body on a stretcher. She told Joe that she couldn't take it anymore, that she wanted him to get out of coaching.

Joe spent most of his nights that week in the solitude of his home office. He didn't sleep much, grabbing winks here and there on his beige La-Z-Boy chair. Sue's pleas didn't entirely fall on deaf ears. When he got emotional thinking about Adam, Joe wondered if maybe he should step down.

The experience was easily Paterno's worst in the 60 years he had been involved with football. Nothing, he said, compared to it.

It hadn't taken him long to figure out that the hit Adam put on Ohio State tailback Jerry Westbrooks was unlike any other tackle in Penn State history. The sense of urgency with which the medical personnel were already working when Joe went on the field offered the first clue. Then there were Adam's eyes. They were filled with such fear; Adam was in big trouble and he knew it. When Joe turned away from Dr. Sebastianelli, who was firmly telling Adam not to move, he kicked the air in anger.

When Paterno looked at Adam, his mind raced back to October 14, 1977. That was the day he walked into an elementary school gym and saw his 11-year-old son David lying motionless on a concrete floor. In the aftermath of Adam's injury, Joe and Sue Paterno would not only wrestle with feelings of guilt. They would also revisit that horrible time when they had almost lost their own son.

* * * * *

The van had been purring along Route 80 on an autumn Friday afternoon. It was filled with the wives of the Penn State football coaches, who were traveling to Syracuse, New York, for Saturday's game.

The light atmosphere that prevailed in the van quickly changed when a Pennsylvania state police car pulled alongside it. "Follow me," an officer said through a megaphone. "I have an emergency message."

Sue Paterno quickly deduced that the message had to be for her. The wives had initially started the trip in a different vehicle, but shortly after they left town, Sue's back started bothering her. She was still in a brace from the surgery that she had undergone in the spring of 1976. When her back started giving her trouble on the opening leg of a drive that took around five and a half hours, she suggested they go back to the Paterno house and get their van. Now, as she and the other terrified women sped toward the news none of them wanted to receive, it dawned on Sue that Joe was the only coach who knew that they had changed vehicles. He was the only one who could have told the police that they were traveling in a sky blue Dodge van.

Like the other mothers in the van, Sue had started doing the accounting in her head right after the police officer had instructed the van to follow him. She figured out where each child was supposed to be that day. Only one of her five kids was not following the regular routine.

And when the van pulled into the police barracks, Sue said, "It's David." He had planned to go to a friend's house after school, and Sue figured something had happened there.

When she called Joe, she learned that a tragic accident had actually happened at school. David and a couple of other students had been sent to the gym to fetch some audiovisual equipment. Sixth-grade boys being sixth-grade boys, they couldn't resist taking a few turns on the trampoline that rested on the stage, even though they had been ordered to stay off it. As they were bouncing up and down, David decided he was going to try to jump through the small opening in the curtain that stretched across the stage. The fact that the drop from the stage to the floor was 15 feet didn't scare David.

Then again, nothing ever did.

He had been jumping off the 10-meter dive at the outdoor swimming pool on Penn State's campus since he was seven years old, and he never shied away from playing tackle football with older kids in the neighborhood. A dog once bit the left side of his face, and the doctor needed 35 stitches to close the wound. His mother fainted as the doctor worked on him, but David didn't cry once. Instead, he kept asking how many more stitches he would need, his excited tone suggesting that the higher the count, the better story he would have to tell at school.

Now, as he jumped toward the narrow slit in the stage, he presumably wanted something else to tell the other kids. Unfortunately, his foot got caught in one of the curtains, and he landed on his head.

Joe had taken his youngest son, Scott, to lunch in town that day, and he had just returned home when he got the call telling him to get to Our Lady of Victory School right away. By the time he got to the gym, paramedics were working frantically on David. Joe rode in the ambulance with him to Centre Community Hospital, which sits in the shadow of Beaver Stadium, and then to Geisinger Hospital, which is about 100 miles east of State College.

When Sue finally got in touch with Joe, the doctors still weren't sure if David would make it or what kind of life he would have if he did pull through. "Just hurry," Joe said over the phone. "We might not have much time."

Sue's knees buckled and her eyes rolled. She dropped to the floor in a heap.

* * * * *

Can't you drive faster?

That was all Sue Paterno could think as they sped toward Geisinger.

The other wives had continued on to Syracuse in the Paternos' van while a state police officer drove Sue to the hospital. A ride that would have been unbearable for any mother who had just learned that one of her babies was near death seemed even longer for Sue. Her watch broke when she fainted, and the hands on the watch were moving faster than usual. Still woozy from the fall and in shock from the news her husband had given her, Sue didn't realize it was broken.

Can't you drive faster?

When they arrived at Geisinger, Sue hurried into an elevator and somehow pushed the button to the floor David was on even though no one had told her where he was. When she got off the elevator she could hear David moaning, and she followed that sound to her son.

David slipped into a coma that night, and the next morning the swelling around his brain was still such a concern to doctors that Joe canceled the chartered plane that was waiting to take him to Syracuse. He sent word to assistant coaches Bob Phillips and Jerry Sandusky that they should handle the game. Penn State beat the Orangemen, 31–24, that day, but Paterno's focus was on getting a far bigger win.

It came the following Saturday when 11-year-old David emerged from his coma on the day of his younger brother Jay's ninth birthday. After opening his eyes, David looked around at his surroundings in the ICU and said through the tracheotomy tube doctors had put in his throat, "I need your prayers."

About an hour later he demonstrated more cognitive skills when Sue pointed to the current day on the calendar that hung near his bed, and David said, "Jay's birthday." David had given him the best birthday present of all said Jay, now a Penn State assistant coach.

David never suffered any long-term effects from the injury that nearly claimed his life, although doctors forbid him from ever playing football. He went on to earn an undergraduate degree in engineering and then a master's from Penn State and currently lives in State College with his wife and two young daughters.

He doesn't remember much about the accident, but the details are still etched in his mother's mind. The date of his accident is still a hard day for Sue. It makes her so uneasy that when David was living in Texas, he would never fly on October 14 because he knew how nervous it would make his mother. If he had to go somewhere on business, he would leave a day early and call Sue the next day. "Everything's fine. I'm not traveling," David would tell his mother. "I know where the Catholic Church is, I'll walk to Mass tomorrow."

David was watching the Ohio State game when Adam was injured. He would send him a card a couple of weeks later, encouraging him and telling him not to listen to the doctors. He also prayed that Adam would be as lucky as he had been.

* * * * *

When Joe flew back out to Columbus, Ohio, on the morning following Adam's injury, the doctors told him that they were just hoping Adam could one day regain the use of his hands. He thought back to the day when a doctor had told him they could save David, but then added, "You may not have the same son."

Remembering all of those lonely hours that he and Sue had spent with their hands clasped in prayer and the cards and get-well wishes that had poured in from across the country, he pulled Andre Taliaferro into a room in the intensive care unit. Grabbing both of Andre's hands, he said, "We need to ask for another miracle."

The next day Paterno addressed his players during an emotional prayer session at the Lasch Building, which serves as the nerve center for the football program. As he stood before the players, the legend looked every bit as vulnerable as they felt. He told them about David and broke down crying. Defensive coordinator Tom Bradley had been a player on that 1977 team, and he had been a coach for Paterno since 1979. But he had never seen him cry.

Paterno would spend the week cringing at every collision in practice and hoping against hope that he hadn't used up all of his miracles.

What he would have given for those "Hellfires of '88" now.

* * * * *

With Adam Taliaferro running a half step behind, the pass sailed just beyond the outstretched fingertips of the Ohio State receiver in the shadow of Penn State's end zone. ABC color commentator Gary Danielson didn't conceal his disgust. "This will be remembered in Happy Valley," he said. "This will be remembered."

The Buckeyes were beating Penn State, 38–6, at the time, and the game had long since been decided. "You're not gaining any experience throwing a bomb with three minutes left in the game. Run the ball. C'mon John!" John Cooper, the Ohio State coach, would later commit a more egregious offense in the eyes of Penn State fans.

It came after Adam had been strapped onto a stretcher, wheeled past his teammates, who were holding hands and praying, and then rushed to the Ohio State University Medical Center. Reserve quarterback Scott McMullen, who had tested Adam with the bomb that had drawn Danielson's ire, completed a fourth-down pass that led to the short touchdown run that capped the worst loss of the Paterno era. *This* would be remembered in Happy Valley, and Penn Staters would direct their anger and outrage at the coach who had never really been embraced by even his own team's fans.

Cooper, who considered Paterno one of his closest friends in the Big Ten, went out on the field to check on Adam after the injury. He could see how concerned the Penn State players were. But in his 24 years as a college football head coach, he had also seen a handful of injured players taken off the field on a stretcher. Every other time, that had proven to be just a precaution. It wasn't until after the game that Cooper found out that the injured player, whose name he didn't even know, had sustained a serious spinal cord injury.

He went to the emergency entrance of the hospital and was taken right back to the capsule in which Adam was undergoing an MRI scan. Cooper went to the next room, where Dr. Gary Rea was studying the MRI reports. From the look on Rea's face, Cooper, for perhaps the first time, realized the gravity of the situation.

"Will he ever play football?" Cooper asked. Later, he would feel like kicking himself for asking that question.

"He may never walk," Rea replied.

Cooper found out that Adam's father was flying in to Columbus, and he dispatched the policemen who guard him during games to the airport to meet Andre. He spent time with Andre that night, returned to the hospital the next day, and was back again on Monday when Adam underwent surgery.

At a news conference following the surgery, a reporter asked Andre what he thought about the pass at the end of the game. As far as Andre was concerned, Cooper had done nothing to put Adam in that hospital. And Cooper had been there for Andre and Addie in their greatest hours of need.

So had Ohio State. An official from the athletic department arranged for the Taliaferros to stay in a nearby hotel, while two-time Heisman Trophy winner Archie Griffin, now an athletic administrator at his alma mater, visited Adam. So did a handful of players.

One of the players who went to the hospital the day Adam had surgery had never done well in that kind of setting. He milled around nervously in the lobby and decided against going into Adam's room. The sight of Adam lying in that bed amidst a web of tubes would have been too much for him, especially since he had been on the other end of the tackle that put Adam there.

Jerry Westbrooks gave a card he had brought for Adam to one of the nurses and left the hospital. Adam and his family never knew he was there.

Neither player knew it at the time, but they had more in common than just a chance encounter in the same cruel twist of fate.

* * * * *

Like Adam, Jerry was a star running back in high school who impressed his coaches as much with his humility off the field as his dominance on it. Like Adam, he had been the football star whom teachers actually wanted in their classes.

Jerry was raised by a strong-willed mother who worked up to three jobs at a time to support him and his two younger brothers. The temptations of drugs were never far from the streets where he grew up in south Florida, but he filled his days with sports and his other hobby, building model airplanes.

Jerry didn't start playing organized football until his freshman year at Pope John Paul II in Boca Raton, but he quickly blossomed into a two-way terror. He bulldozed his way for close to 3,000 career yards and set the school's all-time rushing record.

At the end of his senior season, Jerry somehow found a way to surprise the coaches who had seen him do just about everything on a football field. As the team rode back to Boca Raton following the last game of the season, he walked to the front of the bus and, shaking each coach's hand, thanked them for all they had done for him.

"I've been coaching for 17 years and I've never seen a kid with the same package," said Jeff Fossen, Pope John Paul II's defensive coordinator, who also coached Jerry in track. "I've seen athletes as good or better than him, but I've never seen anyone with his demeanor or attitude. He's a once-in-a-lifetime kid because he's got it all."

Jerry hoped his football talents would allow him to one day buy his mother a house. He also had plans to give back to the school. One day during track practice, Fossen noticed Westbrooks looking around at the rickety stands he hoped to replace one day. "What are you doing?" he asked.

"Just looking for a good place for the sign."

"What sign?"

"One day when I make it this is going to be Jerry Westbrooks Field."

Florida and Florida State each had coveted Jerry as a defensive end, but he had his heart set on playing tailback. When Ohio State offered him a chance to play offense, Jerry committed to the Buckeyes.

Terry Geough, Pope John Paul II's head coach, had been a little uneasy about Jerry going so far away. When the Buckeyes' coach came to visit Jerry, Geough asked him, "Are you going to take care of him? You've got to understand he's as close to my son as they come." Cooper, Geough said, assured him that he would.

But things never worked out for Westbrooks at Ohio State. Jerry was tried at several different positions but had mostly languished on the bench. There always seemed to be a logjam at tailback and Jerry was usually the odd man out.

When Ohio State opened up a big lead against Penn State in the third quarter of the September 23 game, Jerry got some playing time and made the most of it. He scored on a short touchdown run after getting hit by Bryan Scott on the 5-yard line and dragging the Penn State defensive back into the end zone.

No play better illustrated the dominance of Ohio State that day; it was reminiscent of 1994, when Penn State reserve tailback Ambrose Fletcher had jolted a Buckeye tackler on the way to a late touchdown run in Penn State's 63–14 victory. Payback for that game, more than a few Nittany Lions fans felt, was the impetus behind the pass that Ohio State threw after Adam's injury.

On that fateful play, Westbrooks received the ball off an option pitch. The collision sent a sharp pain shooting through his left thigh, but he bounced up immediately because he didn't want his teammates to see that it had hurt. As he passed Adam on the way back to Ohio State's huddle, he had a chilling thought: "This kid's paralyzed."

Westbrooks, who had long yearned to make headlines, never dreamed it would happen this way.

That night he got a call from his best friend and former high school teammate, Brian Taylor. Why hadn't Adam's high school coaches taught him how to tackle? Jerry asked angrily.

Back in Voorhees, New Jersey, Dan Spittal agonized over the same question. He had been Adam's position coach at Eastern High School, and he knew as well as anyone that Adam had broken the first rule of tackling when he lowered his head. But when he thought back to the defensive practices, he clearly remembered preaching to the players to keep their heads up when making a tackle.

Taylor, who was now coaching at his and Westbrooks' alma mater, was also certain that Adam had been properly versed in tackling, and he begged Jerry not to repeat his heat-of-the-moment comments. Jerry didn't say much more about the play, even though Taylor could tell he was upset.

The one thing that comforted Westbrooks in the days following the injury was what he read about it. Adam had bruised his spinal cord, and if it was only bruised, Jerry told himself, that meant it could heal. "I just thank God he didn't sever it," Westbrooks said. He said a prayer for Adam every day, but never really said anything about the play, and he specifically told reporters he would not talk about it.

Jerry would get angry when someone referred to Adam as "that guy that you hurt" even if it was in an innocuous manner. He had never meant for the injury to happen. He had simply been trying to make the most of the limited playing time that had come his way.

Westbrooks hoped as much as anyone that the doctors would be able to put Adam back together.

* * * * *

Jerry Westbrooks had never met Brad Gaines, and the mention of Gaines' name would have drawn a blank stare from the Ohio State tailback. However, if anyone understood what Westbrooks was going through in the days and weeks following Adam's horrific injury, it was Gaines. In October of 1989, he had been on the receiving end of a hit that had rendered Mississippi defensive back Chucky Mullins a quadriplegic. The violent goal line collision changed Gaines' life forever, too.

Prior to that game, Gaines had appeared to be headed toward the same long career that two of his older brothers enjoyed in the NFL. A three-year starter who led Vanderbilt with 67 receptions in 1989, Gaines didn't return for a senior season in which he surely would have been one of the premier fullbacks in the country. He wasn't in a hurry to get to the NFL; he needed to get away from the hit that would haunt him for the rest of his life.

Gaines spent the next seven years bouncing around the NFL and the Canadian Football League. When the Philadelphia Eagles cut him in 1996, he couldn't have cared less. He quit the game for good. "It messed my head up that much," Gaines said. "Football was my life."

Mullins' death in May of 1991 had compounded the guilt that Gaines felt following the accident; the story became not only national but also inspirational. Mississippi, a state where race relations had been viewed by some as an oxymoron, rallied around the black football player. With donations that poured in from all over the state, Mississippi University raised more than $1 million for the Chucky Mullins Trust Fund. The city of Oxford donated land for a special-needs house that was built for the injured athlete.

Mullins, who had vowed to return to school, knew a thing or two about perseverance. He was orphaned at an early age, and many schools considered him too small to play Division I-A football. Mississippi took a chance on him; by his redshirt freshman year, Mullins had worked his way into the Rebels' nickel-and-dime pass defense packages.

The player who addressed his coaches as "sir" and usually addressed opposing wideouts with a teeth-rattling wallop became a fan favorite at Ole Miss. His final hit had been signature Chucky. It stopped Gaines, who outweighed him by more than 50 pounds, and saved a touchdown.

Gaines got to know Mullins following the neck injury, and he became one of his biggest fans. Knowing how badly Gaines felt about the accident, Mullins always tried to make him feel comfortable when the two were together. Their friendship blossomed.

After spending nearly four months in a hospital, Mullins returned to Ole Miss in June of 1990 in a wheelchair and resumed classes. However, on May 1, 1991, he collapsed from a blood clot that had been caused by poor circulation. A couple of days after Mullins slipped into a coma, Gaines got a call from his guardians. He rushed to the hospital in Memphis and rarely left Mullins' side in those final few days. He was with him when Mullins died two months before his 22nd birthday, with a football cradled in his arms.

Even now, Gaines' thoughts are never far from Mullins and the hit that ultimately claimed his life. "It's the first thing I think about when I wake up in the morning," Gaines said, "and the last thing I think about when I go to bed."

In between, the memory of Mullins permeates just about every aspect of his life. Gaines, who owns a health club in Nashville, Tennessee, named his corporation Gaines38, Inc., because *38* is the number Mullins wore at Mississippi. The last four digits in the phone number for Gaines' club, Go Sport and Wellness, are 3800; Gaines had to specially request those numbers. "All of my pin numbers [for credit cards] and all of that stuff, I incorporate that somehow with my lucky number," he said.

Gaines also attends the Mississippi team banquet every year, when the outstanding defensive player from spring practice is awarded Mullins' number. The player gets to wear the number the following season. There is no higher honor an Ole Miss player can receive.

Gaines never got counseling but admits that he probably should have. He grew up with four brothers in a football family, and so he dealt with his grief in his own way. When he first started dating the girl who would become his wife, he told her, "I'll talk about it one time."

And yet he is remarkably open about the experience. Gaines and Mullins were the subject of a book called *A Dixie Farewell: The Life and Death of Chucky Mullins*. He also agreed to let ESPN shadow him during one of the three visits he makes to Mullins' grave every year—Christmas Day, the anniversary of the accident, and the anniversary of Chucky's death. The story fetched ESPN an Emmy Award in 1994.

Every other time, though, Gaines makes the trip alone. He rises in darkness to make the 170-mile drive from Nashville to Russellville, Alabama. He doesn't return until long after the sun has retreated. He takes cleaning products and spends the day reflecting while scrubbing the headstone of Mullins' grave. His family celebrates Christmas on Christmas Eve so he can be at the gravesite the following day.

Gaines, who still keeps in touch with Mullins' family, has two young daughters. He adores them. "Shoot, I don't care if I have any boys," he said. "I'd rather them not play football. I'd rather them not go through some of the things I've gone through." With players getting bigger and faster every year, Gaines said, tragic spinal cord injuries will occur more frequently in the sport in which he now takes only a passing interest. "It's the greatest game to me, to play and to watch," Gaines said, "but it changed my life."

It changed Adam Taliaferro's life too.

Ironically enough, Pat Milligan, the secondary coach at Adam's alma mater, Eastern High School, was a graduate assistant coach at Ole Miss the year Mullins was injured. Milligan had coached the secondary so he got to know Mullins well and spoke of him in glowing terms.

Milligan had never met the kid coaches around Eastern spoke of in such glowing terms, since he joined the staff the year after Adam's senior season. But he would see the southern New Jersey community rally around Adam in much the same manner Mississippi had rallied around Chucky.

CHAPTER EIGHT

From South Jersey, with Love

After moving from Pittsburgh when he was almost two years old, Adam grew up in southern New Jersey, a location rich in football talent throughout the years. It is an area that produced Heisman Trophy–winning running backs Mike Rozier (Nebraska, 1983) and Ron Dayne (Wisconsin, 1999), along with such NFL stars as Franco Harris, Dave Robinson, Lydell Mitchell, Irving Fryar, Deron Cherry, Dwight Hicks, Milt Plum, Art Still, and Kevin Ross. Pennsauken's John Taylor, who caught a final-minute, game-winning pass from Joe Montana to give the San Francisco 49ers a 20–16 win over the Cincinnati Bengals in Super Bowl XXIII, grew up in the same seven-county South Jersey area as did Taliaferro. So did Wildwood's Randy Beverly, who had two interceptions to help the New York Jets stun the Baltimore Colts, 16–7, in the now-legendary Super Bowl III.

Taliaferro was well aware of southern New Jersey's gloried past. He was a student of South Jersey football history, an avid reader on the subject. Someday, he thought, he would be a part of that rich history. When the local newspapers listed a chart of the area players who had made it to the NFL, Taliaferro couldn't help but daydream about the day when his name would be on the list.

There was no reason to doubt him.

As a member of the Voorhees Vikings midget league team, Taliaferro was a legend. He was so good, in fact, that the midget league retired his number.

At Eastern High, the competition got tougher. No matter. Taliaferro still dominated. He averaged nine yards per carry over his final two seasons and became the first football player in the school's history to have his number retired.

A pattern was developing here: gobble up acres of rushing yards, score a lot of touchdowns, have your number immortalized.

From the start, things would be different at Penn State. For the first time since he began playing organized football at six years old, Adam would not be the team's star. And, as amazing as it seemed to those who followed his high school exploits, he would not be playing offense in college.

Taliaferro not running the football? That was like not allowing Jay Leno to crack a joke. It didn't seem natural, didn't seem fair. Taliaferro, however, was the good soldier. He would move to defense and he would do so with grace. Never did he complain. Not once. Adam thought he'd have a better chance to make an impact as a cornerback and, besides, he figured he'd get to show off his running ability by returning punts and kickoffs in future years.

Paterno had told Andre that Adam probably wasn't big enough to absorb the punishment as a college running back, told him that he would be better suited as a cornerback. He had even told Andre that he wouldn't be surprised if Adam played 10 years in the NFL as a defensive back.

Even as a 10-year-old two-way back, Adam was a dominant player. Here he poses with his mother Addie, father Andre, and younger brother Alex. Andre coached the Vikings to a 7–1 season. Photo courtesy of the Taliaferro family.

Adam Taliaferro in the Penn State football program. Photo courtesy of Penn State.

Adam was the cover subject of the Fall 1999 issue of the S. J. Football Preview. *South Jersey has a rich history of producing outstanding football players, and Adam was another one in that long line.* Photo courtesy of Louis A. Chimenti/ Journal Trend Newspapers.

Alex Taliaferro (right) wearing his big brother's practice jersey as he poses with Adam during Adam's sophomore year at Eastern High. Adam scored 62 touchdowns in his varsity career despite missing most of his sophomore season because of a broken collarbone. Photo courtesy of the Taliaferro family.

Adam plays cornerback for the Nittany Lions in the second half of the Septem-
ber 9, 2000, game against Louisiana Tech. The Lions won, 67–17. As a fresh-
man, Adam was a second-string cornerback, but his coaches fully expected
him to be a three-year starter. Photo courtesy of the Taliaferro family.

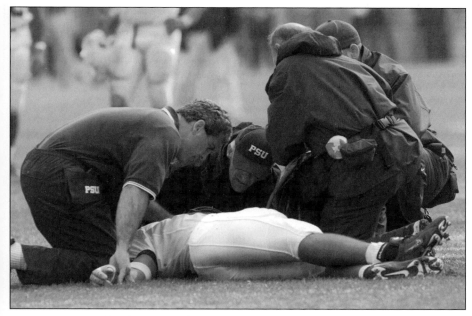

Penn State's medical personnel try to assess Adam's condition immediately after his head-first tackle on Jerry Westbrooks. Nobody yet knew how serious Adam's injury was. Photo courtesy of AP/Wide World Photos.

From left to right, Penn State players Tony Johnson, Eric McCoo, and Larry Johnson bow their heads in prayer for Adam's recovery during a prayer rally at Penn State. Photo courtesy of AP/Wide World Photos.

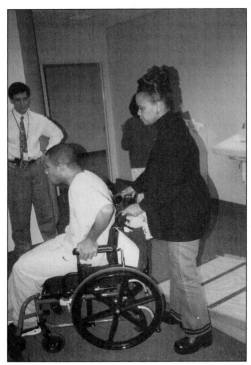

Addie Taliaferro pushes her son's wheelchair, while continuing to believe in her son's determination to rise and walk away from it. Looking on is Magee marketing vice president Ron Siggs. Photo courtesy of Sam Carchidi.

Adam, wearing a gait belt and being assisted by physical therapist Jamie Tomlinson, goes through a walking drill at Magee Rehabilitation Hospital. Tomlinson is observing Adam's gait to see how much it has improved; he is also timing Adam to see how long it takes him to walk a predetermined number of feet. Photo courtesy of Sam Carchidi.

Adam, attached to a harness, walks on a treadmill at Magee. When he first began the drill, Adam couldn't move his legs—five therapists had to move them for him. Here, he is walking by himself. Photo courtesy of Sam Carchidi.

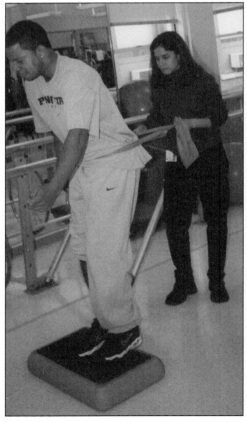

Adam, with an elastic resistance strap being held around his waist by physical therapist Amy Bratta, climbs atop an aerobic step during a workout in Magee Rehabilitation Hospital's gym. This drill is used for strengthening the lower extremities and to help Adam regain his balance. Photos courtesy of Sam Carchidi.

In a moving tribute to their injured teammate, Penn State players line up on the field to form Adam's number, "43." Similar displays of support, in the form of demonstrations, letters, and fund-raisers, came from as far away as Asia. Photo courtesy of the Penn State University Athletic Department.

Adam and Joe Paterno share a light moment during the Penn State coach's visit to Magee. When Adam was injured, Paterno felt he was revisiting a 1977 night-mare, when his then-11-year-old son David fell off a trampoline at his school and fractured his skull. Photo courtesy of Magee Rehabilitation Hospital.

Jen Greenberg began dating Adam right before their senior year of high school. She has been a loving and supportive part of Adam's life through the fun times—such as their senior prom, top—and the hard times of Adam's rehabilitation. Photos courtesy of Jen Greenberg.

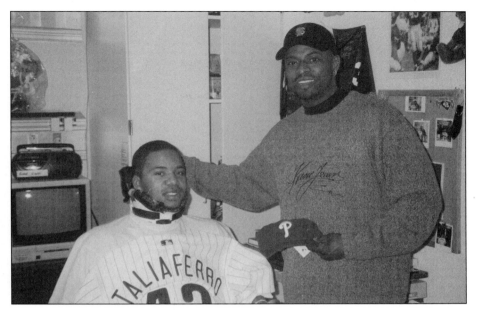

Adam receives a hospital visit from Philadelphia Phillies pitcher Robert Person.
Photo courtesy of Magee Rehabilitation Hospital.

It was a proud moment when the Taliaferro family posed for this photo on January 5, 2001, the day Adam was released from Magee Rehabilitation Hospital. Posing in Room 543 are, from left to right, Andre Taliaferro, Adam, Addie, and 14-year-old Alex, who is wearing his brother's No. 43 Penn State jersey.
Photo courtesy of Magee Rehabilitation Hospital.

Magee staffers take Adam for a joyride on his last day at the hospital, lifting him in the air to salute his remarkable recovery. From left to right are Linda Rizzo, Amy Bratta, Cheryl West, Marygrace Mangine, and Aline King, members of Adam's therapy team. Photo courtesy of Magee Rehabilitation Hospital.

The day Adam was released from Magee was a joyous occasion. Giving the "thumbs-up" on that day are, from left to right, Andre Taliaferro, Penn State athletic director Tim Curley, Penn State football administrator Joe Sarra, Adam, Penn State team doctor Wayne Sebastianelli, Alex Taliaferro, and Addie Taliaferro. Photo courtesy of Magee Rehabilitation Hospital.

Adam, sitting between his father and Dr. William Staas, appears at a press conference on the day of his release. In the background, from left to right, are members of his rehab team: Cheryl West, Dave Wilcher, Amy Bratta, and Marygrace Mangine. Photo courtesy of Magee Rehabilitation Hospital.

With physical therapist Amy Bratta on his left and his father Andre on his right, Adam uses crutches to walk out of Magee Rehabilitation Hospital on the day he was released from the hospital as an outpatient. Andre had told doubters, "My boy is going to walk out of here." On this day, his prediction came true. Photo courtesy of Magee Rehabilitation Hospital.

Adam throws out the first pitch at a Philadelphia Phillies–Chicago Cubs game on April 7, 2001. Photo courtesy of AP/Wide World Photos.

Adam meets Bill Cosby during the halftime of a Philadelphia 76ers–Charlotte Hornets game. Photo courtesy of DN Photo/Yong Kim.

As Adam lay in a hospital bed, barely able to move, that prediction now seemed sadly ironic.

Adam's world had been terribly altered. No longer was his goal to become another South Jersey star who became an All-American and then an NFL player.

Now his goals were more basic: Like being able to go to the bathroom without a catheter. Like being able to hold a fork and feed himself. Like being able to stand without assistance.

Adam was now at Magee Rehabilitation Hospital in Philadelphia. His rehabilitation would be more difficult than any of his two-a-day workouts at Eastern High or Penn State.

But the work didn't bother Adam. He was tireless. His high school coach, Larry Ginsburg, said Adam was the most dedicated player he had seen in his 37 coaching seasons.

The day after the injury, Ginsburg phoned the Ohio hospital to talk to Andre. Rumors were running rampant about Adam's condition, and Ginsburg wanted to get things cleared up. He tossed and turned all night, thinking about Adam. He needed to talk to Andre, needed to get some answers.

Ginsburg, who had retired after Adam's senior year, was stunned when he was able to get connected with Adam. Using surprising detail, Adam told Ginsburg about the impending spinal-fusion surgery. "Don't worry, Coach, I'm going to walk out of here," a heavily sedated Adam told him.

"I couldn't believe how good he sounded," Ginsburg said, "so I just assumed everything was going to be fine."

Now, about two weeks later, lying in bed at Magee, Adam didn't even remember having that conversation with Ginsburg. In fact, he was having a difficult time remembering *anything* that happened in Ohio after he tackled Jerry Westbrooks.

This was the first time Ginsburg had seen Adam since the injury; he looked a lot worse than the former coach had expected. He was frail and continually spitting up mucus. Tubes were everywhere and he was unable to move.

After spending time with Adam, Ginsburg talked privately with Andre. "If there's any possible way that he can make it, he will," he said. "If it only needs work, he's a shoo-in."

Nobody outworked Adam. Nobody. That work ethic, combined with his unique athletic ability, is why Ginsburg referred to him as "the most complete player I've ever coached."

Adam wasn't in any physical pain. The pain was mental. It was generated by the fact that, most of the time, his brain was trying to tell his legs and arms to move, but they weren't responding. The frustration was building.

The first week at Magee was difficult. Adam still felt "out of it" from the medication he was receiving, and he was having problems sleeping at night because he couldn't roll over and get comfortable. His legs refused to budge.

Toward the end of his first week at Magee, Adam, in a wheelchair pushed by his father, was rolled to the rooftop patio. This was a perfect time to enjoy the midday sun and crisp October air.

As he sat in his wheelchair, Adam stared at two men playing one-on-one basketball on the rooftop court. Watching the impromptu game made Adam's mind rewind. Back to the days when he was a star basketball player at Eastern High. Back to the days when he was one of the most heralded running backs the area had ever produced.

Back to the days when he didn't feel like a cripple.

Adam, who was on his way to losing 30 pounds, was feeling vulnerable. He had just finished electro-stimulation treatment, with the hope that it would help get his hands to move.

A few tears trickled down his cheeks.

Andre put his arm on Adam's shoulders. It would be the second of only three times that he would see Adam cry during the entire ordeal. "Son, you've got every right to cry. Go ahead and let it out," he said, "But you know what? Let's look forward because you're going to get better."

Andre hugged his son. Adam couldn't hug back. He was still unable to move his arms.

"That's all right, son. You're going to get there."

When Adam was 13 years old, Andre used to kid his son about his basketball team's makeup. Andre coached that team. They were composed of kids from the suburbs and, to Andre, they didn't have the mental toughness of the kids in his old North Philly neighborhood. "Those kids would kick your butts," Andre used to razz his son. "And you know why? Because for those kids, basketball is their whole self being. They don't have Nintendo and PlayStation. Basketball is all they've got and they wouldn't let some softies from the suburbs kick their butts."

Right now, Adam needed to have the mental toughness of those kids from the city, needed to stay focused on walking out of Magee.

* * * * *

While Adam was getting acclimated to Magee, the South Jersey football community was rallying behind him. Ginsburg, the former Eastern coach, spearheaded the rally.

Ginsburg wanted to do something to help Adam and the family, but he felt helpless. What could he possibly do? What could *anybody* do? Wherever he went, friends would ask the same question: is there some way that we can help?

Ginsburg, a kindly, gray-haired man with an easygoing manner, had an idea. He talked with some South Jersey coaches and asked if they could have their players hold up four fingers on each hand (thus making a *44*, the number Adam wore at Eastern High) while the national anthem was being played before games. Adam had worn No. 43 at Penn State because No. 44 was taken by one of the team's veterans, but around South Jersey, he was still known as No. 44. The coaches embraced Ginsburg's idea. Pretty soon, the teams in Eastern's Olympic Conference were making the *44* gesture, along with some teams out of the conference.

Watching 100 teenagers solemnly hold up fingers while the anthem was being played was an emotional sight. Ginsburg, 64, got teary-eyed when he saw it. He was not alone. "And they didn't just hold them up; they held them up *high*," Ginsburg said. "They meant it."

Adam was adored in South Jersey, not so much because he led the area in scoring as a junior and senior, but because of his genuinely humble and sincere personality. "People love him," Ginsburg said. "Wherever he goes, people take to him."

Which is why the pregame tribute spread throughout the area. Tim Gushue, the Shawnee coach, was happy to ask his team to hold up their fingers every game, happy to keep Adam in his team's thoughts and prayers. Adam, Gushue said, had become Shawnee's symbol for perseverance and hope; he had become the team's symbol for never giving up.

Since his injury occurred on national TV and had been followed closely by the networks, Adam was getting support from folks all around the country. His high school teammates who were at various colleges were taping *44* and *AT* to their lockers and wrists. Players who didn't even know Adam were scribbling his name or number on a piece of their college equipment. Adam's Penn State teammates wore *43* on the back of their helmets and named one of their defenses for him: "Tally," short for Taliaferro. Adam was always in the thoughts of the Penn State players and coaches. Always.

Others were also thinking of Adam. The Ohio State University Medical Center sent a seven-foot signed card. Thousands of letters and cards were being sent to Magee and to Adam's home. Some were from the West Coast, some were from as far away as Pakistan and Israel.

Closer to his home, the preschool children that Addie taught were showing their support. Addie had taken a leave of absence to be with her son. The children missed "Miss Addie," missed her smile, missed her effervescent personality. They wanted to comfort her and Adam. They created homemade cards and drew Adam in his No. 43 Penn State jersey. It was Crayola crayon art at its sincere best, Addie thought.

There were also hundreds of cards from grammar school students from the area. The cards were filled with innocence . . . and misspellings. "Adam, you are my herow!" wrote one. One little boy sent a photo of himself and told Adam he planned to graduate from Penn State in 2015.

Addie would look at the cards when she needed a pick-me-up.

There was even a heartfelt letter sent by actor Christopher Reeve, who became a quadriplegic after a 1995 horse-riding accident. The letter was dated October 11, 2000:

Dear Adam:

I heard about your injury and just wanted to drop a note to let you know that you will get through this. You are getting the best of care, and, from what I know about you, you are an incredibly determined young man. There are more people rooting for you than you can imagine.

I was once where you are now. It seems surreal. It seems like your life has been turned upside down. I remember being so angry that this happened to me. I remember the frustration, and especially, I remember the fear. You are done with surgery and about to begin rehabilitation. You'll learn new ways to do the same old things. Most importantly, you'll discover who you are.

I was also an athlete in my free time and had based my acting career on motion and my body. It seemed like a split second changed all that. But it didn't. There is something about you that won't change. You'll always be you. Your life may be different than you imagined it to be. But you are still the same man. So, to quote your father, "Let's go forward."

You should know that the Christopher Reeve Paralysis Foundation funds research for a cure. It is no longer a question of "if" but "when." So on those days when you're really down, know that hope is on the way. I not only believe that it will

happen, but I'm determined to make it happen. In the meantime, push yourself in your rehabilitation as hard as you pushed
yourself for football. Let people help you. Remember that your
life holds so much more than you can imagine. Keep going.

Sincerely,
Christopher Reeve
(dictated)

Adam felt honored that someone like Reeve took the time to send him
a letter. Addie taped it to Adam's hospital room wall so others could
read it. It made him feel proud. So did the bags full of cards and letters
that he read whenever he needed a boost.

Adam had also been given videotapes of the prayer services that were
held for him at Penn State and in South Jersey. Unlike the cards and letters, he found the videotapes depressing. "It was like watching my own
funeral," he said. He watched for only a minute or two, then turned the
TV off.

* * * * *

Now that his life was out of danger and he was at Magee, Adam was able
to get visitors. There was a constant flow of well-wishers to his room.
Friends and relatives were always there. So were several Philadelphia
sports celebrities, including former Eagles coach Dick Vermeil; 76ers
president Pat Croce and 76ers Tyrone Hill, Todd MacCulloch, and Craig
"Speedy" Claxton; former Flyers goalie Bernie Parent; former Eagles
quarterback Ron Jaworski; and Phillies pitcher Robert Person. Several
Eagles players also stopped by, including Donovan McNabb, Brian
Dawkins, Troy Vincent, and Bobby Taylor.

There was even a visit from Tigger. Actually, it was Chaz Brown,
dressed in an orange and black Tigger costume that he had purchased
at a mall as a way to boost Adam's spirits. Several of Adam's other high

school teammates were with Brown, who was the only one wearing a tail. "He knew it was me," Brown said, "because I guess I'm the only type of guy who would do that."

Chaz lived two doors away from Adam in Voorhees and they had been close friends since sixth grade. They hung out together, played youth and high school football together, even went to a Penn State football camp together before their senior year.

Adam may have been shy and reserved around adults, but not when he was around Chaz (whom he affectionately called "Bubba") and his friends. They had great chemistry and seemed to feed off of each others' personalities. It wouldn't be unusual for Adam to greet Chaz by putting him in a headlock and asking, "What's up, man? Give me a kiss." It was just the playful nature of their personalities. They could bust on each other without either one getting upset.

So when Chaz walked into Adam's hospital room dressed as Tigger from *Winnie the Pooh*, Adam knew who was behind the costume. "What's up, Bubba?" he asked, trying to contain his laughter.

Tom Bradley, the Penn State defensive coordinator, didn't wear any goofy costumes when he visited Adam at Magee. But he had the same intentions as Chaz: to keep Adam's spirits high.

Bradley had been having a difficult time sleeping. He had been living with the guilt of putting Adam into the game at left cornerback. He had been living with the helpless look of fear on Adam's face as he lay on the ground at Ohio Stadium. When Bradley went to visit Adam in early October, it was the first time he had seen him since that fateful day in Ohio.

"How you doing, Adam?" Bradley asked.

"Hey, Coach. How are you? You look tired."

"I look tired? What about you? Let's worry about you."

Bradley choked back tears. In a roundabout way, Adam was telling him, "Don't feel sorry for me. I'm more worried about you guys." Penn State had just dropped a 25–16 decision at Minnesota and the team record had slipped to 2–5. "Tell the guys not to get down," Taliaferro told Bradley. "Tell them we can get the next five."

Before Bradley left, Adam felt his left toe moving. He pointed it out to Bradley. "Oh, that's great!" Bradley said. He was telling a little white lie. He hadn't seen any movement but he wasn't about to tell Adam, wasn't about to discourage him.

Darren Drozdov didn't want to discourage Adam, either. "Tell him if he ever needs someone to talk to," Drozdov said, "I'm here." Drozdov was a star football player at South Jersey's Oakcrest High; then in the eighties he went on to play nose tackle for the Denver Broncos. He later found a niche as a professional wrestler before dislocating his spine and fracturing two disks while executing a routine move in a 1999 World Wrestling Federation show in Uniondale, New York. The flamboyant Drozdov, who became so popular that he had his own "Droz" dolls sold in stores, underwent four hours of spinal-fusion surgery and later did rehabilitation work at Magee.

When Adam suffered his injury, Drozdov was still in a wheelchair and, a year after his wrestling mishap, still had no feeling in most of his body. His injury was similar to the one suffered by Adam, and the doctors had painted a bleak picture of his case. "It's a waiting and hoping game, basically," he said.

Adam wasn't someone who wanted to wait; he was a doer. He was getting antsy to start his rehab work.

* * * * *

Andre and Addie were spending most of their time at the hospital with Adam. Addie would stay from 8:30 A.M. until Alex would get home from school. Andre, a national accounts manager for the Alcoa aluminum company, would take the late-afternoon shift and stay there until Adam fell asleep near midnight.

Alex had quit his youth league football team because he wanted to spend time with his brother and because he knew it would ease his mom's concerns. She had too many things on her mind without having to worry about her youngest son getting injured, he thought.

Trying to assist Adam had become an almost round-the-clock occupation, so Andre was happy to take Alex to the store to buy some paintball equipment one afternoon. It was nice to spend some time with his 14-year-old son, nice to be able to talk to him and see what he had been feeling.

Andre wasn't prepared for what he heard. "It should have been me that got hurt, Dad. Not Adam," Alex said. "He was going to be a star. It should have been me."

Andre was jolted. "No, no, no, son. That's not the way it works," Andre said. "Adam has experienced some good times in football and, unfortunately, this is a bad time. But he'll get past this."

Alex was still stunned at the sight of his brother. When he went to Penn State, Alex thought, he was built like solid steel. Now he seemed so weak, so frail, so helpless. At least Alex no longer feared that his brother would die. Having him close to home where he could visit had helped those fears subside.

Adam's injury brought Alex and Adam closer together than ever. Alex suddenly felt like Adam's protector, like his older brother's guardian. He thought he might one day be his brother's caretaker. In the solitude of his bedroom, where figurines of NBA and NFL players were tacked to a wall, Alex could envision himself pushing Adam around in a wheelchair and taking care of him. Even if it meant he couldn't go to college, so be it. Taking care of his brother was more important. While visiting Adam at Magee, Alex thought about what life would be like when his parents got older and could no longer take care of their two boys. "Adam will live with me and, whatever I have to do, we'll make it," Alex thought. "Nothing is more important than family."

* * * * *

Following Adam's injury, Dan Spittal had the burdensome task of trying to keep Eastern High's football team on an even keel. Spittal didn't feel like coaching, didn't feel like teaching. He was consumed by thoughts of Adam. "How is he doing? Will he get better? Is he going to live? Is he going to walk?" Those thoughts zoomed in and out of Spittal's mind.

Like their coach, the players were in a daze. The upcoming game that week against Overbrook seemed so inconsequential. It was Adam that was on their collective minds, not some football game. And with members of the local and national media descending on the high school, it was difficult to think about anything except their fallen former teammate.

The first school day after the injury, Spittal called the football players into the high school auditorium to answer questions about Adam's condition and to comfort the emotional young men. Spittal told them Adam needed prayers. He knew prayers weren't allowed in school, but he didn't care. "Anybody that doesn't want to be involved with this," he explained to them, "can leave." No one left. Assistant Coach Don Olsen led a prayer, and Spittal updated the team on Adam's condition.

Spittal was the offensive coordinator when Adam played there; now he was the head coach. Spittal had become a religious person over the past 10 years, reading passages from the Bible each morning. Spiritually, he said, he had started to gain focus.

And then Adam broke his neck. Suddenly, Spittal started questioning his faith. "I said, 'God, you know what? I know I ain't so smart and I know you're in charge, but holy shit. Why him? He didn't do a bad thing to anybody. And I'm going to be patient, but I'm pissed off at you.'"

Spittal shared those thoughts with Andre. "He better reveal to me damn quick why He did this," he told Andre.

Privately, Spittal's prayers were tinged with bitterness. It had been a particularly rough time for him. He was still recovering from the recent death of one of Eastern's longtime assistants, Ernie Oldenburg, a beloved "old school" coach who had been especially fond of Adam.

Spittal would open his Bible, read a passage, and then start asking questions about Adam's injury. "I know, God, you know what I'm thinking and I still ain't happy with you because that wasn't right. There are a lot of asses walking around having a lot of success. Why, God, are they doing that and you give this kid the worst blow he could ever have? I'm still not right with it."

Maybe, Spittal reasoned, Adam will do something for God down the road. Maybe that was the reason for the injury. "But I'm not smart enough to figure out a reason. Maybe some religious theologian could. I'm just a high school football coach and a dad and I can't figure that out yet."

During his early days at Magee, Adam was still flat on his back, virtually unable to move. Addie would brush his teeth every few hours to keep his mouth fresh. Every so often, she would feed him broken off bits of a plain bagel or gummy bears that Ginsburg, his former head coach, had brought.

Spittal looked at Adam, a player he once projected as a first-round NFL draft pick, and knew this was going to be a long and grueling rehabilitation. "I think in this society, we want a problem solved in a half hour, like a TV sitcom," he said. "Well, this wasn't going to take a half hour."

The week after Adam was injured, Spittal said, reminded him of when he was 13 years old and his dad died of a cerebral hemorrhage. "I never felt like that since that time," he said. He had a sick feeling in his stomach. An empty feeling.

Spittal knew that, in high school, Adam had been taught to tackle with his head up. But things happen on the field in fractions of a second that cause players to make adjustments. Sometimes they don't have enough time to get in the correct position. That was the case when Adam tackled Jerry Westbrooks.

When Spittal saw Adam at Magee, he told him, "I loved how you came up and attacked him on the play." Keeping things positive. That was the theme here.

Spittal, a muscular 42-year-old who grew up in blue-collar Johnstown, Pennsylvania, was having a difficult time staying positive when he said his prayers. God had tested the Taliaferro family and everyone who was close to Adam. Spittal still couldn't understand it. "God knows I'm pissed off and I don't care," he said. "Maybe that's good. Maybe you can tell God you're pissed off and He probably says, 'Well, I don't care . . . I did it because . . . I'm not telling you for another 18 years, 4 months, and 16 days."

If he wasn't religious, Spittal said, he doesn't know how he would have handled the crisis. "When my dad died, it was like, 'Why did I grow up without a father and why did my mom grow up without a husband?' I don't know. It's tough to live with. You question it."

After Adam's injury, the first time Spittal felt some peace was when he attended the prayer rally that was held at the Rev. Khan's church in Lindenwold, New Jersey. The Rev. Khan talked about how one woman had taken prayer out of the schools in the sixties—and how one young man, Adam, had put prayer back into the schools in a matter of weeks.

"Schools were praying for him," said Spittal, whose team dropped an emotional 18–13 decision to Overbrook in its first game after Adam's injury. "Football teams all over South Jersey were praying for him before and after practices. Are you allowed to do it? I don't know."

On the practice field, Spittal would ask for a moment of silence for Adam, then would lead a prayer. "He was always our strength," Spittal told his players. "So now let our strength be his."

There was never a reference to God. "So we kind of circumvented the religious rule," Spittal said. "One young man caused prayer to come back to school."

CHAPTER NINE

Feeling Home at Magee

Addie knew she was going to like the Magee Rehabilitation Hospital on Adam's first day there. The reason for her optimism was Dr. William E. Staas Jr.

Addie liked his upbeat nature. Staas examined Adam, came out from behind the curtain with a smile on his face, and winked at the Taliaferro family. It was almost like Staas was the Wizard of Oz, telling the Taliaferro family that Adam's journey was going to have a happy ending. "It's going to be OK," he told them.

Adam still couldn't move most of his body, but Staas' words had a soothing effect. "He gave us hope," Addie said.

A slight man with distinguished gray hair and a pleasant disposition, Staas has an air of wisdom about him. Some doctors talk over your head. Not Staas. He has an artful way of simplifying medical terms, which helps patients and their loved ones understand their situation and feel at ease. He is deeply respected at the hospital, not only for his knowledge but also for the way he makes everyone feel important. He treats opinions from other workers—whether they are nurses, therapists, or fellow doctors—with the utmost respect; Staas makes everyone feel like a valuable member of the team. And he helps patients, no matter how dire their diagnoses, feel like there is a chance that they can recover.

Staas knew at an early age that he wanted to work in the field of medicine. He was 13 years old, to be precise. It was then that his best friend, who was also 13, died of leukemia. Suddenly Staas' world was turned upside down. No longer did he feel invincible, like most teenagers. It was at that point that he made a vow to himself: he would spend his life trying to cure the sick. Maybe he wouldn't find a cure for leukemia, but he would find a way to help people.

Now 64 and the longtime president and medical director at Magee, Staas took an instant liking to Adam. He liked Adam's positive nature, liked the fact that his goal was to someday walk out of Magee. Staas, the "Prince of Hope," had a similar goal for Adam.

The first day Staas examined Adam, he performed a pinprick exam and tested his toe to see if Adam could determine if it was up or down. He checked his strength and reflexes. "He was able to feel when I touched him. I didn't have to make guesses," Staas said. Other doctors might not have been able to get the same results in earlier tests because Adam had been heavily sedated at that time. "Now," Staas said, "his head was perfectly clear." The positive pinprick exam led Staas to believe that Adam's strength would return, as would his ability to walk.

These were guesses, but they were *educated* guesses.

Being able to get out of bed and into a wheelchair made Magee a much more pleasant environment for Adam. He felt as if he had regained a little sliver of freedom, a little piece of his old life. Good vibes seemed to be everywhere.

There were, however, some people whose good intentions didn't quite mesh with the Taliaferros' positive outlook. For instance, there was one volunteer—a middle-aged woman confined to a wheelchair—who rolled herself into Adam's room during his first week at the hospital. She meant well, explaining to Adam that she had been paralyzed in a car accident but that she had two children and a fulfilling life. Addie returned from the adjacent restroom just in time to hear the woman's "encouragement." "It's not really hard being paralyzed, dear," the woman told him. "You have to accept it. You can still go on."

If this scene had been a cartoon, smoke would have been coming out of Addie's ears. She bristled at the woman's "pep talk" and asked her to *please* leave Adam alone. How dare she talk about how easy it is to spend your life in a wheelchair, she thought. How dare she assume that Adam would not walk again. Addie asked the nurses to make sure that the woman didn't return to Adam's room. "No offense to her. I appreciate what she was trying to do," she said. "But not right now."

One of the nurses, away from Adam's earshot, said, "Well, Mrs. Taliaferro, there are certain things you're going to have to accept."

Addie went on the offensive. "I'll accept it when I know it's going to happen," she said, "but his injury is incomplete, so we don't know if he's going to walk or not going to walk."

There were also activities at Magee that challenged the Taliaferros' determination to stay upbeat. One such instance was a class designed to show disabled patients how to get in and out of a bathtub from their wheelchairs. Addie found the class too depressing. It was for patients who would spend their lives in wheelchairs.

"Why am I here, Mom?" Adam asked her.

"I don't know," Addie said.

Before the class ended, Addie had seen enough. She pushed Adam back to his room, determined not to allow him to attend any more wheelchair classes. She didn't want him even *thinking* he would be in a wheelchair forever. "If he needs it in the future, we'll come back," she told a nurse in private.

In the next few days, Addie could sense that some hospital workers thought she was in denial and needed help. She told the nurses and doctors to make sure they never told Adam he wouldn't walk. She wanted him to focus on the positives.

Like Addie, Andre was feeling uncomfortable about having his son exposed to so many people in wheelchairs. Before Adam was admitted to Magee, Andre took a tour through the hospital. "This is messed up," he thought to himself. "What's my boy going to think when he gets here and sees all these people like this?"

Adam, of course, was one of those people. But Andre didn't see it that way. The other patients were disabled. They were in wheelchairs. They were going to have a difficult time walking again. Adam was someone who was only having a temporary setback, Andre thought.

Andre was startled by the hospital's cafeteria; only a few people were standing in the checkout line. Most were patients in wheelchairs. Adam would sometimes join those lines in the coming weeks. In a wheelchair.

* * * * *

Addie and Andre continued to spend as much time as they possibly could with Adam. After dropping Alex off at the school bus stop, Addie reached the hospital at around 8:30 each morning. She would stop and pick up breakfast, usually pancakes or a biscuit and egg, for Adam and herself. She would heat the meals in the nurses' microwave and then carefully feed Adam—just as she had when he was an infant—as he sat in his hospital bed. Adam was regaining his appetite and he enjoyed the breakfasts, which he ate while watching ESPN's *SportsCenter*. Andre would relieve Addie at around 3:00 P.M. so she could go home and be with Alex when he returned from school. Andre would stay until around midnight and occasionally sleep at the hospital. "I did the day shift, Andre did the night shift," said Addie.

One of Addie's acquaintances told her she was too consumed by Adam's injury and that she needed a break, needed to go to a movie or out to dinner, needed to get away from the straining situation for a few hours. "You're letting this eat you up, Addie."

"Sister, when you've walked a mile in my shoes, then you come talk to me," Addie snapped. She was happy being with Adam seven days a week. She couldn't imagine leaving him to get a "break," couldn't imagine leaving him to go to work, let alone to go to a restaurant. She didn't care if the family struggled a little financially. If they had to eat pork and beans every night, Addie thought, that's what they would do. Nothing was more important than Addie and Andre being with their son as much as possible, whatever sacrifices it took.

Addie saw sadness in the eyes of some of the other young patients in the hospital. She thought that sadness was caused by more than just their physical problems: it was because their mothers and fathers weren't with them.

That wasn't going to happen to Adam. Addie and Andre wouldn't let it.

* * * * *

When Adam arrived at Magee he was having problems trying to sit up, and he had minimal shoulder and arm movement. He had an occasional flicker in his left leg and was able to bend both elbows and lift his wrists slightly, but no other parts of his body were moving.

Marygrace Mangine met with Adam during his first day at Magee. She and Amy Bratta were the physical therapists that Paul Tighe (the man who broke his neck while diving into a swimming pool in 1996) had recommended to Andre. Both were assigned to Adam. Dr. Staas referred to the therapists as "physical terrorists." He was only half kidding. Mangine and Bratta each stood only 5'5", yet they would push Adam harder than his coaches at Eastern High or Penn State ever had.

Marygrace Mangine has thick glasses, dark hair, and a sunny disposition. As an occupational therapist, she would oversee many areas of Adam's "retraining," including teaching him to get into a bathtub and wash and to wipe himself after using the bathroom. "It's not glamorous," she said, "but someone has to do it." At that time, Adam could not do any of it. He had no hand movement, so he couldn't even pick up the phone. Mangine supplied him with an adapted phone holder that he could pick up with his arms.

Using the knowledge she had gained through past clinical experiences, Mangine had to form a plan for her role in Adam's recovery. After assessing Adam's upper extremities that first day, she was not as optimistic as Dr. Staas. She graded Adam as an ASIA-B; patients in that category frequently don't walk again. Adam, she was convinced, would be in a motorized wheelchair for the rest of his life. She had worked with other patients who were in the same classification—C-5, ASIA-B—during her 6½ years at the hospital. None of them had ever walked again. If Adam wanted to be as independent as possible, she thought, he might be able to one day push a manual wheelchair. But because of his arm and hand limitations, she thought he'd be better off in a motorized wheelchair.

At the end of Adam's first week at Magee, Mangine's opinion hadn't changed. Because she knew the Taliaferros were sensitive about Adam using a wheelchair, she gently broached the subject with him. "If I put you in a power chair, you can get around the hospital. It doesn't mean you'll be in it for life," she told him. Adam consented.

The decision turned out to be beneficial. Someone pushed Adam when he was in the manual chair, but that didn't stop him from trying to generate some movement himself—and that attempted pushing was causing shoulder problems. Once he got into a power wheelchair, he rarely had shoulder pain.

For the next six months (the first three of which were spent as an inpatient) Mangine and Bratta were Adam's confidantes. They were pleasant, professional, and always seemed to know how to keep Adam's spirits up. Adam felt as if they were his older sisters, as if they could read his mood and knew when to push him in therapy—and when to ease off.

Bratta, a slender 29-year-old with long brunette hair, has an easygoing manner that she developed while growing up in Illinois. She is a focused, goal-oriented individual and has run in marathons and half marathons. She had been at Magee for four and a half years and knew from looking at Adam's charts that he had an uphill journey ahead of him. The fact that Adam was young would help him in his recovery. But walking? That seemed highly questionable to Bratta. Still, she was impressed by his openness, by his friendliness, and by the incredible support he was getting from his family.

Three days after Bratta met Adam, he was finally able to move his left big toe again. The toe had moved sporadically at Jefferson, and the Magee therapists had been anxiously watching to see if that movement would return.

Adam's first week at Magee was dominated by evaluation tests. The second week included a lot of stretching in Magee's gym, which is where he would spend most of the next three months. The gym is three-quarters the size of a football field. It includes two dozen navy blue mats placed on wooden frames, about two feet off the tiled yellow floor, where patients exercise. The room also has universal weights, dumb-bells, voice-activated computers for patients who can't move from the neck down, and lots of colorful, oversized balls and hula hoops used for exercise therapy. There is a washer and dryer that patients can learn to operate. There is a doll lying in a brown wooden crib that is used as a training aide for learning how to pick up a baby. There are chrome parallel handrails that are used to assist patients trying to walk. The gym also includes a functional kitchen used to retrain patients on how to use their fingers and hands in that part of a home.

On an average day in the gym, patients are at different stations doing different workouts; as many as 20 empty wheelchairs line one of the walls, and the sound of Top 40 music fills the air as patients diligently go through their routines.

During Adam's second week at Magee, the therapists worked differ-ent parts of his body that had begun to move. Mangine showed him exercises that would help him with self-care tasks, such as feeding and grooming, while Bratta educated him on how to get in and out of a chair and how to transfer to a bed. After a week, he could transfer out of a wheelchair with two people assisting him by pushing off with his arms. His legs still weren't working.

Adam had frequent bouts of dizziness during his first few weeks at Magee because his body wasn't used to being in an upright position. He didn't have movement in his legs, so the muscle action wasn't pumping blood back to his heart efficiently; this caused the dizziness. When the feeling subsided, Bratta would put him through a rigorous set of drills that included rolling, balancing, and breathing exercises as well as leg stretches. Six weeks earlier, all of these tasks were mundane, done without thought. Now they required every bit of Adam's determination.

When Adam entered Magee, he had no movement in his hands. But weeks of electro-stimulation, a technique for electrically stimulating the muscles in the forearm to open and close the hand, had started to kick in. By the end of October, some of his hand movement had returned.

After three weeks at Magee, Adam was making considerable headway. Different parts of his body had flickers of movement. The "circuits" were connecting. The spinal cord, in Dr. Staas' layman terms, is like a sophisticated electrical wire with many circuits running through it. Some control feeling, and in Adam's case, there wasn't much injury to them. The ones that were affected the most severely were the ones that controlled strength and movement. Adam's body was repairing and retraining those "circuits."

During this time period, Adam enjoyed telling his visitors about his progress in physical therapy and weight lifting. "Here's a kid who used to bench-press 300 pounds and he had just made his first big jump in physical therapy," said Tim Gushue, the football coach from rival Shawnee High. Gushue, along with his wife, his 11-year-old daughter, and his assistant coach, visited Adam one Saturday night. "He had gone from a 2½-pound dumbbell to a 5-pound dumbbell and he told us about that and it was just so inspiring," said Gushue. The weights were cuffed to Adam's wrists or upper arms. It took every ounce of his strength to lift the five pounds. Going from 2½ pounds to 5 pounds made Adam feel as if this was the start of something big. Gushue listened to his enthusiastic voice and couldn't help but feel uplifted by the way Adam was dealing with his life-altering injury.

Jerry Segal was also inspired.

Segal knew all about life-altering injuries. In 1988, he was paralyzed when his spinal cord was inadvertently nicked during surgery in California. His injury was similar to Adam's: C-5 and incomplete.

Like Andre, Segal had an outgoing and positive outlook; the two formed a strong bond almost immediately after meeting. Andre was checking out Magee when one of the hospital administrators introduced the two men. Segal, a Philadelphia attorney whose talkative nature lights up a room, is now walking with the aid of arm crutches. He spent several months rehabbing in Magee and was so devoted and thankful to the hospital that he started an annual golf tournament that, in its first 12 years, raised $2.25 million for Magee's patients. He frequently does volunteer work at the hospital, motivating paralyzed patients with stories of his own recovery.

Segal told Andre that, before he arrived at Magee, doctors at two different hospitals told his wife that he would never walk again. "From what I understand, your son has the same injury I had," Segal said. "There's no reason he can't walk out of here. To me, this is the best place in the world."

Talking to Segal helped Adam understand some of the things he himself was going through. For instance, Adam was shivering when Segal first visited him. Jen was gently stroking his forehead, and Adam had a blanket pulled up to his chin, even though the room seemed extremely warm to Segal. He told Adam that the chills were due to his injury. "I went through them, too," he said, leaning on his metal arm crutches. "You get different sensations because the spinal cord works that way." Segal's spinal-cord injury had fouled up his thermostat, he said. Even now, 12 years after the injury, he still couldn't distinguish between hot and cold from his shoulders down. He used to have a specially designed mat in his shower that told him if the water was hot, warm, cool or cold. His wife insisted he use the mat after too many showers that left him strawberry red because he couldn't tell he was being scalded by hot water.

Segal's stories made Adam feel more comfortable with his condition. "I'm going to be the biggest pain in the neck you've ever had," he told Adam the first day he met him. "If they tell you to do 20 reps, I'll tell you to do 100. I would always do more and that's what you have to do. And when you're in your room watching TV, don't just relax. When your legs start to move, put weights on them while you're watching TV and make them stronger, and squeeze putty with your fingers to strengthen them. I want you to bust your tookus."

Adam nodded. He wasn't intimidated by this chatty little 59-year-old man with grayish hair and a Norman Vincent Peale outlook. He was drawn to him. "He knew what I was going through," Adam said, "and for him to be so optimistic and say I'd get through it, it gave me a lot of confidence. He made me feel good."

The feeling was mutual.

Segal visited Adam two or three times a week until, on December 8, he had to leave for Florida, where the warm weather helps him to function better and improves his physical-therapy sessions. Before returning from the "Sunshine State" in early May, he phoned Adam once a week.

Segal was amazed at Adam's drive and disposition. "He never blinked," Segal said. He meant that Adam never felt sorry for himself. "He never complained about the cards he was dealt. From the moment I met him, he had the attitude, 'OK, it happened to me. What do I have to do to get well?'"

That attitude reminded Segal of somebody else: himself. When he was injured, the steroid that had been administered to Adam was not yet available, so the swelling in his spinal cord was more severe and more damaging. Yet four months after he was admitted, he walked out of Magee with a cane.

He told Adam about the support he received from his wife and children, told him about the wonderful rehabilitation staff at Magee. Segal believed the support he had received from his family and from Magee's staff was one of the two main factors that had aided his rehabilitation.

The other factor was his attitude. "I wasn't smart enough to quit," he said. "I was convinced—and I still am—that there's nothing in this world I can't do."

The more time Segal spent with Adam, the more he could sense that the two had more in common than the titanium plates in their necks.

* * * * *

Adam's early days at Magee brought out a variety of different emotions in his visitors. Some were inspired. But just as many were saddened.

Andre looked at his son lying in bed and wished he could trade places with him. "I had my career. I don't need my body as much as he needs his," he thought. He had always thought his son would play in the NFL someday. And even if he didn't make it to the pros, he was going to be a three-year starting cornerback at Penn State. Why, Andre wondered, couldn't it be me stuck in that hospital bed?

Andre and Addie are very orderly people. That is evident in their impeccably decorated house and in their tight focus and direction. From the naming of their family members—they all start with the letter A, including their pet shih tzu, Archie—to the study habits of their children, this is a family with a strong sense of order and discipline.

Now their life had been turned topsy-turvy.

Friends tried to console Andre by telling him that the injury was part of a plan that God had for Adam. Andre prayed every night: "God, I don't understand. If there was a plan, couldn't He have gotten to me some other way?"

Judy Caruso was brought to tears by her visit with Adam.

Caruso, whose son Jordan played at South Jersey's Shawnee High and was a senior offensive lineman at Penn State, visited Adam shortly after he was transferred to Magee. She had become friendly with the Taliaferro family. She had attended some of Adam's high school games and later tailgated with Andre and Addie at Penn State. She had even groomed and watched their dog.

As she walked into the hospital room, Adam was wearing his neck brace, barely able to move. Addie would brush his teeth every so often. "He was literally a vegetable who could talk," Caruso said. When she left and drove home, she was in tears. As a football mom, she knew that life without sports would be painful to Adam. But that was secondary. "He has such a long road to get back to normal, never mind playing football," she thought, tears trickling down her cheeks.

Jen was also starting to get depressed. She made the trip from Rutgers to Philadelphia every weekend and spent time with Adam in the hospital. They watched Penn State and NFL games in the hospital lounge. They made small talk and dreamed about the day that Adam would be able to get on his feet.

In private, Jen cried a lot. How could this have happened to Adam? Why did it happen to him? What had he done to deserve this? She was feeling bitter.

But Adam, who had to wear diapers during the day, wasn't. Jen couldn't understand how he could be so mentally strong, how he could accept such a cruel twist of fate. "How come you never cry?" she whispered to Adam by his bedside. "How come you're never down?"

Again, Adam never blinked. "Well, I'm going to walk again, and they tell me I'm going to have a second chance and there's no reason to cry," Adam said. "I look around and see people who are never going to walk again. I'm going to have a second chance."

Adam Taliaferro, his neck broken and his NFL dreams shattered, felt lucky.

* * * * *

With each passing week, Adam developed function in another body part. First his left leg, then his left arm, next his right leg, then his right arm. There was nothing the therapists could do to make a muscle work if it wasn't working, but when the muscle came back, they could work it and make it stronger.

Adam was getting stronger and more functional at a rate that astounded even the optimistic Staas. "Usually, the progress is month to month," said Staas (who, coincidentally, graduated from South Philadelphia High in 1954 with Larry Ginsburg, Adam's high school coach). "With him, it was week to week and, in some cases, day to day."

Said Andre: "It seemed like he could move something different almost every day."

In therapy, Adam reeducated his muscles to the lessons he had mastered as an infant and toddler. "He had to relearn everything," Mangine said. Adam was twitching his foot, bending his ankles, pulling up his legs.

Geri Zelazny, one of the nurses who had cared for Adam and had gently held his hand during one of his trying moments at Jefferson Hospital, visited Adam each week to watch his progress. Zelazny had been in Adam's company dozens of times, but he had always been in a bed or a wheelchair. "When are we going to meet each other eye to eye?" she asked him one late October afternoon, a little more than five weeks after his injury.

Adam, seated in a wheelchair, started to brace himself up as if he was going to stand. He couldn't do it. "They tell me I can't do that," he said.

"Do you know why?" Zelazny replied. "If you get up and you can't stop yourself, you're going to kiss the ground. *That's* why they don't want you to do it."

Adam smiled devilishly. One of these days, he hoped, he would stand eye to eye with Zelazny.

CHAPTER TEN

A Buddy for Life

When Adam left home for Penn State, Addie Taliaferro ironed every piece of clothing that she later packed neatly into his suitcases. She grumbled about it at times, sure, but Addie loved taking care of Adam. And, as with many mothers when their child first leaves home, she struggled with the post–high school transition much more than Adam did. She talked to him every day while he was at Penn State and always fired the same motherly questions at him: Are you eating right? Is everyone treating you OK? Andre never said anything about the bloated phone bills that started arriving at their house in Voorhees, New Jersey. He knew she made those calls more than just out of parental concern. Addie missed Adam more than she had ever thought she would.

There were times when she would go sit on the wooden deck out-side of her family room and watch Adam's childhood unroll before her very eyes. Didn't it seem like yesterday that she was dressing five-year-old Adam in a Philadelphia Eagles uniform for Halloween? Her heart would ache just like it had on the night she watched Adam collect his high school diploma. Where had the years gone?

The house seemed empty without Adam. So empty that sometimes Addie would take a small TV set into Adam's bedroom, set it on the dresser, and plop down on his bed. His scent was still on the pillowcases that she refused to wash, and it made her feel close to the son who was exploring his new life 200 miles away. "I really had Adam withdrawal," Addie said.

Now Addie had Adam back full time, and the circumstances surrounding that change had left her on the brink of a breakdown. Those days in Ohio were the darkest she had ever known, but she quickly pulled herself together. Still, there were times when she came close to violating the "no sadness" zone she and Andre had instituted in Adam's hospital room in Philadelphia. Some days she would look out the windows at Magee and get that same forlorn feeling she had experienced while sitting on her deck a couple of months earlier.

She would flash back to those autumn nights when she sat in her car in the dimly lit parking lot at Eastern High School. The hot chocolate that she sipped out of a white Styrofoam cup would warm her as much as the crackle of the PA announcer's voice that wafted through the slightly cracked window. When Adam was doing what he loved most, Addie was happy—even if she couldn't bear to watch.

Now football was as gone as Adam's childhood years, and he was fighting just to walk again. Some days, Addie would have to fight to keep herself together, too.

That's where Andre came in. He was so positive, so upbeat, and so sure Adam would walk again that it couldn't help but rub off on Addie. "I really don't know what I would have done without Andre," she said. "He would kind of help me get through some days."

She wasn't the only one.

Penn State Coach Joe Paterno had been very emotional the day after Adam's injury, and the person who comforted him was the one who should have been falling to pieces. "Adam's father helped me, I didn't help him," Paterno said. "He said, 'Look Coach, it will be all right, it will be all right.' He was the strong one, I wasn't."

Paterno wasn't the only one to see that strength. "Andre Taliaferro is the most optimistic person I have ever met," said John Lombardo, the team doctor for Ohio State's football team. "Far and away."

"There was never a moment when Mr. Taliaferro didn't express the feeling, 'My son will make it, my son will walk again,'" Ohio State Coach John Cooper said. "I'm telling you he was an inspiration."

He certainly was to one of the doctors who rode in the ambulance with Adam. Jeff Laubenthal was serving a one-year medical fellowship at Ohio State, and he hoped to become a doctor for a collegiate sports team when he was finished in Columbus. His training had prepared him for a worst-case scenario such as Adam's, but the approximately half-mile ride from Ohio Stadium to the Ohio State University Medical Center had shaken him nonetheless. He couldn't stop thinking about the awful silence after Adam said, "I can't be paralyzed. I just can't be paralyzed." Since the extent of the injury had not yet been determined, Laubenthal and the others could only tell Adam to remain calm.

When Laubenthal visited the hospital the next day, he met Andre, who shook his hand, looked him squarely in the eye, and said, "My son's going to walk back to Ohio State. Thank you for what you've done." Andre's conviction made a convert out of Laubenthal, even though the medical reports he had seen painted a bleak picture.

The assuredness that Andre always projected comforted everyone around him. He couldn't quite explain its origin. He rejected the suggestion that the perseverance he had needed to survive the rough streets of north Philadelphia had prepared him for this. Maybe Andre had seen enough of Adam's athletic exploits to know that all Adam needed was a sliver of a chance to walk again. Maybe Andre figured that if there was any justice in this world, Adam would walk away from the injury that had already claimed his promising football career. Whatever the reason, a feeling had lodged deep in Andre's gut that Adam would recover, and he held on to that belief as tightly as if it was a winning lottery ticket.

In private, however, Andre had his struggles, too. There were times when he didn't want to talk to the doctors because he didn't want to hear what they had to say. And there were those fleeting moments when he became overwhelmed by the long odds doctors had given Adam or simply the sight of Adam not being able to move. Andre was sure that if Adam spent the rest of his life in a wheelchair, seeing his son that way would put him in an early grave.

Fortunately, the guy who everyone else seemed to lean on had someone to prop him up as well.

That person was Joe "Buddy" Sarra, a tough and tender gridiron lifer who had long labored behind the scenes in the grand production that is Penn State football. Sarra, 63, is mostly bald, with snow-white hair on the sides of his head. He has a bit of a stoop and walks with a limp that is the result of an old football injury. A product of hardscrabble western Pennsylvania, he embodies that fabled football area as much as anybody. He is tougher than a double shift in a coal mine. After making a point, he often crunches the words "Know what I mean?" together; in his gruff manner, it comes out sounding like "KnowhadImean?"

Sarra also has a bit of the absentminded professor in him. When he was still a coach, he regularly crammed 30 hours of work into a 24-hour day, obsessed over details (like any coach worth his whistle); because of this, he frequently forgot names. He compensated by calling everyone "buddy," a nickname he still uses so often that it has become *his* nickname in the Penn State football community. One of his grown sons even named his dog Buddy so Sarra could get the poodle's name right.

Jordan Caruso experienced that endearing absentmindedness when he briefly played for Sarra on the defensive line in the spring of 1998. Sarra would call Caruso at night to see if he or his roommate, Bob Jones, also a defensive lineman, had any questions about that day's practice. Even if Caruso told Sarra that Jones wasn't there, Sarra would call back a couple of minutes later, forgetting that the two were roommates.

"Buddy," Caruso would say, "I just talked to you."

"OK, buddy," Sarra would say, "that's not a problem."

Sarra moved into the role of administrative assistant following the 1999 season. His myriad duties led to organizing pregame tailgates and close interaction with the parents of the football players. That is when he developed a friendship with Andre Taliaferro. The two had met during Adam's official recruiting visit to Penn State the previous year, and the bond they had forged during that weekend continued when Andre and Addie attended Penn State's first four games. Sarra quickly dubbed Andre "the senior senator from New Jersey," because Andre is as quick with a smile as he is with a handshake and can work a room as well as the most seasoned of politicians.

In the weeks and months following the injury to Adam, Joe Sarra would become the chief adviser to the "senior senator from New Jersey." He would also become Andre's closest friend.

* * * * *

In 1967, as a second-year coach named Joe Paterno was putting his stamp on Penn State football, Joe Sarra was changing the way players at a small high school in southcentral Pennsylvania approached the game. That season provided a telling snapshot of the man who would later become as loyal a foot soldier as Penn State has ever had and a central figure in Adam Taliaferro's recovery.

Sarra's first preseason at Southern Columbia High School probably felt like boot camp to the players. They practiced three times a day and spent their nights sleeping in the school gym. When they weren't practicing, Sarra was drilling them during chalkboard sessions. He would scrawl Xs and Os on the board and players were called forward to explain their responsibilities for that play. Memories of that camp were no doubt on Bill Rider's mind when he later told people that he had "survived Joe Sarra." Rider, a senior two-way starter on that team, meant it as the ultimate compliment.

A funny thing happened that fall. The program, which struggled perennially because it played in a conference with much bigger schools, held its own. By the end of a highly respectable 5–5 season, the players who had cursed the arrival of the brusque coach with the funny western Pennsylvania accent would have tackled an oncoming pickup truck for him.

The Southern Columbia players didn't see just the tough side of Joe Sarra that year. It was not uncommon for him to pile players into his car on weekends and drive them all over the back roads of Pennsylvania, West Virginia, and Ohio to visit colleges. He also helped players fill out financial aid forms. Sarra helped Rider get to a small college in Ohio; Rider would later become a teacher and high school coach and then an administrator. To this day, he is as loyal to Joe Sarra as he was during his days as an undersized defensive end at Southern Columbia.

After a successful high school coaching career, Sarra moved into the college ranks. Following a lengthy stay at Lafayette College in eastern Pennsylvania, he arrived at Penn State in 1986. That year he coached the linebackers, the heart and soul of a team that went 12–0 and won the national championship.

Sarra quickly earned a reputation as one of the staff's most tireless workers. For years, Sarra's family hadn't been able to coax him into taking a vacation (when he finally relented he took work with him) and, true to form, when he was a coach he sometimes slept in his office. At that time he may have been the only person who put in more hours than fellow workaholic Joe Paterno. And he proved to be every bit as tough on the players as his boss.

Sue Paterno, who frequently tutors players, witnessed the evidence of that once. In the late eighties she worked with a linebacker whose punctuality apparently needed as much work as his punctuation. He was frequently late to his tutoring sessions, and the tardiness grated on Sue, who, like her husband, keeps a tight schedule. The student would always apologize, but sometimes that would make Sue even madder. She once became so infuriated after the player again offered repeated apologies that she had to leave the room. "Yes ma'am, yes ma'am my ass!" she fumed.

Just then Sarra walked around a corner and asked her what was wrong. When Sue told him, he went into the room. He came out after a few minutes and told Sue everything would be OK.

"I'm so sorry. I'll never be late again," the player said when Sue reentered the room. "I don't want Buddy mad at me." True to his word, he was never late again. He would earn a bachelor's degree and then go on to get a master's.

Years later, the toughness that Sarra had exhibited in that room could still be seen on the playing field. During spring drills in 1998, Penn State, as it does every year, opened up one of its practices for high school coaches to observe. Before one drill, in which the defensive linemen exploded out of their three-point stance and hit a tackling dummy, Sarra introduced the players to the hundreds of coaches who were watching (naturally, he got most of the players' hometowns wrong).

Sarra held the bag and exhorted the players: "C'mon, hit the bag hard! Punch 'em in the mouth." When Jordan Caruso hit the bag, the top of his helmet accidentally smashed into Sarra's face and split open the bridge of his nose. Blood trickled down his face, but he made no attempt to wipe it away or move from the hazardous spot. "Just keep going," he said to the wide-eyed players. "Punch 'em in the mouth."

"He is," Caruso would later say, "as old school as they get."

Sarra also has a tender side that seems as embedded in him as that western Pennsylvania grit; the essence of that side can be gleaned from a chance encounter that took place during one of the countless recruiting trips Sarra made from Penn State to the Pittsburgh area. The road that winds its way down through the mountains of central Pennsylvania and connects State College to the western part of the state often becomes treacherous during winter. One night Sarra was returning from Pittsburgh when he had to pull over on the side of the road due to snowy weather. There were already three other cars there, also waiting for the storm to let up. After stopping his car, Sarra made sure everyone else was OK. The drivers of two of the cars told him they were going to forge on, but the frightened lady in the third car asked Sarra if he would wait with her until a salt truck passed through and made the roads a little less slick. Sarra agreed, but after awhile he told her that they would be better off driving and finding her a safe place for the night. He had her drive in front of him in case she ran into trouble. He followed her to a motel and, when she said, "I'll pray for you," Sarra learned she was a nun. He went into the motel and tried to get her a room but there were no vacancies. Sarra asked the person at the front desk about setting up sleeping arrangements on a sofa for the woman in the lobby. Instead of driving back to State College, he folded his tired body into a small chair and stayed with the woman as she slept on the nearby couch.

The next day, when Sarra got to the office—he had driven straight there, of course—he joked with the other assistants that he had slept with a nun. It was vintage Sarra. He didn't think twice about all he had done for that woman. Helping people seemed to be a reflex for him. That's why it came as no surprise to those who know him that Sarra emerged as a constant and calming presence when Andre and Addie's world was coming apart.

Sarra volunteered to stay behind in Columbus the day Adam got hurt. He ended up flying back with the team, then went home to pack for his return trip to Ohio. "You're the best person to do this," his wife Barbara told him. She would barely see him over the next two weeks.

Sarra became Andre's most cherished confidante, in part because he helped see the Taliaferros through their lowest moments. On the morning of Adam's surgery, Addie became so overwhelmed with anxiety that she fell to the floor in the Taliaferros' hotel room in Columbus. Andre, who was as worried about his wife as he was about Adam at that point, called Sarra and Herm Wood, a longtime friend who had flown to Columbus, to the room to help him get Addie back on her feet.

In the following weeks, Sarra would pick up Andre time and time again. When Andre became frustrated—whether it was at a meeting or in an informal discussion with the doctors—Sarra always added an objective voice that Andre would later appreciate. "Mr. T, don't you think we ought to listen to them?" Sarra would say. "They've got knowledge."

"No, Coach, that's not what I want to do." Sarra wouldn't push, and a couple of hours later Andre would find himself seeking out the doctors with Sarra in tow.

As close as Andre became with Sarra, he still called him "Coach Sarra." That proved to be fitting, too, since that is how Sarra approached Adam's recovery. Listening to and trusting the people who would guide Adam through therapy was the same as listening to a coach, Sarra believed. The rehab sessions that Adam sweated through had the same aim as the weight-lifting sessions he had gone through as a player: to get stronger and ultimately get better.

Sarra also believed firmly in projecting a positive attitude to Adam; that is one of the reasons why he was so embraced by the Taliaferros. If players sense any doubt from their coaches, it can lead to disastrous results. Sarra felt the same way about Adam's recovery. That's why he and Andre started using snappy sayings, such as "Pray for Adam. Bet on Adam." While Adam was at Magee, Sarra frequently flew down to watch his therapy sessions. That always seemed to bring out the coach in him; the only thing missing from those days when he cheered Adam on was an exhortation to "Punch 'em in the mouth!"

Sarra became such a fixture at Magee that he was soon staying in the spare bedroom in the Taliaferros' basement. He would call Addie before his trips and jokingly tell her to make sure his bed was ready.

Nobody looked forward to his visits and the phone calls that came every day more than Andre. "He came in at a time when we were flat on our butts," Andre said. "He was really a source of comfort for me. I'm falling down, my wife is falling down, and he's the guy that's really holding us up emotionally. He was always there. Always."

That is something Andre will never forget. "I'm the kind of person when you do me a favor and especially do something for my kids, I'm yours forever," Andre said. "That's how I feel about him. There will never be anything I can't do for him."

Andre and Addie weren't the only ones who came to see Joe Sarra in a different light. When Adam first went to Penn State during the previous summer, Andre had asked Sarra about getting his son a job. As an administrative aide, Sarra's responsibilities include helping players who stay at Penn State over the summer to get jobs. Adam didn't get to Penn State until the middle of July, however, and with preseason practice only a month away, he wanted to concentrate on working out and getting to know his new surroundings. He also wanted to sleep late, which is why he started dreading the phone calls that seemed to come every day from Sarra about this job interview or that opening. Adam finally had Andre call Sarra and tell him that it was OK if Adam didn't work.

When practice started, Adam continued to see Sarra as the father that he and the other players thought they had left behind when they got to Penn State. "You'd see him in the locker room after practice and all of the guys would try to hide from him because you knew he was coming after you," Adam said. "He always had this big list of names with him of guys who had missed class or guys who had missed lunch or something. So everybody was trying to duck him."

Adam found that impossible to do while he was at Magee, but it didn't take long for his perception of Sarra to change. The guy who had frankly been a pain in his rear came to be appreciated by Adam more than he would have thought possible. "He's a great guy," Adam said. "He's been there from day one. He's not a young guy and he's made these trips back and forth. He's a cool guy."

* * * * *

It hadn't quite been *Planes, Trains and Automobiles*—the 1987 comedy about a businessman who desperately enlists every method of transportation available in an attempt to return to his family for the holidays—but Jarid Brookins' trip home was certainly a circuitous one. He took a four-hour bus ride from Tallahassee, Florida, to Jacksonville, hopped a flight to Raleigh, North Carolina, and then rode in a car for seven hours back to Voorhees, New Jersey.

The framed picture sitting on his desk in his dorm room at Florida A&M had provided the impetus for Brookins' trip. Taken at Eastern High School's prom, the photo shows Brookins, Adam, and Justin Barton posed in their tuxedos while making *S* signs with their hands. That was a reference to Sturbridge Lakes, the housing development where the three good friends lived.

When Brookins looked at that picture, taken in much happier times, tears would sometimes fill his eyes. In the weeks following Adam's injury, he found it hard to concentrate on anything else. One day, he called home and said, "Mom, I have to come back."

Brookins had to fly out of Jacksonville to get to Raleigh because of the short notice. In Raleigh he met up with Barton, Khary Sharpe, and Darryl Scott. The four then drove home for the first group visit Adam would receive from his high school friends.

Sharpe and Scott were playing football for Duke, but the Blue Devils had a bye the weekend of October 6. Barton played for North Carolina, but he was redshirting his freshman year, and he, too, had received permission to go home that weekend.

Adam had some reservations about the visit. He hadn't seen most of his high school friends since he left for Penn State, and he knew they wouldn't recognize him. The muscle he had worked so hard to put on that summer had been stripped away in a matter of weeks. And Adam, who had always been the most active person in his group of friends, now got tired talking; he frequently had to pause in between sentences.

When Adam was wheeled into one of the visiting room at Magee, Scott was so shaken by his appearance that he couldn't bring himself to talk to his former backfield mate. He sat on the other side of the room while the others made a big circle around Adam.

Once, Adam had been able to calm Scott's fears during a high school game. Two years earlier, Coach Larry Ginsburg told Scott at halftime of a playoff game that he would start the second half at quarterback. He had primarily played on defense that year, and his stomach started turning somersaults. But on the way back to the field, Adam walked up to him and said, "Give me the ball and we'll be OK."

Those words had been so reassuring to Darryl. Now he couldn't offer any in return to Adam. The reality had hit him like a blitzing linebacker: Adam really couldn't walk.

Brookins also struggled with what he saw during that visit. Adam looked so skinny and weak. His voice was barely audible and he had to keep spitting into a small cup, which Andre held for him, to get rid of the mucus that would build up in his lungs.

Fearing he might get emotional, Brookins (called "Rod" by his friends) walked away from the group momentarily. Pretty soon, though, Adam was asking for Rod. Brookins walked over to Adam's wheelchair and leaned in close. "How are the girls down in Florida?" asked Adam.

Brookins cracked up.

That moment illustrates how easy Adam made it for the hundreds of people who visited him at Magee—not to mention his parents, who stayed with him every day, and the nurses and physical therapists who worked with him on a regular basis. Most visitors initially entered Adam's room with a queasy feeling; they were not sure what they would see. But Adam quickly disarmed that uneasiness with his upbeat attitude, a demeanor that was devoid of any self-pity, and the infectious smile that his insidious injury had not been able to change.

When Jordan Caruso hobbled into Adam's room a couple of weeks after getting hurt in a mid-October game, Adam immediately asked, "How's the knee?" The concern Adam showed for Caruso nearly left him speechless. Hadn't he come to see how Adam was doing?

When Tim Gushue visited, he also thought he would have to cheer the young man up. But like so many others, he left Adam's room downright cheery. "We felt like we were walking 10 feet in the air," Gushue said.

Michael Kirschner knew the feeling.

A 1966 graduate of Penn State, Kirschner became close to Joe and Sue Paterno through his involvement with the school's library (the Paternos are perhaps its biggest benefactors) and other work as an alumni. During Adam's stay at Magee, Kirschner became Exhibit A as to the effect of Adam's magnetic personality.

Kirschner, who lives in suburban Philadelphia, got a call one day from Sue Paterno, who asked if he would visit Adam at Magee on the Paternos' behalf. There will be a time, Sue said, when the visits from celebrities come few and far between. She and Joe wanted Penn State to have a consistent presence there.

But what started as a favor to the Paternos quickly turned into what Kirschner called a favor to himself. He marveled at how positive Adam always seemed to be and noticed that when someone sent Adam cookies he always made a point to share them with his roommates.

Kirschner observed Adam's effect on others as well. One day while he was visiting, two teenage girls stopped by Magee hoping to see Adam. One of them said she had met Adam at a dance a couple of years earlier, but he didn't remember her. He told the people at the front desk to let the girls up to his room anyway. He spent the next half an hour talking to them, displaying that uncanny ability he had to make whoever was around him feel like a close friend.

A Penn State contingent always visited Adam on Thursdays. Athletic director Tim Curley would haul in the bags of letters and get-well cards that had been sent to Penn State. When told of the progress Adam had made that week, he would thrust his right fist into the air and say, "Yes!" Wayne Sebastianelli, Penn State's team doctor, and Joe Sarra were on those trips as well, and Kirschner became a regular during the Thursday visits.

One night he was having such a good time that he got home an hour and a half late for dinner. "I just didn't want to leave Adam's room," he told his wife, Patty.

"Well, why are you spending so much time there?" she replied. Kirschner knew words wouldn't do, so he took her on his next visit. She left Magee smitten with Adam, and Kirschner had his absolution for missing dinner.

In the following weeks, he would call the Paterno house, as excited as could be, whenever Adam made any progress. By then, visiting Adam was no longer a favor Kirschner was doing for the Paternos. "If I had a third son, I'd be happy if it was Adam," Kirschner said. "He may be one of the most positive human beings I have ever met. He doesn't know what negative means."

As Joe Sarra might say, "KnowhadImean?"

CHAPTER ELEVEN

Making Lemonade . . . and a Miracle

Until late October, only relatives and some close friends had been informed about how Adam was progressing at Magee. A few comments from his high school coaches, who had been visiting Adam, made their way into the newspapers but, for the most part, the public was in the dark.

Rumors were rampant and wide-ranging. Adam is going to be a vegetable, went one. Adam is going to walk one day, went another. The Taliaferro family wanted to end the rumors.

At the same time, Penn State was getting flooded with phone calls and e-mails asking about Adam's condition. Jeff Nelson, the school's sports information director, phoned Andre and suggested that it was time to hold a news conference.

Replied Andre: "You know what? I'm ready." Ready to tell the world that Adam was in the process of beating astronomical odds. Ready to explain that some doctors had underestimated his son. Ready to spread the word that Adam was going to walk one day. "Let's do it," Andre told Nelson. He couldn't wait. This was a chance to show everyone that his boy was on his way back.

About 40 media members attended the November 1 press conference at Magee. It was the first time the public had seen Adam, via TV and newspaper cameras, since his injury 39 days earlier.

Adam, sitting in his motorized wheelchair and wearing a neck brace, had a wide grin on his face as he raised both arms and greeted friends and the media with a shy wave. He was flexing his arms and fingers, moving his legs, and smiling.

Andre choked back tears. "As you can see, sitting here today, through God's grace and mercy, he's on the road to recovery," Andre said. "He's movin' and groovin' and he's on his way back. We're going to walk out of here someday."

Dr. William Staas, Adam's attending physician, agreed with Andre's assessment. Staas, president and medical director at Magee since 1977, said it was just a "matter of time and practice" before Adam was walking again. "Every day, there's another muscle working that wasn't working," Staas said. The muscles critical to walking were working. Adam, who had been at Magee for just 27 days, was getting stronger and his feeling was improving.

"When I first got here, I couldn't move anything," said Adam, dressed in a gray, long-sleeve Penn State sweat shirt and matching sweat pants. "Now they've got me moving my legs and my arms and everything."

Adam was composed during the press conference. His father wasn't. He continually dabbed at his moist eyes. He was oozing with pride, like a man whose wife had just given birth to their first child. "A lot of people said they thought my boy wouldn't walk again, but I want everyone to see the whole story," Andre said. "We have a miracle in progress."

Staas said Adam's mental makeup was partly responsible for his amazing strides. "Adam sees lemons," Staas said, "and makes lemonade. He doesn't see the negative, he sees the positive." The broken neck, of course, was the ultimate lemon. "Adam is a strong person, not just physically, but mentally and psychologically," Staas said. "He sees this as an opportunity—a word he used with me very early when he came here."

Adam's career as a football player may be over, Andre said, "but he's on his way to walking again, so who cares? One door closed, but 10 more have opened up. He's had a chance to meet some great people."

On the football field, Adam had an invincible aura about him, which the injury took away. Now that air of humble confidence seemed to be returning. At the press conference, it was obvious that he was starting to regain control of his life. "People say that if I get through this, I can get through almost anything," Adam said.

There was still lots of work to do, still numerous hurdles that had to be cleared, Staas cautioned. Adam, after all, still couldn't stand without assistance. But all signs, he said, were pointing toward a recovery. Staas said Adam had approached his rehab with "the mind-set of an athlete." He was setting goals and going after them. "And in about two more months, it's possible he'll walk out of here."

A little later, Staas stunned everyone, including the Taliaferro family, when he said it was "quite possible" that Adam would be able to play football again by the next year. "If he were my son, I wouldn't let him play," he said. "He might be able to play next year, but I wouldn't recommend it. Of course, he doesn't have to listen to my recommendation."

"He will," Andre said, drawing laughs from relatives, friends, and the media. "He will."

Adam said he planned to be with the Nittany Lions at their 2001 opener against visiting Miami on September 1—not as a player, but as one of the guys. He said he hoped to lead the team through the football tunnel and onto the Beaver Stadium field.

It was a feel-good press conference and, when it was over, many members of the grizzled Philadelphia media—folks who have a reputation for being harsh critics—applauded.

Adam Taliaferro had turned them into Silly Putty.

* * * * *

After the press conference, Adam went home for the first time since his injury. The visit was brief. He was accompanied by Magee staff members who wanted to see how the Taliaferros' home could be made accessible for Adam when he left the hospital for good, hopefully in a few months.

It was the first time Adam had been in his Voorhees home in almost four months. When he had last been there, he was excitedly packing to go to Penn State. He was full of hopes, full of expectations.

Now he had to be helped into the house in a wheelchair. Andre and one of the drivers from Magee pulled Adam and his wheelchair up the steps to his second-floor bedroom.

Marygrace Mangine and Amy Bratta walked around the inside and outside of the house, evaluating how it could be made wheelchair accessible—which seemed ironic in light of the fact that Dr. Staas hoped Adam would be walking in perhaps two months. Within a few weeks, a brick walkway was built in the backyard to make it easier to move a wheelchair. Electric stair glides were installed on the two sets of indoor steps. Portable ramps were purchased to make it easy to transport Adam to and from the house.

The Taliaferros and the Magee crew stayed at the house for about two hours. Adam wasn't disappointed to leave. He felt restricted at home because it wasn't wheelchair friendly. He wanted to return to Magee, wanted to continue his rehab because "I want to get better and get back on my feet."

That night, clips of the press conference were shown on news telecasts. Trish Power, the Jefferson nurse who saw Adam move his leg and toes on October 2 and thought it was a sign that he would recover, watched the coverage and couldn't help feeling a sense of pride. "When I saw him moving his leg on TV," she said, "it made me feel vindicated." It was Power who had earlier told Adam that his toe and leg movement signified that he didn't have permanent spinal-cord damage. It was

Power who disagreed when doctors told her Adam's movement might be involuntary.

Power, a Catholic with short brown hair tinged with red highlights, wasn't a very religious person before she took care of Adam. "Adam changed my life," she said. "I didn't always have a strong faith until I met Adam. Now I go to church regularly and now I get more out of the Mass. Adam did that."

Adam has a profound effect on people—all kinds of people. Those of different races and varied backgrounds, those who are established in their professions, like attorney Jerry Segal, and those who are struggling to find their place in society. They gravitate toward him.

Addie was amazed at how the wheelchair patients drifted toward Adam; it was as if he had a secret formula for getting out of the wheelchair. Two of those patients were young, paralyzed men: Luis, from Camden, New Jersey, and James, from west Philly. A gunshot wound paralyzed James, while Luis was injured when he fell off a dirt bike. Both were rehabbing at Magee.

Adam didn't feel depressed being around people in wheelchairs, especially Luis and James, men in their early twenties. He drew strength from their positive attitudes. "They seemed to know how to handle it," he said. Luis and James would maneuver their wheelchairs down to Room 543, Adam's temporary home, and entertain him and his mom with animated, humorous stories about their lives on the inner-city streets. Luis, who had a fondness for tattoos, would punctuate the stories with sound effects. James seemed to know just when to chime in. If they had been a comedy team, critics would have said they had perfect timing. They had a knack for spinning a good story; so what if they were probably exaggerating some of the details? "They were the funniest guys I've ever met," Adam said. "They were in wheelchairs but they had as much fun as anyone I've ever seen. I never saw them down and they'll be in wheelchairs the rest of their lives. I don't know how they deal with it."

Before being released from Magee, Luis and James presented Adam with a Penn State football they had purchased on one of the hospital's bus trips to a mall in Cherry Hill, New Jersey. They had signed the ball and passed it around for the hospital staffers to sign as well before giving it to a genuinely appreciative Adam.

After they left, Addie shook her head. "Adam," she said, laughing, "you're loved by everyone!" The outgoing young men stayed in contact with Adam after they left the hospital. "We became good friends in a short amount of time," Adam said.

* * * * *

Mangine and Bratta had Adam on a grueling schedule. He had been as stiff as a board when he entered Magee but was now gaining function at a stunningly quick rate, so he didn't seem to mind the unforgiving rehab regimen.

Dr. Staas had seen other patients become unwilling participants when they had to take orders from female therapists. Adam, however, thrived on it. "They were the ones who were really the driving force behind this," Staas said.

Staas told Adam he was proud that he didn't object to taking orders from women. Adam smiled and gave Staas a puzzled look. "Why should I be upset about taking orders from women?" is how Staas interpreted his expression. "You don't get that from young males," Staas said. "Typically, they get intimidated by women. Adam had no chauvinism, and I think that gives me some insight into what kind of husband he's going to be and what kind of father."

Mangine said Adam's upbringing was a major contributor. "From my experiences, it seems that males who grow up in an African American background are used to obeying their mothers. The mother is the one that controls the house," she said. "That's how you learn respect."

Mangine earned Adam's respect through the way she treated him. She became Adam's therapist *and* his friend. Some therapists don't agree with that method. They think you can't get results unless you show the patient you have the authority. But that isn't Mangine's style. She develops a rapport with her patients, finds out their likes and dislikes, finds out what makes them tick. She becomes their friend, someone who wants to make them feel that they are on the same level.

Bratta, who, like Mangine, had never heard of Adam before his injury, has a similar philosophy. "You build a personal relationship so you know what motivates them and when they're not feeling well," she said. "You want to know what to expect and how to read them." The two therapists learned to read Adam perfectly.

By late November, Adam was able to move his legs up and down. He'd playfully lift them off the bed and pretend he was going to give Jen a kick. "He was my medicine to feel better," Jen said. "He was helping *me* get through this."

Adam's mental makeup and emotional discipline stunned Staas. "He's as close mentally to a Green Beret as I've ever seen," Staas said. "He's used to working hard and applying himself." Adam never whined, never said he couldn't complete a task, never felt sorry for himself, Staas said. "He's very disciplined. If you say to him, 'I'd like you to do this,' he doesn't say, 'No,' or 'What?' He says 'OK. You want me to do it 10 times? I'll do it 12. I'll do it 15. I'll do it and keep doing it better.' He takes pride in what he does; he's very mature and disciplined for someone 18 years of age. You don't see that in folks at that age. It's something that you see in later years, with more experience." All these things, Staas said, helped to "prevent an incomplete injury from becoming complete."

A lot of Adam's mental toughness, Staas said, could be attributed to his supportive family. And to Adam's ego. "He's not an egomaniac, but he has a strong ego," Staas said. "There's a difference." Adam, the doctor said, doesn't think he'll succeed; he *knows* he will.

The therapists kept Adam's mind off his physical problems and improved his finger movement by playing cards, checkers, and other board games with him. The electro-stimulation had worked wonders on his fingers, especially those on his left hand. He was now able to use his fingers to make phone calls. Late at night, he would tell Andre it was

OK if he went home. As soon as he left, Adam pulled out his cell phone and dialed his friends. He wasn't tired because he took naps during the day; he would sometimes stay on the phone until 3:00 in the morning. "I don't know who got the phone bills," he said, "but I know they had to be crazy."

* * * * *

"Adam! Stop it, Adam! You're going to hurt yourself!"

Addie's words were stern, but they were also tinged with just enough compassion to let Adam know that she was happy he was able to enjoy himself. Adam, in a playful mood, was going for a joyride. He was the pilot. His motorized wheelchair was his vehicle. "You're scaring me with that thing, Adam," Addie said.

"I'll be OK, Mom."

Adam had become adept at working the wheelchair's joystick. He rolled out of his hospital room and into the hallway before putting the wheelchair on its highest speed. He couldn't return kickoffs or interceptions, so this was the next best thing. He would zoom around the hallways and then come to an abrupt stop.

Jen's laughter couldn't drown out Addie's pleas coming from Adam's room. "No playing around, Adam! You're scaring me!" Adam would travel so fast that Jen, running from behind, couldn't catch up with him. He'd stop the wheelchair and let her catch up.

"Ready? Hold on," he said. Jen would steer the wheelchair as Adam motored along, sometimes bumping into the walls.

"Jump on, Jen." She would hop on the back and Adam would cruise around the hallways.

"This is just how we'd have fun," Jen said, "because there was nothing to do in there." In order to have time alone, they would ride the elevator from floor to floor, over and over and over. Sometimes they'd go outside to the rooftop deck, but the weather was turning cold.

Sometimes they'd go to the cafeteria where Adam, who had become a celebrity because of the publicity his story had generated, would spend hours listening to other patients' hard-luck stories. And sometimes they would just cruise around on his wheelchair.

While Adam was going for a joyride, his Penn State football team was going in reverse.

The week after his injury, Penn State achieved an emotional 22–20 upset over Purdue, a win that would be the highlight of the season. As the Nittany Lions rushed into each others' arms, reserve safety Russ Manney, a senior from Wellsboro, Pennsylvania, pulled off his helmet, walked to the 50-yard line, and rested on his left knee. His teammates followed, gathered around him, and formed a circle while holding each others' hands. Manney, his head bowed, offered a prayer of thanks. "Take care of that boy in Philly," he said at one point. "Send him home so he can walk out of the tunnel again."* It was the end of an emotional day. Penn State would have few other reasons to celebrate on its way to a 5–7 record, the second losing season in Joe Paterno's 35 years as its head coach.

Adam would watch some of the games on TV, but he was having a difficult time being a spectator. He was excited to see his Penn State teammates, telling Jen personal stories about a lot of the players as they watched the games together in the fifth-floor hospital lounge. But after watching for a little while, he would lose interest. "Want to go for a walk?" he would ask.

Jen was surprised that Adam didn't want to watch most of the games.

"I'd watch to see where I would have been playing," Adam said, "and it hurt to see someone else playing where I used to be." It also hurt to see someone make a tackle; it made Adam second-guess himself and wonder why he had his head down when he made his career-ending tackle. "But as soon as I'd think about that, I'd realize it could have been worse than it was," he said. "As soon as I'd think, 'Why did it happen

* Quote courtesy of the *Penn State Daily Collegian*, from an article appearing October 2, 2000.

to me?' I'd switch it around and not worry about it and say, 'You still have a chance to walk.'"

After turning the TV off, Adam and Jen would wander around the halls. Sometimes they would return to watch the end of the Penn State game. Sometimes they would just drift around the hospital and mingle with the staff and other patients.

*   *   *   *   *

During the same week that Adam had his upbeat news conference at Magee, a Hudson County, New Jersey, grand jury cleared Penn State quarterback Rashard Casey of criminal charges. Back in May, Casey had been accused of assaulting an off-duty police officer outside a dance club in his hometown of Hoboken. After Casey was charged, his attorney, Dennis McAlevy, and Paterno maintained his innocence. And when the grand jury cleared him, McAlevy blasted reporters who had criticized Paterno for his stance on the matter. "May they burn in First Amendment hell," he told *The Philadelphia Inquirer*.

Casey wasn't indicted and could concentrate on football again. Adam, meanwhile, was making extraordinary progress. Folks in Happy Valley were smiling.

As the weeks went by and Thanksgiving inched closer, it seemed Adam was on target to walk out of Magee someday. His family was looking toward a joyous Thanksgiving, a development that had seemed unrealistic just a month earlier. The Taliaferro family felt blessed and thankful for all the assistance and support that had come to Adam and themselves.

Perhaps they should have been most thankful toward Wise Young, the doctor who invented a steroid called methylprednisilone during the eighties. When given within a few hours of an injury, this drug helps restore some lost body function. Young's invention was injected into Adam's system about 30 minutes after his spinal-cord injury.

Gary Rea, the surgeon who performed Adam's spinal-fusion surgery in Ohio, said it wasn't clear how much the steroids helped in this case. "Did it make a difference? I don't know. Did it hurt anything? No. If it happened again, would you want him to have steroids quickly? Yes."

But Wayne Sebastianelli, the Penn State doctor, thought the steroids played a key role. Methylprednisilone isn't an anabolic steroid that will "juice" somebody up or increase their muscle mass. It is a steroid compound used to control inflammation and swelling. "And what that does," Sebastianelli said, "is decrease secondary damage caused by further loss of blood flow." As things swell, he said, you pinch off the little capillaries and blood vessels in body parts and spinal tissue; the nerve roots are just so soft that any type of pressure at all will completely shut off blood flow through that part of the nerve where the spinal cord is located. When these tissue cells die, they release poisonous enzymes that can cause further damage, Sebastianelli said. Methylprednisilone controls the enzyme inflammation and secondary damage, which consequently helps the blood flow through that part of the spinal cord.

Steroids aren't the cure-all for a spinal-cord injury, Sebastianelli said. "A lot of things have to go right besides the steroids. But if you get the steroids in a patient within four hours of the injury, they stand a much better chance of getting some recovery than if they got them after four hours. And I think that's where the difference is in this kid. I think if he was lying in a field somewhere in a car and wasn't found for three or four hours and had his neck rolled back and his body twisted and there was all that tension on the spinal cord . . . well . . ." If that had happened, the swelling would have continued and Adam probably wouldn't ever be able to *think* about walking again. But it didn't happen in a car on a deserted road. It happened on a football field, near the Penn State sideline. It happened where the appropriate personnel knew how to manage immobilization, transportation, and equipment removal.

Lying in his hospital bed, Adam was thankful that his injury occurred near the Penn State sideline. "If I would have gotten hurt in the middle of the field or the end zone, I could have moved around and hurt myself even more," he said. But because he was injured near the Penn State sideline, the Nittany Lions' medical staff was able to immobilize him in less than 30 seconds.

There is a lot about the spinal cord that is still unknown. Culturing spinal-cord tissue and injecting it into patients is among the many research projects now underway, Sebastianelli said. He doesn't profess to be an expert in the ever-changing spinal-cord field. But he does think that, 20 years from now, there will be more patients making spinal-cord advances than ever. And he does know that Adam definitely would not have walked if he had suffered the same injury during the late seventies and eighties, when Sebastianelli was in training.

CHAPTER TWELVE

Tunnel Vision

Thanksgiving turned the Taliaferro house into what Addie called "Grand Central Station," but she didn't mind a bit.

Adam had progressed enough that he received permission to return home for the holiday. His friends were also home, and they kept the doorbell at the Taliaferro house ringing as Addie prepared a Thanksgiving Day feast. Adam was in a wheelchair, but he looked much more like the Adam they knew before his injury.

Darryl Scott dropped by the house. Adam was heartened. "I haven't seen you in awhile," he said. Scott had actually visited Magee during his friend's first weekend there, but he had been too distraught to talk to Adam. "I was there in October," Darryl said.

"Yeah, my mom told me, but I don't remember seeing you," Adam said.

On Thanksgiving, the friends who visited Adam inevitably ended up in his younger brother's bedroom to try a PlayStation2 game. They were just doing what Adam would have been doing had his legs allowed him to climb the stairs.

As happy as she was to have Adam home, Addie couldn't help but feel a little bit sorry for him. Confined downstairs in a wheelchair, he cut a lonely figure watching TV in the family room. Days like these had become Adam's reality. Even though his recovery was speeding along, the time dragged, especially when he only had brief rehabilitation sessions. It was almost as if the hands on clocks had five-pound dumbbells tied to them.

It hadn't been that way prior to his injury. About two months earlier, on the plane ride out to Ohio State, Adam sat next to senior tight end Tony Stewart. The time goes so fast, Stewart told him. Adam nodded. Heck, he was already trying to figure out where the time had gone.

Those first days after the freshmen arrived on campus already seemed like a distant memory. He couldn't help but laugh when he thought about it. They had been the stars of their respective high school teams, and they arrived at Penn State as all-conference, all-state, and even All-American in more than a few cases. They spent those first couple of days sizing each other up.

That wariness had prevailed between Adam and Gerald Smith, a blue-chip cornerback prospect from Maryland, when they had first met during the previous spring as high school seniors. Each had attended the Blue-White game, Penn State's annual spring scrimmage, and both knew they would compete against each other for playing time the following fall. They didn't talk much until they sat together and watched the scrimmage. Then the walls that had been constructed by their competitive natures came tumbling down. "We started to get to know each other better, and he's a good guy," Adam said. "He seemed like one of my friends from high school. He wasn't a cocky guy or thought he was better than anybody." Both spent at least part of the summer at Penn State, and they became close friends. By the time the season started, they were studying their playbooks together and talking about the days when they would be the Nittany Lions' starting cornerbacks.

A different yet predictable catalyst had brought the rest of their class together: the arrival of the rest of the team to preseason practice. That's when the high school hotshots got daily reminders that they were starting over, that freshmen at Penn State don't have the exalted status they enjoyed in high school. Actually, they have *no* status of which to speak. They don't get a mention in the team's voluminous media guide and aren't even listed on the official roster.

During the first full-squad meeting, each freshman has to stand up and list his high school honors. Naturally, the returning players who have endured this initiation ritual have a lot of fun with it; they gave it to one of the freshmen pretty good that day. Some of the upperclassmen had noticed that fullback Paul Jefferson bore a resemblance to the World Wrestling Federation megastar "The Rock," who has a signature saying: "It doesn't matter!" The other players seized on that, and every time Jefferson recited one of his awards, voices shouting, "It doesn't matter!" would echo throughout the room.

Adam got through that meeting OK, and even laughed at himself when the freshmen had to sing "I'm a little teapot" at a team pool party. In fact, his adjustment to major college football went as smoothly as was possible. Even the dislocated thumb he sustained during a preseason scrimmage didn't force him to miss much practice time, and he was one of the few freshmen to make the traveling squad.

He enjoyed life away from football, too.

School had always been pretty easy for Adam, so he didn't get overwhelmed by the demands of football and his class work. Far from it, in fact. During the mandatory study halls players attend at night, he sometimes found himself working ahead just to pass the time. Prior to the injury, he was on track to make the dean's list.

Like the rest of his classmates, he also found time to have fun.

Gerald Smith roomed with wideout Tony Johnson in the fall, and Johnson, who had gone to nearby State College High, turned into a tour guide for Smith, Adam, and his roommate, J.D. Benson. Like most freshmen, their newfound freedom meant going to parties and making late-night forays for food. They usually ended up at the McDonald's in downtown State College, which really does resemble Grand Central Station at

2:00 A.M. during weekends. One night, they decided they were tired of McDonald's and looked for something else. They found a nearby pizza place that sold slices for a buck. They happily munched on the pizza and basked in their new discovery. This was college.

Adam doesn't remember ever getting homesick, although there were times when he would get restless and leave his dorm room at night. He would wander around downtown State College, finding something new almost every time.

The injury had interrupted all of that and seemingly hit the pause button on a life that had been in fast-forward.

Adam sometimes called Smith, who would tell him about a party he had attended recently and some friends he had made. Adam couldn't help but feel a little left out.

Not that he was ever far from the thoughts of his teammates. Stewart organized a photo shoot in which the players lined up in a "43" formation on the field at Beaver Stadium, and Penn State sent the picture to Adam. Teammates and coaches also called and visited regularly, as did athletic director Tim Curley and Dr. Wayne Sebastianelli. But it wasn't the same as being at school with them.

It had been the same way with his high school friends. Justin Wolk, one of his former classmates, always seemed to be at the hospital. So did numerous other high school friends, including some of his ex-girlfriends. Adam had wanted nothing more than to go out with his buddies when they visited him in Magee; the plans they made only reinforced the fact that Adam was stuck in a hospital bed.

It would be the same way on Thanksgiving. His friends were planning to enjoy the Philadelphia nightlife after their respective family dinners. Adam, meanwhile, would have to go back to Magee and endure another uneventful weekend. "I just wanted to go out and do what everybody else was doing," Adam said. "They understand I'm hurt, but they don't understand the other part about sitting there all day and being bored and that's when I wanted to get out and get better."

And get his life back.

* * * * *

Letters sent via mail and the Internet continued to pour into Penn State after the public became aware of the remarkable progress Adam was making. One particularly heart-wrenching story found its way to Andre.

It came from the relatives of a high school boy in Alabama. The boy played baseball and golf; he also wrestled during the winter months, primarily to stay in shape for the other two sports. One day in practice, his coach demonstrated a takedown move on him and accidentally broke the boy's neck. It looked like the teenager would spend the rest of his life as a quadriplegic. Stories like that reminded Andre, who later got in touch with the family, how lucky Adam was.

Just before the November 1 news conference at Magee, Andre had been pulled aside by Ron Siggs, the hospital's affable marketing vice president. Siggs told him about another football player who, like Adam, had been paralyzed while making a tackle. It had happened about a month after Adam's injury and it involved a player from Siggs' alma mater, the University of Washington. Siggs told Andre about it in case any reporters mentioned it during Adam's news conference.

"Let's give him a call," Joe Sarra said. Andre agreed, and shortly thereafter he got in touch with an older brother of Curtis Williams, the Washington player who had sustained a serious spinal-cord injury in an October 28 game. He had only been able to blink his eyes in the days that followed.

Of all the stories Andre had heard, none would resonate more with him than what had happened to Curtis Williams. Like Adam, Williams' life had been altered forever after he dipped his head while tackling a hard-charging running back. And, like Adam, Williams' best football had appeared to be ahead of him before he sustained that spinal-cord injury.

After rushing for over 1,400 yards and 31 touchdowns as a senior at Bullard High School in Fresno, California, Williams arrived at the University of Washington in 1996 as a prized tailback recruit. He also arrived at a time when Corey Dillon, who later became an NFL star, had yet to crack the starting lineup. Because of the depth the Huskies had in their offensive backfield, Williams spent his first couple of years shuttling from position to position, trying to find a way to get on the field.

By the beginning of the 1999 season, he had found a home at free safety. He started all 11 games there; at the end of the season he won the award for the defense's most ferocious hitter. He moved over to strong safety in 2000 and continued to deliver punishing hits while patrolling a secondary that held Miami's All-American wideout Santana Moss to one catch for seven yards in Washington's 34–29 win against the Hurricanes.

The 5'10", 200-pound Williams possessed the same intimidating aura as Penn State's fearless safety James Boyd, and he had developed into an NFL prospect. An NFL career would allow Williams to support his young daughter, Kymberly, who lived with his ex-wife in Anchorage, Alaska. Kymberly was watching the October 28 game when Williams met Stanford running back Kerry Carter in a helmet-to-helmet collision. She walked into the kitchen and announced, "My dad fell down and he won't get up."*

Williams had torn the ligaments that hold the C-1 and C-2 vertebrae together. He also ended up with a contusion on his spinal cord. Carter, meanwhile, walked away from the hit. In the weeks that followed, Williams would not show much improvement and had to breathe with the aid of a ventilator. His spinal cord had not been severed, but because of the severity of the injury, his long-term prognosis wasn't nearly as promising as Adam's.

Andre's heart ached for David Williams, the older brother who would come to care for Curtis. He also knew that as bad as he sometimes felt about Adam losing football forever, his family had been lucky. That is why Thanksgiving had a different feel for Andre than in years past. "Now, you kind of embraced the real meaning of what it really meant," Andre said.

* Quote courtesy of the *San Jose Mercury News*, from an article appearing April 24, 2001.

While Andre, Addie, Adam, and Alex had dinner with their relatives, Jen's family was experiencing the powerful emotions that a holiday can evoke. Her father said grace, adding some prayers for Adam's recovery. "We pray that Adam will get better and walk again soon," he said before he suddenly became choked up. When the rest of the family looked up, they realized they were crying, too. They giggled at each other and then cried some more.

* * * * *

Back at Magee, Adam's routine included practice-walking on a treadmill in a small room on the fifth floor, around the corner from the gym and his hospital room. At first the therapists moved Adam's legs for him, trying to retrain the muscles. But a few weeks later, in late November, the therapists weren't moving his legs. Adam was. The therapists were at his side to catch him if he fell.

That room became Adam's torture chamber. A black and red canvas harness was strapped around his torso and shoulders. The harness was clipped to a metal plate hanging from a beam in the ceiling. Below Adam was a motorized treadmill. Addie was seated a few feet away, working the buttons that control the machine's speed. This drill was incredibly challenging and draining to his already beat-up body.

Adam was just barely able to move his legs on his own. His sneakers rubbed back and forth on the treadmill's rubber mat as it moved at a slow speed, two miles per hour. Adam was expressionless as he looked into a mirror while moving. His eyes were focused as he breathed deeply. He grunted and groaned, struggling to keep up the pace. "Doing great, Adam," said Amy Bratta.

Adam breathed more heavily. His left leg was moving easier than his right one. The injury had done more damage to his right side. His right foot began to drag. "Pick up your foot," Bratta said. Adam, his gray Penn State T-shirt swimming in perspiration, grimaced. He would rather be doing two-a-day football workouts with the temperature near triple dig-its. But he didn't complain. Whatever instructions Bratta and Marygrace Mangine gave, he followed.

Occasionally his feet would tangle and he would clumsily stumble as his legs flailed. The therapists would grab him, put him back in position, and keep him on his merry way.

"Step up and swing your arms, Adam," said Bratta in a voice a lot calmer and sweeter than any of his previous football coaches. "C'mon, step, step, step." They were baby steps. But they were steps, nonethe-less, and they would lead to bigger ones. Steps that numerous medical people had thought would never be possible.

Adam was a guinea pig of sorts. He was part of a research project sponsored by the National Institute of Health, which is testing the the-ory that spine-injured patients will walk sooner—and better—if they bypass the use of leg braces and go directly to walking without them. The project, which will last five years, had been underway for about a year when Adam joined the program. Roughly a dozen patients have taken part in the study at Magee, Dr. Staas said. Some have been suc-cessful, some haven't. "But Adam's particular progression was dramatic, when you consider how he first started on the treadmill and how much assistance he needed," Staas said. When he first started on the treadmill, four or five people were assisting him, literally moving his legs for him. Not now. Now he was moving his legs by himself, with one or two aides by his side.

"I call him Miracle Boy," Addie said.

* * * * *

By mid-December, Adam was regaining so much function that, for the first time since his injury, he was able to dress himself without assis-tance. "I can't believe I just put my pants on!" he said with Mangine next to him. His freedom was returning. The catheter had been out for more than a month. Although he still needed someone to give him a shower, he was able to go to the bathroom without assistance and to stand and move all his fingers.

Geri Zelazny, the Jefferson nurse who had never been face-to-face with Adam, finally got her wish one afternoon as she saw him doing a walking exercise in the hospital hallway. They were about the same height, and Zelazny flashed back to Adam's arrival at the hospital, flat on his back and unable to squeeze her hand.

"I got it now, didn't I?" she said. She meant that, at long last, she got to see Adam when he wasn't in a hospital bed or a wheelchair. Adam grinned proudly. Words weren't necessary.

Adam was making so much progress that he was allowed to go home for a weekend in mid-December. He returned to his alma mater, Eastern High, to watch the Vikings' season-opening boys basketball game against highly touted Camden on December 15.

A standing room only crowd of 1,500 fans jammed into Eastern's gym. Eastern's players wore "A.T." patches and chanted "A.T." during huddles in honor of him. Eastern lost, 76–61, but the game seemed secondary. "People ask me what's the most important thing about this year," said Eastern basketball coach Dave Allen after Dajuan Wagner scored 36 points to engineer Camden's victory. "It's not winning games; it's not winning championships. It's to see him walk."

Even Wagner, the Camden guard who was generally regarded as the top prep player in the nation, couldn't steal the show from the spectator who sat in the wheelchair next to Eastern's bench. It was the first time Adam had returned to Eastern since his accident. As his father wheeled him into the gym 25 minutes before the 4:00 P.M. game started, Adam received a standing ovation. About 15 minutes later, after numerous well-wishers had greeted him at courtside, public-address announcer Pete DeFeo introduced Adam to the adoring crowd. "He's a special member of the Eastern family," DeFeo said. "His dedication and hard work often inspired others when he was a student here at Eastern. Today, his hard work and faith inspire people around the country."

The fans, some in tears, stood and applauded as Adam was wheeled to center court by Andre. Wearing his familiar Penn State gray sweat suit, Adam waved and smiled. Eastern presented him with a "44" basketball jersey. Camden's coach, Glen Jackson, gave him a fruit basket and a Camden jersey. The coach and Wagner then each hugged the Penn State freshman.

Love was everywhere. Adam was greeted by swarms of friends, teachers, and fans at halftime. Everyone, it seemed, wanted to squeeze him and tell him how proud they were of his determination. One of his grammar school teachers, Harold Little, kissed him on the forehead. One classmate shook his hand, looked around at the outpouring of love, and proclaimed, "This is like a family reunion."

Eastern's nurse, Shirley Martinsek, planted a big kiss on Adam's cheek. Adam had served as her aide during his senior year. She was furious when Adam was injured. It didn't seem fair, didn't seem possible. But throughout the entire ordeal, she said, "Nothing was ever bad in Adam's eyes. He always found something good. In fact, he calmed other people down. We cried, we got angry, and he said, 'Everything will be fine.' He's a delight."

Having Adam next to their bench was special said Lance Evans, a junior guard who led Eastern with 28 points. "I just wanted to play as hard as I could for him," he said. "He'll be an inspiration all year. He'll probably be an inspiration for the rest of my life."

Adam was basking in the adoration that everyone was showing him. "It was great to see a lot of old faces," he said. "It brought back the good times. And the times are starting to get better now."

As he watched the Friday afternoon game, Adam would do a weight shift every 15 minutes: bracing his hands on the wheelchair's arms and gently lifting his body a few inches to prevent sores on his butt. He could walk with crutches but needed someone to balance him. He could stand with support. And he was getting stronger: he had gained back 15 of the 30 pounds he had lost.

Adam was looking forward to hanging out with some of his friends in a nonhospital setting. He would stay overnight at his Voorhees home for the first time since his injury, then return to Magee after the weekend and continue to work toward leading Penn State through the football tunnel and onto the field for its 2001 opener. Adam had tunnel vision. "When it happens," said Allen, Eastern's basketball coach, "I'll take the four-hour ride to be there."

A lot of people in the area were feeling the same way, including Adam's unofficial rehab coach, Jerry Segal. Segal, the attorney whose own handicap didn't deter his unbridled enthusiasm, continued to visit Adam regularly. Based on the amount of function that Adam was regaining, Segal believed that Adam would soon be walking out of Magee. He also felt that down the road, Adam would indeed lead Penn State onto the field for its 2001 opener. "When you come out of the tunnel, I want to be in the stadium to see it," Jerry told him.

"Oh, no. You're going to be *with* me," Adam replied.

Jerry's eyes filled. Getting back on his feet was one thing. Helping someone else get back on his feet was something else. It was a feeling that gave him much more satisfaction than any of his court cases, a feeling that grew stronger as each day passed and Adam improved. September 1, the University of Miami at Penn State: Jerry had it marked on his calendar. It would be, he figured, one of the proudest moments of his life.

* * * * *

It had been six weeks since Adam climbed atop a treadmill with five therapists bracing him and pushing his legs back and forth to show his muscles how to walk. Each day there seemed to be gradual improvement. There were days when his legs shook violently from fatigue, when they collapsed and he was literally caught by his therapists. But that was to be expected.

Now, 10 days before Christmas, Adam's therapy included a new wrinkle: walking with crutches as a therapist stayed by his side. It was a struggle. His brain was telling him one thing, his legs were telling him something else. Trying to coordinate his thoughts with his movement was one of Adam's most difficult assignments. But not nearly as difficult as his next hurdle: walking without crutches.

It was a few days before Christmas, and Team Adam had congregated in a small hallway parallel to the gym. Adam had been paralyzed in front of millions of viewers. Now, three months later, as he attempted to take his first unassisted steps since the injury, there were only a few hospital staffers by his side. "It was scary," Adam said.

Bratta and Mangine were there. So was Linda Rizzo (one of the physical therapists' assistants), advanced clinician Cheryl West, and rehab attendants Dave Wilcher and Fritz Louis-Jean. Adam had been walking with crutches, canes, and ski poles, but the therapists were helping him with his arm movements. Now he was trying to go solo. Bratta had asked him if he wanted to attempt to take a few steps by himself, and Adam had consented.

He gingerly took a step, then another; then, with his arms flailing, he lost his balance and started to wobble backward. He was caught by a few members of the team, and they laughed and cherished the moment. Wilcher rubbed Adam's closely cropped dark brown hair, and the others applauded.

Never mind that he had fallen. Never mind that he was physically exhausted. Adam had taken two steps *on his own*. "It felt like a totally new thing, like something I had never done before," Adam said. "It was so much easier with the canes." But so much more rewarding without them. "It was a great feeling."

It was the proudest moment of Adam's young life. Forget about his five-touchdown game against Lenape in 1999, or his five-touchdown, 265-yard rushing effort against Shawnee in that same season. "Not that football is easy, but football didn't take as much effort as it did to get back to walking," he said. "This was the biggest achievement I ever reached."

The news of Adam's accomplishment quickly circulated around Magee. Dr. Staas smiled proudly when he met with Andre. He shook

Andre's meaty hand and patted him on the shoulder. "I guess you got your Christmas present a little early this year."

Andre nodded. The first time he had seen his son in the Ohio hospital, he wondered if he was going to die. On that emotional September night, "I would have been satisfied if he was a paraplegic and could move his arms," Andre said. Back in late September, Joe Paterno was just hoping Adam would gain enough strength in his hands to one day push his own wheelchair. Now Adam was moving all of his body parts and seemed to be on the verge of walking out of the hospital. "It's a miracle," Paterno said.

Adam's steps were choppy and his gait was wobbly. He struggled with his balance with each inch he negotiated. But there were still steps, *his* steps. And in the coming weeks after New Year's, the two steps turned into five, the five steps turned into ten, and the ten steps turned into twenty.

Before Christmas, Paterno and several of his Penn State associates attended a holiday party at Magee and visited with Adam in his hospital room, which had a four-foot Christmas tree standing in the corner. The tree, sent by an unknown fan, was decorated with some blue Penn State Christmas ornaments. Adam surprised the group, which included Paterno, Joe Sarra, Sebastianelli, Curley, and one of Paterno's close friends, Michael Kirschner, by handing them gifts that Andre had purchased. They were miniature plastic Penn State helmets decorated with No. 43 stickers and a heartfelt "thank you" message to the men for their support through the entire ordeal. Andre had written the message with a marker. Adam, whose right hand could barely open, struggled to sign his name on each helmet. The gesture produced a few teary minutes in Room 543. They were tears of joy, tears of appreciation. Tears signifying that this nightmare was slowly coming to an end.

Adam was freed from his neck brace on December 20 and was getting ready to return home for two days. This was a different kind of Christmas for the Taliaferro family. A special Christmas. A Christmas they would always remember. Adam was on the verge of walking, and he would spend Christmas Eve and Christmas Day with his family at home before returning to Magee.

The week before the holiday, Andre said the family still hadn't done any shopping. "We are not focused on material things," he said. "Everything is focused on getting him on his feet, getting us well again. This is the ultimate Christmas present. We haven't even thought about gift giving. The key thing is, I've got my son back."

Addie and Andre did eventually get to the mall. They went separately, since one of them was always with Adam. There were plenty of presents for Alex under the tree. Adam got what he wanted: a pair of black Jordan sneakers and money to buy clothes.

Adam himself had managed to do some Christmas shopping from the hospital. Kirschner had asked him if he could pick up something at the store for him to give to his parents. Adam asked if he could buy some Christmas candles. Kirschner picked out some Frosty the Snowman candles that were put under the family's Christmas tree. "It was a normal Christmas," said Adam, mindful that the three months before the holiday were the most *abnormal* days the family had ever experienced.

A few days after Christmas, the Taliaferros were getting ready to go to the mall. Adam planned to spend some of his gift money and have a leisurely day with his family. Adam loved going to the mall, loved looking at sneakers (a fetish of his, according to Addie) and meeting with friends. The attention he received made it even more enjoyable. He had become a celebrity; his mug had been all over TV, all over the newspapers. When he was driven somewhere, people would stop in the car next to him and give the "thumbs up" sign. When he went to the mall, even strangers would stop him and offer encouraging words. They would explain how inspirational he was and how thrilled they were to see his progress. "It was like he was an icon or something," Addie said. "It shocked me the way people treated him."

On this late December day, however, Adam wasn't feeling like a celebrity, an icon, or a heroic figure. He was feeling like a cripple.

His family was ready to go to the mall, but had to wait for him. It seemed to take him forever to get dressed. Everything was a struggle. It was such a hassle for him to put on his navy blue Penn State coat. Andre held it so Adam could put his arms through the sleeves, but his right arm got stuck and he had a difficult time getting it loose. A simple task had turned into a major production.

"Leave me alone for a while, Dad," he said.

It was only the third time Andre had seen Adam cry since the day he broke his neck. "Whatever you want, son."

It was difficult for Andre to watch his son cry, but he could understand Adam's feelings. It had been a hectic time. Friends and relatives were constantly calling and stopping at the house. Adam loved seeing them and talking with them, but he needed some time to himself. The media was constantly on the phone, too. Everyone, it seemed, wanted a piece of him. "It was like he was on display and he felt overwhelmed," Andre said.

Adam sat in his wheelchair in the family room, close to the spot where he had been interviewed live on network TV during halftime of the Blue-Gray football game on Christmas. It took a half hour for the frustration to pass. When it did, Addie and Andre helped him put on his coat. They headed to the mall. There were sneakers to look at.

CHAPTER THIRTEEN

Miracle on Race Street

Magee's glass doors slid open and out stepped Adam, walking gingerly with the aid of two metal arm crutches. Amy Bratta and Marygrace Mangine, the therapists who had pushed him like drill sergeants, were at his side along with Andre, Addie, and Alex, who was wearing a No. 43 Penn State jersey. Relatives, friends, Penn State personnel, and other hospital workers walked close behind. Two dozen cameras documented each step and Adam, wearing a gray Penn State sweatshirt and jeans, smiled proudly. When he had arrived at Magee 91 days earlier, Adam had only a little more movement than a department store mannequin. Now he had movement in all of his body parts and was walking with crutches, about to head home.

Each step seemed like a miracle. Each step seemed like it was right out of some tearjerker. But this was real life. This was modern medicine at its very best combined with a little luck, a lot of determination and grunt work, and prayers from around the world. About 40 people, including many hospital workers, stood on a balcony at the

Philadelphia rehabilitation facility, cheering and whistling as they watched Adam walk toward the family's black sport-utility vehicle. On the ground, seven of Adam's former football teammates stood and clapped. So did about 50 other people, who lined the narrow street. The applause echoed down Race Street after the Taliaferros got into the car and drove away.

The grueling inpatient rehab was finally complete. Adam would now live at home and visit Magee as an outpatient five days a week until he improved his hand and shoulder movement and could walk without assistance. Dr. William Staas said he believed Adam would be walking without crutches or assistance "within weeks."

"This is a beautiful day," said Larry Ginsburg, Adam's high school coach. "When you saw where Adam was when he first came here and where he was today, well, it's beyond words."

Before Adam's dramatic exit, an emotional news conference was held inside Magee. "I want to thank God, foremost," said Andre, sitting next to his son at a long table covered with a thicket of TV and radio microphones. "When people said this wasn't going to be possible, we prayed and He said yes. This was definitely a case of divine intervention."

"I never thought of it as a nightmare. I thought of it as a freak accident that happened to occur to me," said Adam, adding that he planned to take classes at Penn State in the summer.

The calendar said it was January 5, 2001, but Adam made it feel like Thanksgiving. He thanked the personnel at Magee, the Penn State staff, and his family and friends for their unyielding support. "I was never alone," he said. "Someone was always there to push me and keep me going."

Kim McCulley smiled as she sat in the back of the room and watched the news conference. An intensive care nurse at Ohio State University Medical Center, she had been one of the first people to treat Adam after his injury. He made such an impression on her that she traveled to Philadelphia to see him. Adam, who was heavily medicated in Ohio, didn't remember her. Heck, he couldn't remember much of anything about Ohio. McCulley felt a sense of pride as she looked at the new, rebuilt Adam and remembered the broken-down version she had seen in September. She remembered feeling sorry for Adam prior to meeting him for the first time. Doctors had not painted a happy picture. "I think my heart broke before I ever saw him," she said. "His prognosis wasn't good." Now he was fielding questions from the media about his recovery and would soon walk out of the brick building and regain some of his freedom.

Adam thanked everyone for their love and support. He even thanked strangers. He talked about the thousands of get-well cards and inspirational messages that people had sent. He said he got his positive approach from his parents "and everybody who's been there for me. I mean, from the point that I got injured, there's always been someone there. All my friends and people I didn't even know came to visit me." And those who couldn't visit sent cards. The Taliaferros had two closets at home filled with cards and letters. "It makes you feel good when you see thousands of people caring for you, and you want to get better for them," Adam said. "I'm just thankful basically to the whole nation for supporting me. I definitely couldn't have gotten through this experience alone."

Adam drew laughs when he praised Alex. "My little brother over there," he said, smiling, "he's actually been nice to me through all this."

Andre was also in a thankful mood. "I want to thank those angels who masquerade as therapists," he said. Then, as he began to thank Penn State administrative assistant Joe Sarra and athletic director Tim Curley, his voice cracked with emotion. He stopped to compose himself, wiped his eyes, and took a deep breath before continuing. There were more tears when he thanked Penn State's doctor, Wayne Sebastianelli, a man who would kiss Adam on the forehead every time he visited him at Magee, a man Adam said "saved my life on the field" on that infamous September day. "Dr. Sebastianelli," Andre said, "treated Adam like he was his son."

Dr. Staas pointed out that "everything fell into place in an idealized system. If we had dreamed of a perfect care system for somebody who was injured like Adam was, we got it. And that's why he's here today and that's why he's able to do what he's able to do."

Numerous friends and relatives were at the farewell press conference, including Andre's younger brother, William, who had been a regular visitor at the hospital. Seven former Eastern football players—Darryl Scott, Jarid Brookins, Justin Barton, Khary Sharpe, Chaz Brown, Patrick Smothers, and Larry Evans—sat near Adam. "We all saw him do miracles on the football field for four years in high school," said Scott, the former Eastern quarterback who was now a freshman at Duke, "and I felt he could do one more miraculous thing."

"When I heard what happened, I knew we were talking about Superman, so I knew he was going to walk again," Brown said. "I'm just waiting for him to fly."

"He's an inspiration," Brookins said. "Whenever I have a problem, I say, 'How can I complain and be so selfish when I see what he's going through?'"

"I know he wanted to come out with us when he was home before," Smothers said, referring to Adam's brief return to Voorhees for the holidays. "As soon as he gets back on his feet, he's never coming back home."

Addie shook her head and laughed out loud. It felt good to let it out.

After the news conference, Adam returned to his room before getting on the elevator that would take him down to the first floor and his grand exit. As he was about to leave Room 543 for the last time, one of the aides asked him if he wanted to take a wheelchair to the elevator. "No, I'm walking out of here," he said.

Those words would forever be etched in the mind of Curley, the Penn State athletic director, who was standing in the room near Adam. Curley loved the sound of those words.

Using crutches, Adam negotiated the extremely long hallway to the elevator. When he got to the first floor, he walked through the lobby and out the front door. He was oblivious to the multitude of TV and newspaper cameras. All he saw was his freedom, his future. "That was incredible because two weeks before that, we weren't sure he was going to be able to walk," Curley said. "That whole part was special. To see his team of nurses and therapists, to see what Magee had done for him and what he had done for Magee."

As Adam walked out of the hospital on a crisp winter day, the applause grew louder with each step. Adam, against all odds, was headed home on his own two feet.

* * * * *

Jen didn't know whether or not to attend the press conference. Adam left it up to her. She wanted to be there, but she was nervous that a reporter would ask her a question on camera. She decided not to attend, but later regretted it. "I didn't want to be the only one who wasn't part of the family who was there," she said. "Adam didn't know his friends were going. They just showed up. I would have gone with them if I knew they were going."

After leaving Magee and going to lunch with his family, Adam was dropped off at Jen's house, located less than a mile from the Taliaferros' home in Voorhees. It was a special day. Adam, at long last, was out of the hospital and it was Jen's 19th birthday—four days after Adam had turned 19 on New Year's Day.

They watched a lot of TV sitting on her couch. "It was just such a relief to be together," Jen said. "We flipped through the channels, and it seemed like every channel had him on it, so we just watched him the whole night on TV. It was like, 'Wow, this was you earlier today and you're sitting right next to me.' I felt so honored that he got out of the hospital and was spending the time with me. It was neat."

Adam, who had been greeted warmly at his high school's six-month reunion a few days after Christmas, had also been over at Jen's house the previous week. Michele Greenberg, Jen's mom and a registered nurse, watched Adam walk in on his crutches and couldn't help noticing that his legs were quivering. "It broke my heart," she said. "He was shaking and we had to push him in the room and sit him down. I realized that, even though he was starting to walk, just how devastating it had been to his body and how slow a process it was."

Adam improved by leaps and bounds in the next few weeks. His balance was getting better. He was able to feed himself, able to stand up on his own, able to walk with crutches. He still had limited control of his right hand, which he couldn't open all the way. That would take several more months of therapy before it was close to being normal, doctors said.

* * * * *

Three days before the farewell news conference at Magee, Ginsburg visited with Adam as he went through a tiring workout at the hospital. Ginsburg, Adam's high school football coach, had been vacationing in Florida, and it was the first time he had seen Adam in a little over two weeks. "Look at that! That's amazing. Amazing!" Ginsburg told Adam as he pushed himself up from a sitting position and stood. Before Ginsburg had left for Florida, Adam couldn't stand and, most of the time, the therapists had been moving his legs for him.

With his former coach watching, Adam had an intense look as he went through several grueling drills with Mangine. He did a series of exercises designed to reprogram his muscles and build his endurance. In previous weeks he had been reeducating his muscles on how they should be working. Now they were working and Mangine was pushing them to move faster. "It's a lifelong recovery, but he's gained a lot more in three months than a lot would have because he's an athlete and because he's so determined," she said. "A lot of recoveries occur when you're motivated, and he's had that motivation from the beginning."

The mental aspects of Adam's athletic career aided his recovery more than his physical condition, Dr. Staas said. "The training he went through here was similar, at least in principle and discipline, to what he went through in his athletic career in football and basketball," he said. "We became an extension of his coaching experience."

Adam's athletic ability didn't help restore his nerve tissue, but it may have helped keep his lungs strong through the dangerous early stages, Dr. Sebastianelli said. During the entire recovery process, the doctors did all they could, Sebastianelli said, "but ultimately it was up to God whether or not he would walk again. I think we had a lot of prayers answered here."

* * * * *

As Adam huffed and puffed on the treadmill, his gait was improving. He was much less wobbly than he had been during the previous week. He was two weeks into his outpatient workouts at Magee and, on this day, Joe Sarra was urging him along. "You're doing fine, buddy," said Sarra, who had flown in from State College to get a firsthand look at Adam's progress. "You're doing fine."

Adam started to struggle with his balance. He had been on the treadmill for 12 minutes and he was starting to feel fatigued. His legs turned into jelly and he collapsed toward the floor; two female therapists caught him as he screamed and grunted. "Arrghh!"

He composed himself and tried to stand up straight, but his legs were shaking too violently; it took him a minute to regain his balance. "That's OK, Adam," said Addie, sitting behind the panel that controlled the treadmill's speed. "You're doing great, doing great."

The treadmill was restarted. Adam walked for a few more minutes. "Keep it up, buddy," Sarra said. Adam breathed heavily, like a pregnant woman on the verge of delivery. Each exhale seemed to be in rhythm with the rubbing noise created by his sneakers bouncing off the rubbery treadmill mat. He was pushing himself to the limit, and Addie's head was bobbing up and down to the drumlike beat when, suddenly,

Adam's legs gave out again. This time, three therapists lunged to grab him, and Adam's right foot momentarily got stuck in the treadmill mat. "Oh, man!" Adam yelled.

Addie sat there expressionless as the medical personnel attended to her son. "How can you be so calm?" asked Dave Wilcher, a rehabilitation attendant.

"Adam knows I love him," Addie said.

Wilcher smiled. "Your boy almost came back here—in-house," he said.

After a short break, Adam began a sprint-walking drill in which two aides held a belt harness that was attached near his waist. Adam walked briskly. His control was a little wobbly, but it was better than it had been the previous day.

Sarra stood at the other end of the hallway, about 50 feet away. Adam headed toward him. "Come on, buddy. Get to the finish line," he said. "You can get here." He reached Sarra. The therapists turned him around and he started walking in the other direction. This back and forth was repeated over and over.

Adam was walking with the help of the therapists, but at home he was more daring. He had tried to walk without assistance in his family room; each step was accompanied by a violent wobble that made Addie think he was going to fall to the carpeted floor. "No, no. Not my clean walls, boy!" she had shouted the previous day, as Adam lost his balance and braced his hands against the wall to keep from falling. Addie couldn't help but laugh.

"You look like Spider-Man," she told him.

Spider-Man. Superman. Miracle Boy. Adam was getting lots of nicknames. And lots of support. Even after he was released from Magee as an inpatient, Dr. Sebastianelli still came to visit. During a mid-January trip, he delivered what had become his signature greeting to Adam: a kiss on the forehead. He kissed him because he wanted to show Adam how much he cared and he did it on the forehead because he knew that, initially after the injury, that was one of the few places Adam could feel it.

Andre had been deeply moved by this gesture while Adam, thinking ahead, pictured Sebastianelli planting one on him in front of the other players when he returned to Penn State. "Mom, he has to stop this," Adam said jokingly.

A few months earlier, Sebastianelli had literally screamed when Andre phoned him near 2:00 A.M. and told him Adam had moved his toe. When the farthest body part from the injury moved, Sebastianelli thought it meant that everything in between could start moving at any time. It was as if electrical current had just made it through a war zone all the way to the bottom of his body.

Sebastianelli now looked at Adam, standing in his family room, and marveled at just how much progress he had made since he first wiggled his toe. Adam showed Sebastianelli how he was walking with crutches, then put the crutches down to demonstrate how he could take a few steps without them. "I knew at that point," Sebastianelli said, "that it was just a matter of time before this kid was jogging again."

And a matter of time before he was leading Penn State out of the tunnel and onto the football field for its 2001 opener. "Do you know how many times I've seen that in my mind?" asked Sue Paterno, the coach's wife. "Initially, I saw him with hand crutches and then I progressed to no crutches and holding on to Andre and Addie. Now I have him running."

* * * * *

A little more than five months after Adam's injury, Andre took a business trip to California. He returned with a stark reminder of how differently things could have turned out for Adam and the Taliaferro family.

After finding out in early November about the spinal-cord injury sustained by University of Washington safety Curtis Williams, Andre got in touch with Williams' older brother, David. Curtis, like Adam, had emerged from a helmet-first tackle unable to move. Curtis, like Adam, had not cut or severed his spinal cord. But his injury was much higher on the spinal column than Adam's and that made his odds of ever walking again a lot more daunting.

The paths of these two young men diverged sharply following their life-altering tackles, which had happened within five weeks of one another. By the time Curtis got permission to attend Washington's January 1 game against Purdue in the Rose Bowl, about two months after his injury, he still could not move. He was breathing with the assistance of a ventilator.

Williams, who had been flown into Pasadena, visited with his coaches and teammates before the game. Clad in a purple Washington game jersey with a commemorative Rose Bowl patch sewed onto it, Williams watched the game from a box seat, a nurse by his side the whole time. Inspired by his presence, Washington outlasted Purdue, 34–24. It was the same team an emotional Penn State squad had beaten the week after Adam's injury at Ohio State.

Andre kept in touch with David Williams. In late February he called David—by then Curtis had come to live with him and his wife in Fresno—and told him he had an upcoming business trip to California. Andre, who racked up frequent-flyer miles like points on a pinball machine, had recently started traveling again. "When I get out to California," Andre said, "I'd like to see you."

Andre flew into northern California specifically so he could visit with the Williams family; he rented a car and drove to David's house. He got there at about the same time David was steering his car into the garage. As he followed David into the house, Andre heard a dull suctioning noise that nearly brought tears to his eyes. He didn't have to see anything to know that Curtis' tracheotomy tube was being cleared of mucus or anything else that might hamper his breathing.

When Andre saw Curtis, he walked over to his wheelchair and gently hugged him. "Hey, how are you doing?" As he and Addie had with Adam, Andre tried not to convey any of his sadness to Curtis. He made sure he looked directly at Curtis when he spoke to him. Curtis had lost

40 pounds since the injury, and he sounded as frail as he looked. He asked Andre how Adam was doing in a voice that was barely audible.

Andre, as outgoing a person as there is, would have launched into a dissertation had anybody else asked him that question. But when he looked at Curtis, feelings of guilt washed over him. How could he tell Curtis that Adam was already walking without any assistance? That every day now he seemed to reclaim another piece of his life? Curtis should have been getting ready for the NFL draft while finishing up school. Instead, he needed a nurse to care for him around the clock; with each passing day the outlook for him ever getting out of his wheelchair grew dimmer. It didn't seem fair, especially since Williams had a three-year-old daughter from a previous marriage to support. As Andre talked with Curtis and his brother, he couldn't help but think how lucky he was. "Man," Andre later said, "I realized what I just missed." Andre did what he could to offer Curtis hope. He answered his questions about when Adam first started moving and walking.

Later, David expounded on a theory that held Andre in rapt attention. He told Andre that it had been raining the day his and Curtis' lives changed forever. He was convinced the slick field at Stanford Stadium had played a major role in Curtis' injury. David had played football at Fresno State in the early eighties; he surmised that because of the wet field, Curtis had not been able to get proper footing prior to the tackle he made on Stanford running back Kerry Carter. That is why, David said, he hadn't been able to get his head up in time.

As positive as Andre had been throughout Adam's recovery, he found himself at times groping for a reason as to why Adam had lowered his head before tackling Jerry Westbrooks. Adam had always been a smart player as well as exceptionally talented, and Andre had a hard time accepting the fact that Adam's athletic career was over because of an uncharacteristic mental mistake.

As he listened intently to David, Andre thought back to Penn State's game at Ohio State. The start had been delayed by flashes of lightning, and rain had soaked the field prior to kickoff. Andre left that night convinced that the wet field had somehow factored into Adam's career-ending injury, too.

The only thing that made more of an impression on Andre during his visit was seeing the hardships and the uncertain future that had almost become his family's reality. With their mother battling Alzheimer's disease, David had assumed care of Curtis. The tremendous burden that came with that responsibility was as etched on his face, Andre thought, as it had been noticeable in his voice.

"The thing that got me when I looked at him," said Andre, "was the sadness he had for his brother."

* * * * *

Why did Adam come back so quickly while, months after Williams' spinal-cord injury, he still could not move? Adam thought about that sometimes. He also thought about all of the people he had seen during his stay at Magee—people who were confined to a wheelchair and, barring a cure for paralysis, would never walk again. "Out of all the people who are there paralyzed, why did I come back so quick?" Adam asked.

When Joe Paterno pondered that question, his mind flashed back to his own son, David, who had made a full recovery following his near-fatal trampoline accident in 1977. As Paterno saw it, there was one common denominator between Adam and David's situations: both had countless people praying for them. "I know a lot of people don't want to believe there's such a thing as miracles anymore, but it's hard to believe that there isn't some kind of force up there, that when so many people are concerned about somebody that it doesn't have an impact," Paterno said. "To me, I keep thinking I've been involved with some people that I care for who have literally had somebody step in and create a miracle."

Sue Paterno also believed that a higher power had played a role in Adam's recovery. One frosty day in late January, she sat in the Corner

Room, a popular restaurant in downtown State College, and talked about all of the letters the Paternos had received in the weeks and months after David had returned home. She was struck by how many of them had come from people who had questioned their religious beliefs and had stopped going to church. David's miraculous recovery, they wrote, had restored their faith in God. "We didn't know the people and they didn't have to write and tell us," Sue said, "but I'm inclined to think that, maybe the world being what it is, it was time for a public miracle." For that same reason, Sue said, "I think God picked Adam."

This much is certain: Adam had embraced religion for the first time during the months leading up to his accident.

His friends from home had picked up on a few signs of Adam's subtle transformation. One night, when Adam had returned to Voorhees after spending part of the summer at Penn State, he and Chaz Brown were getting ready to eat dinner. Chaz said a private blessing, as he does before his meals. What surprised him is that Adam also bowed his head in prayer before the two munched on some chicken wings. Brown also spied a Bible sitting on a coffee table in the Taliaferro's house, something he had never seen there before.

Patrick Smothers, another one of Adam's high school teammates and a close friend, visited Adam at Penn State over the summer; he too found himself surprised by something. While Adam was showing him around campus and then State College, he pointed out the church he had been attending. Church? Adam?

"I hadn't really gone to church too much," Adam said.

That started to change when he arrived at Penn State in July. Larry Johnson, the Nittany Lions' defensive line coach and a deeply religious man, handed out schedules for Bible study. One day Adam, his curiosity piqued, found himself tagging along with some of his teammates. He became a regular at the weekly sessions and started attending church on a regular basis as well.

Adam soon gained a different perspective on the physical gifts that had earned him a football scholarship to Penn State. "It made me think that you just didn't get there on your own," Adam said. "Someone else had to be helping you to get where you are."

When school started in the fall, Adam continued to attend the Bible study sessions. He also became a regular at the church services that are held before every football game. Less than a week before he got hurt at Ohio State, he met with Tim McGill, the team chaplain. McGill shared his thoughts on God with Adam. He also gave Adam a pamphlet on how he should be living his life, which they reviewed together.

That life took an unforeseen detour at Ohio State, and Adam wondered if a higher power had helped get him back on his feet too.

CHAPTER FOURTEEN

Maxwell Club Magic

During his 15 punishing years as an NFL quarterback, Ron Jaworski was known as a fiery, vocal leader—a trait that later made him a natural as an ESPN broadcaster as well as a coveted motivational speaker. So Jaworski seemed out of character when his voice cracked and he struggled to address the sellout crowd at the 64th annual Maxwell Football Club awards banquet in late February. He bit his lip hard and tried mightily to get the words out. Instead of words, he got tears. They swelled and spilled as he stood at the podium of a plush Philadelphia hotel ballroom.

Adam Taliaferro had left Jaworski speechless.

Jaworski is president of the Maxwell Club, which is named after the late Robert "Tiny" Maxwell, a kindhearted, 6'4", 240-pounder who played collegiate football and later became a highly respected college referee and sportswriter. Maxwell promoted sportsmanship and gentlemanly values. The football club, founded by Maxwell's close friend Bert Bell, was named in his honor in 1937; one of its goals is to promote Maxwell's high standards. It is the oldest football club in America.

Adam was about to receive the Maxwell's newly created Spirit Award. An hour before Jaworski introduced him, Mark Schweiker, the lieutenant governor of Pennsylvania, told the audience Adam was the perfect choice. Schweiker commended Adam in a rapid-fire, deeply sincere delivery:

> I know if Bert Bell was here looking at Adam, he would say, "My Lord, this is exactly what I had in mind when I said, 'Let's do something to remember what Tiny Maxwell was all about. . . .'"
>
> And so [Adam] turns to his mom and dad that day in Columbus, he turns to those doctors that day in Columbus, and he comes back to Philadelphia and says, "There's courage and guts in my heart. There's determination in my mind, and I've got some incredible effort yet in this body. And I'm going to walk again." Now I don't know about you, I don't know what your take is on the purpose as to why we gather [here]. Yes, it is social. But I think in large measure it's just to sit here for a short time tonight and think back to that fourth quarter and realize that, in a couple of minutes, he's going to walk to this microphone and you're going to say to him by handing over this remarkable trophy, "Your spirit is incredible. Your courage is incredible. Your determination is incredible."

Schweiker was just getting warmed up:

> And we're not only going to recognize a fascinating story of success on those high school football fields in New Jersey, success on those Big Ten venues that are all over midcountry, but really his success in the spiritual fields of recovery. I don't know about you . . . over and above the fine eight people who

will be recognized for their contributions to the game tonight, I've got to believe that the Tiny Maxwell Award will never stand so tall as it does tonight when he makes his way and is given the opportunity to address you, by virtue of the award you have given to one Adam Taliaferro, that great Penn Stater.

The audience applauded loudly, and Adam sheepishly nodded from his seat, about five feet to Schweiker's right. "Thank you," Adam said as he smiled.

Schweiker wasn't done. He knew the awards ceremony was going to be shown on national TV, and said he hoped "every parent and son and daughter has an opportunity to see him receive this tonight." He said he hoped parents would have "a chance to tell their children, 'If you can be one-tenth of what Adam has been over the last couple of months, you will be a fine person and someday a great leader.' That makes for a very special moment and like you, I'm excited for the opportunity to enjoy it tonight."

About an hour later, that moment had almost arrived. Jaworski was trying to introduce Taliaferro, trying to tell the audience that this amazing Penn State freshman cornerback had defied the doctors' numbing predictions: that he would never walk again because of a frightening tackle on September 23. "Nothing is more special," Jaworski told the 1,000 spectators, "than the honor I have now."

The crowd stopped sipping from their glasses, stopped dabbling with their strawberry cheesecake, stopped their small talk with friends. Suddenly, without warning, an almost eerie stillness permeated the ballroom. The jovial atmosphere of the evening turned solemn, turned respectful. The room, lit by dozens of chandeliers, became as quiet as a church. It was as if even the paintings of the football greats that hung on the posh walls were snapped to attention. Taliaferro, sitting between Philadelphia Eagles Coach Andy Reid and Kansas City Chiefs President Carl Peterson, a few feet from where Jaworski was standing, smiled politely as the old quarterback tried to regain his composure.

"This year, the Maxwell Club has created a new award," he continued. Again, he paused. Again, the tears started to build. "It honors an athlete whose courage and perseverance reflect the highest value of the game."

Jaworski, who quarterbacked the Philadelphia Eagles to the 1981 Super Bowl, stopped and dabbed at his eyes. So did many on the dais; which provided seating for football luminaries such as Don Shula, Chuck Bednarik, Tom Brookshier, and Peterson. They could relate to Jaworski's sentiments. It seemed that the people behind the paintings could too—guys who tried to block out the fear of injury when they played football. Guys who knew that one hit could end their career, or their life.

There was a painting of Eagles great Pete Retzlaff, of Jim Plunkett throwing a pass for Stanford in 1971, of Fran Tarkenton scrambling for the Vikings in 1975. There was Archie Griffin (who, coincidentally, had visited Adam in the Ohio hospital after his injury) running the ball for Ohio State in 1975 and Ed Marinaro breaking loose for Cornell in 1971. The Ghosts of Players Past—Terry Bradshaw with hair, Walter Payton with grace, Andy Robustelli with a nasty scowl on his face—were everywhere in the room, the paintings hanging from the cranberry red wallpaper and rich oak paneling giving the room the feeling of some fancy men's club. There was Ken Stabler firing a pass for the Raiders in 1976, Tommy McDonald gaining yards for Oklahoma in 1956, Norm Van Brocklin passing for the NFL champion Eagles of 1960, O. J. Simpson breaking loose for the Bills in 1976, Dave O'Brien throwing a bomb for TCU in 1938.

If the players in the paintings had been at the podium, they probably would have been as emotional as Jaworski was as he continued his introduction:

> Adam Taliaferro represents the highest values of the game, and a whole hell of a lot more. He was a star athlete at Eastern High School in Voorhees, New Jersey. Rushed for 3,227 yards and 62 touchdowns. There wasn't a major college in

America that didn't want Adam on their roster. That's the kind of player he was; that's the kind of *person* he was. Every big-time program in America wanted this young man. He accepted a scholarship to Penn State University, and this season, playing as a *freshman* at Penn State—a freshman, a true freshman—he suffered a fracture of the fifth cervical vertebra in a game at Ohio State.

Jaworski adjusted his glasses. He was starting to get choked up. Each word was more difficult to deliver. "The doctors didn't think Adam would ever walk again." He paused and repeated himself. "After that serious injury, the doctors *did not think he would ever walk again*. But in the five months since that injury, Adam has written a comeback story that is both miraculous and inspirational."

Now Jaworski could no longer talk. His children had attended the same South Jersey high school as Taliaferro, so he felt a special connection to Adam and his family. He wanted to say more, wanted to tell everyone that Adam was his hero. But those words would have to wait. Jaworski was too overcome with emotion to continue speaking. He would let the pictures do the talking. "Please roll the tape," he said.

Two large movie screens at each end of the ballroom showed Ohio State's Jerry Westbrooks, wearing a bright red jersey that contrasted starkly with the shock of green grass, running the ball in the closing minutes of the September 23 game. Never mind that Penn State was hopelessly behind: Adam was in dogged pursuit.

The announcer's voice gave the grim report: "Pitches it back to Westbrooks at the 20, and Westbrooks is down for a loss." The screen faded to black for a few seconds. It was symbolic: during that time, Adam's football career had also faded into darkness. "Adam Taliaferro is down for the Nittany Lions," said the announcer as the next clip showed the cornerback lying on a stretcher on the field.

The entire video lasted one minute and 35 seconds. There was Adam, wearing a neck brace and sitting in a wheelchair at Magee, explaining how he couldn't feel anything when he first made the hit. "I tried to get up and tried to move my arms and . . . nothing. My body had just shut down."

There were clips of Andre and Addie, explaining the fear that had engulfed their lives. There were clips of Adam lifting weights and doing exercises at Magee accompanied by grunts, groans, and a determined demeanor. And then there was Adam, explaining, "This is my life right here, and I go into it every day just like it's a battle. I may not be able to play football, but I'm just hoping I can keep pushing forward and walk out of here soon."

When the video ended, Jaworski tried to resume talking, but his words were difficult to hear because, by now, all 1,000 people were standing and applauding. Most had moist eyes and clapped until their hands turned red. As the cheering escalated, Jaworski raised his voice so he could be heard. Sensing the crowd wanted Adam at the podium, he raced through the words. "Last month, Adam walked out of the hospital and he's going to walk up here to accept this award. Adam Taliaferro."

Adam, dressed in a black tuxedo with a gray printed vest, stood and walked to the podium a few feet away. Jaworski threw his arms around him. "Thanks a lot," said Adam, an earring glistening in each ear, as the fans stood and continued to applaud wildly. "Thanks a lot." Brookshier, the former NFL defensive back who was the night's master of ceremonies, patted Adam on his right shoulder as he glanced around the reverberating room.

Andre and Addie stood and wept openly. This may have been their proudest moment, knowing their son had touched so many hearts. Addie wiped away the tears and worried that Adam would be too brief, that he would just say "thank you" and sit down.

Adam, however, composed himself and delivered a heartfelt speech. "I'd like to start off by thanking God because, without him, I wouldn't even be here today," he said. He thanked the Maxwell Club for creating the Spirit Award and presenting him the trophy. "I'm just honored to be here."

The room became quiet as he talked about his spinal injury:

> From that day, September 23, it was one of the toughest bat-
> tles of my life, trying to get back. But there's no way I could
> have done it alone. I had a tremendous amount of help from
> everybody, including my parents, who were there from the
> time I woke up to the time I went to sleep. They were right
> there by my side.
>
> I see I have the Penn State family here. I thank Penn State,
> and Coach Sarra has been our right-hand man. He calls every
> day and he's been there for me. He's like a part of the fam-
> ily now. It's just overwhelming to see the amount of people
> who've sent cards and cared for me. There have been times
> when I was in my room at Magee and I'd be bored and I'd
> have 100 cards to read, and that's gotten me through the day,
> and I'm just tremendously thankful. I mean, I've made great
> friends with people and I've met so many great people.
> There's not even words that can describe the way that peo-
> ple have cared for me so much.

He then thanked his therapists ("They kick my butt every day, but it's
worth it") and the doctors, especially the ones who were on the field
when he was injured. "Without them doing the right thing, I wouldn't
be on my feet right now."

Adam smiled. He seemed comfortable being at center stage. The fact
that the Maxwell Club banquet, including his speech, would appear on
national TV didn't make him nervous. Not after what he had been
through.

"It's partly me, but it's been a group effort," he said. "I mean, the doctors at Ohio State, the doctors at Penn State, everybody. The people at
Magee.

"I really don't have anything else to say," he concluded, finishing his
two minute and 15 seconds of sincere eloquence. "I'm just one of the
most blessed people in the world right now. I consider myself lucky,

and hopefully by September 1, I'll be able to run out that tunnel and help us beat Miami."

As he headed back to his seat, Adam received another long standing ovation. In the coming months, there would be plenty more.

* * * * *

Some of the other Maxwell award winners mentioned Adam during their acceptance speeches.

Raiders quarterback Rich Gannon, who was named the club's NFL player of the year, said he and several teammates watched an ESPN piece on Adam from Oakland's training room and that "there were several tears in our locker room. Not only are you an inspiration to the people in this room, but you're an inspiration to NFL players across the country." Gannon played his high school football in Philadelphia and then starred at tiny Delaware. He had beaten long odds, too, going from a Division I-AA school to the NFL. Gannon continued:

> It brought a tear to my eye because I can relate to your story, not from a physical standpoint but from the toughness that you displayed. And I think if you look at my career and the way it's gone in the 13 years I've been in the National Football League, I've been in four different cities and it hasn't always been easy for me. And I've prided myself on being a tough kid from Philadelphia. And although you're not from Philly, you're from across the river, you're a tough kid, and I think the best days are ahead of you. You're a great example to myself and a lot of people in this room.

In most conversations before and after the banquet, Adam was the subject. Shula, the winningest coach in NFL history, grasped Adam's still-weak right hand and offered his congratulations. So did Drew Brees, the Purdue quarterback who was named the Maxwell's college player of the year, and whose team had lost to fired-up Penn State the week after Adam's injury.

Chuck Bednarik, the NFL Hall of Famer who was the last of pro football's 60-minute men, had a unique perspective on Adam's recovery: "I survived 30 missions over Germany in a B-24 bomber in World War II," he said, "and he survived something similar. This was tantamount to that. This was a miracle."

* * * * *

In his high school yearbook, Adam was voted Most Likely to Become Famous. He didn't want to get his fame this way, but there he was, a media star for the next several months after he walked out of Magee. He was on local TV and radio shows. He wrote a first-person story for *The Philadelphia Inquirer*. He got a standing ovation from a sellout crowd as he was introduced during halftime at a 76ers' game on January 15, and he received a long embrace from comedian/actor Bill Cosby, a Philadelphian, near midcourt.

Prior to his introduction to the crowd, Adam watched a wheelchair basketball game that was held at halftime. He couldn't believe the athleticism that the players, known as the Spokesmen, displayed. The team included players with sad tales. Guys like Tony "Stinky" Norris, a former South Philadelphia High star who was drafted by the NBA's Portland Trailblazers. Norris seemed to have a bright future before he was shot during a gun fight between police and two men who were holding up a bar in 1979. Norris, an innocent bystander and 22 years old at the time, was caught in the crossfire on that February night. Two bullets lodged in his spine, practically guaranteeing he would not walk again. Now he was playing for the Spokesmen, the wheelchair team sponsored by Magee and the 76ers.

"Just wheeling a wheelchair is tough enough, and to be able to move and dribble a basketball is unbelievable," Adam said. "Those guys are strong and it takes a lot of heart because you can fall out of the wheel-chairs. Those guys have such good spirit. They inspire me."

Adam watched them play and thought that, if he wasn't so fortunate, this could have been him. Andre had a similar thought. He had developed more compassion and respect for people in wheelchairs. "When I see them now, it's different," Andre said. "Before, you used to see them and say to yourself, 'Oh, that's sad,' but you kept on. Now, you *feel*. You *really* feel for those folks. When I see Curtis Williams, that hurts me because that was almost my son. It really bothers me when I see him because you feel like you've been given something that maybe he didn't get. You want to see that boy recover."

Adam's injury and his recovery changed Andre forever. He has vowed to continue his volunteer work for the disabled for the rest of his life. He will share Adam's story with them and try to bring them hope, try to bring them some sunshine.

* * * * *

Standing ovations were becoming almost the norm for Adam. He received another one when he returned to Happy Valley on February 24 and was introduced to the crowd during halftime at a Penn State–Michigan State men's basketball game. "It's great to be back," Adam said. "It's been five months. It feels like five years."

Then on April 7, Adam threw out the ceremonial first pitch—he struggled, because he had a difficult time gripping the ball with his not yet totally functional right hand—to the Phillies' Robert Person before a Phillies–Cubs game at Veterans Stadium. And, yes, there was another standing ovation. "I'm sorry I had to get hurt," Adam said, "But in being hurt, the care that people have shown me . . . I'm grateful. I'm truly grateful."

Person said he had "broke down inside" when he visited Adam at Magee in November. Five months later, he was stunned to see the improvement Adam had made. Person kept a photo of him and Adam, taken during his Magee visit, atop his locker for inspiration. "To see him walk out there and throw the ball, it was just exciting," Person said. "I was going to make sure I caught that ball even if I had to dive for it."

Person said Adam is never far from his thoughts. "I haven't skipped a day of working out since I met him," he said. "I take a little more pride in doing my workouts now. Any time that you think you're tired, you've got a little nagging injury, or you think you don't want to do something, just think about Adam."

Adam's newfound celebrity status also included the filming of his story for the Discovery Health Channel along with an appearance at Magee's "Night of Champions" on May 11. The night included a dinner, a silent auction, and exhibitions by wheelchair athletes. Proceeds benefited Magee's wheelchair sports programs. Adam was listed as one of the headliners along with two Hall of Famers: former Philadelphia Flyers goalie Bernie Parent and former Philadelphia 76ers forward Billy Cunningham. A year earlier, Adam had still been in high school; now he was signing autographs and sharing the spotlight with two of the most revered sports figures in Philadelphian history.

Adam has also been nominated (by Magee) to be one of the 2002 Olympic torchbearers. A contest is being held to select about 2,000 torchbearers throughout the United States; individuals who best exemplify the spirit of the Olympic movement will be chosen. Magee, understandably, felt Adam was a natural.

* * * * *

Justin Barton has a claim that few can make: he once absolutely leveled Adam Taliaferro on a football field. It happened early during their varsity careers at Eastern High School and Barton, like a fisherman who has reeled in a big one, never tires of telling the tale.

Adam caught a punt during practice. When he didn't signal for a fair catch, Barton, who would leave Eastern standing 6'6" and weighing more than 300 pounds, buried him. "It wasn't a normal jump up after a hit. He stayed down for a little bit," Barton said. "He still won't admit it, but there's really no denying it."

Barton loves to tease his childhood friend about that hit; that's a bit ironic considering that he always saw himself as something of a bodyguard for Adam. The two grew up playing basketball, Adam as the speedy guard and Justin as the big man who took care of the grunt work inside. Barton also anchored the offensive line that blew open holes for Adam at Eastern. That massive line coupled with Adam's ability to dip, dart, and dash rarely let opponents get a clean shot at him.

Barton earned a football scholarship to the University of North Carolina; as his freshman year in Chapel Hill wound down, he experienced some feelings that he would have trouble putting into words. They were triggered at the beginning of March—Adam was walking without any assistance at that point—when he found a weight-lifting glove in a friend's dorm room closet. Following Adam's injury, Barton had written Adam's initials and high school number on the inside of the glove.

Now, when he looked at that glove, guilt washed over him. The feelings were no more rational than those of Penn State defensive coordinator Tom Bradley, who had blamed himself for Adam's injury because he put him into the Ohio State game at left cornerback instead of right cornerback. Still, like Bradley's emotions, they were too powerful for Barton to ignore. "All through elementary school and middle school and high school I was there. Not that he needed protection, but I was always there to protect him," Barton said. "I would block for him in football and help him in basketball. Finally, I'm not there to protect him and he gets hurt. I don't know how to explain it."

He could explain the profound sadness he felt when he got a phone call from Adam one night after he had returned from study hall. Was it true, Justin had asked him, that he couldn't play football anymore? When Adam said yes, Barton's sleepy brown eyes filled with tears.

He was not the only one who would mourn the death of Adam's football career. About a month later, Addie was in a grocery store when she ran into the grandfather of one of Adam's former high school teammates. He asked about Adam and then started to cry.

"Don't cry," Addie said, "because you're going to make me cry."

The man said he couldn't believe Adam's football career was finished. It just wasn't right. "Please don't say that," Addie said, "because we don't know why things happen. Just be happy for Adam. Don't cry."

That scene spoke volumes about the promise that had been cut down on that fateful September day at Ohio Stadium. From the time Adam took his first carry as a pint-sized tailback for the Voorhees Vikings, his career seemed destined to end up in the NFL.

Larry Ginsburg, the head coach at Eastern High School during Adam's years there (who has since retired), sent a handful of players to the NFL over the years, including Chris Canty, a first-round draft pick with the New England Patriots in 1997. Adam may have been the best player that Ginsburg ever coached. His work ethic, desire to improve, and willingness to listen to coaches put his career on a fast track as much as his natural ability did.

It didn't take long for the coaches at Penn State to see those same traits, and Adam emerged as one of the few players in his class who would contribute as a true freshman. How much did Adam impress the coaches? Bradley compared him to Courtney Brown and LaVar Arrington when they were freshmen. Both players would leave Penn State as consensus All-Americans and became the first and second picks, respectively, in the 2000 NFL Draft. "When a guy like Arrington comes through the door, you say, 'Hey, NFL.' A guy like Courtney Brown, Adam was that type," Bradley said. "You knew someday he was going to play on Sundays. He wanted to learn so badly and just had the great feet and great understanding of the game. He wanted to be out there, had that kind of confidence in his abilities, just the type of person that makes your program and defense better because he's a guy you don't have to worry about."

Adam was, in fact, the kid Joe Paterno had in mind when he waxed poetic about what he called "The Grand Experiment." Paterno had long held the belief that just because a kid played major college football didn't mean he couldn't excel academically and socially as well. Adam had been doing just that before he got hurt. "I think he had all of the instincts to become one of the really good corners we've ever had," Paterno said. "He had all of the things you're looking for in a kid to excel at that position."

The progress Adam made at Magee Rehabilitation Hospital was so remarkable that Dr. William Staas left open the possibility of him returning to football, though he had quickly added that he wouldn't recommend it. Dr. Gary Rea, the neurosurgeon who had performed the spinal-fusion surgery on Adam at Ohio State University Medical Center, had been more blunt when asked if Adam could play football again. "Would bullshit be too strong?" Rea asked.

Adam joked with the coaches about one day returning to the team as a third-down wide receiver, but he knew the risk was too high. He knew his playing career was over. What concerned those closest to Adam was how he would deal with it when he wasn't suiting up in the fall. "Something like this where your career is about to explode and this happens, I think you may need some counseling," said Dan Spittal, who had been an Eastern assistant coach when Adam was there. "It's tough. You're a racehorse, you're built to run, you're born to run, and now you can't run? What do you do?"

Nobody worried more about that question than Adam's mother. Addie knew how deep her son's passion for football ran. She had been the one who, at Adam's insistence, drove him to midget league practices in the pouring rain. She had seen him doing sit-ups in his bedroom after Eastern football games no matter how badly he had been beat up. She had been exasperated with Adam when he wouldn't eat what she cooked because of the diet he was following in preparation for Penn State. Now she fretted over how Adam would deal with life after football.

Penn State had assured her that Adam could still be an integral part of the team. The Nittany Lions coaches had talked to Adam about assisting them with the defensive backs, though his responsibilities had not yet been defined. "Addie, every time you look at the TV, you'll see Adam underneath my armpit," Paterno told her.

"I better!" she replied.

When she and Andre had initially dropped Adam off at Penn State, Addie had marched up to Paterno and bluntly told the legendary coach that he better keep his promise to take care of her son. "You're a tough lady," Paterno said.

Addie made it clear that she would be closely monitoring the situation this time, too. "I want him to be a part of that team," Addie said. "I don't mean being a water boy, I want him to do something. Not suiting up is going to crush him. I don't want my son up there depressed. My son got hurt giving it his all on the football field, so I think he deserves something back in return."

Only time would tell how much of a return Adam might get from coaching. He knew how close he had come to spending the rest of his life in a wheelchair, a proposition he still couldn't fathom, and he knew how lucky he had been to escape that fate. How much his perspective would change when Magee Rehabilitation Hospital was 200 miles away and he was standing on the Penn State sidelines with 100,000 cheering fans, not even Adam knew. "I went all out and can't look back and say I didn't do enough or regret anything," Adam said. "I don't think it will really hit me until I get back up there and it's football season again."

Nobody better understands what Adam may go through than David Paterno, the coach's son. David made a full recovery from his fall from a trampoline in 1977, and the accident that almost claimed his life did take football away from him. That loss may have seemed insignificant in light of what could have happened, but for an 11-year-old boy who had always told people he would play football in college, nothing could have been more unfair.

Miracle in the Making

* * * * *

As a kid in gym class, David Paterno could do pull-up after pull-up while others could barely do one. Blessed with a stout body and thick legs, he could shimmy up a rope so easily that it looked like he was sliding down it backward. His natural physique is such that to this day people take one look at him and assume that he works out regularly.

Nothing excited him more as a kid than running with a football tucked under his arm. It didn't matter if it was the older kids in the neighborhood chasing him or even the Suhey brothers, Paul and Matt, who both played for Penn State in the late seventies and whose family was close to the Paternos. David seemed to have no fear.

That was not all with which he was blessed. "He was the best athlete in the family," Joe Paterno said. "No question about it."

David's athletic course was forever altered by that fall from the trampoline. A sixth grader at the time of the accident, he fractured his skull in the fall. His doctors forebade some activities; unfortunately for David, football was at the top of a relatively short "can't do" list. "But I can! But I do!" David would insist to doctors. "When I play in the neighborhood I do well against the older kids!"

Two years after the accident, David still couldn't accept the ban on football. One day his mother took him to the hospital for another opinion. He had been rushed to that same hospital after his October 14, 1977, accident. The hospital is 100 miles east of State College; on the drive there David chattered nonstop, convinced that the doctors would let him play football. He had even brought a tape recorder along to get proof that his mother was just being overprotective.

After a series of tests, David did not get the answer he had been positive he would hear. He didn't say a word on the drive back to State College. Sue Paterno was almost as crushed as her son.

The Paternos did come up with a compromise: David could play soccer. His response: "Whoopdedoo." He did end up playing, but it wasn't the same as football. He quit playing on his high school team during his senior year. His love for football had been so strong that he never could commit himself to another sport.

"I was resentful about it being taken away, so in rebellion I probably didn't put it behind me and commit myself to the next thing," David said. "No, I didn't develop a drinking problem or a drug problem or anything like that, feeling sorry for myself. But I didn't have any passion to be a good soccer player or a good runner, I just kind of went halfway about stuff. Who knows? Maybe I could have gone to college and played soccer but I always thought I was a natural for football."

David had rebuffed his father's offer to become a ball boy following his accident, and through the years he kept the football program at arm's length, even though he got his undergraduate degree and a masters at Penn State. By contrast, his younger brother Jay grew up around Penn State football, was a reserve quarterback for the Nittany Lions in the late eighties, and is now an assistant coach on his father's staff.

David does not attribute his distance from the Penn State program to bitterness. His life simply took a different course after football ended for him. The passing years have lent a healthy perspective to his experience: "I had a wonderful, full, happy, healthy life even though I never played college ball," David said.

His message is one that might be beneficial to Adam.

CHAPTER FIFTEEN

Completing the Circle

"You are the most beautiful sight I have ever seen!"

Adam Taliaferro stopped. So did the throng of reporters and TV cameras that were tailing his much-publicized return to the Ohio State University Medical Center in mid-April. Adam could only offer Alice Herman a quizzical stare in return.

Back in late September, Herman, a chaplain at the hospital, sat by Adam's bed at night, praying and gently wiping away the tears that rolled down his face. Now he stood before her with a look that turned apologetic because he didn't remember her. It was a beautiful sight indeed, especially since Herman hadn't expected Adam to walk again when he left the hospital.

When Herman spotted Andre in the entourage, she said, "I remember you!"

"I remember you, too!" Andre said, his arms swallowing the petite woman with whom he, Addie, and Joe Sarra had spent hours praying. When the Taliaferros left the hospital in September, Andre had said

Adam would one day walk through the same doors he had exited on a stretcher. Now that they had followed through on Andre's vow, the hospital staff feted them as if they were visiting dignitaries.

Andre had been waiting for this day for a long time. The trip was a chance for his family to express their gratitude and to exorcise any lingering demons from the horrible days that followed Adam's injury.

Like Andre, Adam wanted to thank those who had helped make his miraculous recovery possible in person. He also hoped the mid-April visit would trigger any memories from the time he had spent there. As the scene with Herman illustrated, however, he remembered virtually nothing from his five-day stay at the hospital. Andre was shocked when Adam later told him that he didn't even remember Andre being in Ohio.

For their return trip, the Taliaferros flew from Baltimore to Pittsburgh, met up with Sarra, and caught a connecting flight to Columbus. Andre was adamant that Sarra make the trip with the family. Even after Adam started walking again on his own, Sarra and Andre talked on the phone at least once a day. By now he was part of the Taliaferros' family.

Kim McCulley, a nurse who had cared for Adam at Ohio State University Medical Center, met them at the airport. McCulley had grown so attached to Adam that she later visited the Taliaferros in New Jersey. Now, as McCulley spotted Adam, she could hardly believe her eyes. With his eyes covered by a pair of sunglasses and a shiny "43" medallion hanging from his neck, Adam looked like any 19-year-old kid. His walk revealed barely a trace of his spinal-cord injury. McCulley had seen him only three months earlier but the progress he had made since then astounded her. McCulley gave Adam a hug and told him how good he looked. She drove the Taliaferros and Sarra to their hotel, the same one they had stayed in during their previous trip, and the group soon made its way to the hospital.

During a tour of the intensive care unit, Adam visited a patient who had been paralyzed by a gunshot wound. The kid, who was around Adam's age, talked so softly that Adam had to read his lips to understand him. It served as the first of several reminders during the trip of how lucky Adam had been.

Andre and Addie felt lucky when they saw the anxious, tear-streaked faces in the waiting room of the intensive care unit. It wasn't too long ago that they had been in the same situation, when time had stopped and tragedy's long reach had turned total strangers into kindred spirits. "You realize those folks are going through the same thing you were going through," Andre said.

Adam ran into Dr. Gary Rea, who had performed his spinal-fusion surgery, as the neurosurgeon was coming out of the operating room. Adam would not have known Dr. Rea from Dr. Dre, the famous rapper. Rea, for his part, barely recognized Adam. It was the big group that followed Adam, along with the TV cameras, that gave him away. "You look a lot better standing," Rea said to Adam.

Adam thanked Rea, who was wearing sky-blue scrubs, for performing the surgery. "That's what I spent all of those years in school for," he said. Rea later added, "If you look at all the spinal-cord injuries, maybe 5 percent of them do quite well. The real problem is, you don't know; you flat don't know. Several young, healthy patients die every year from similar injuries."

At a news conference that afternoon, Rea thanked Adam for reminding the people there that the work they do is important. McCulley, meanwhile, reminded Adam in front of reporters that, on the day following his injury, Adam had wanted to watch football. He grinned sheepishly.

Adam and his family concluded their whirlwind day at the Woody Hayes Athletic Center. They met Jim Tressel, the coach who had taken over for the fired John Cooper. During a team meeting, Adam thanked all of the players who had visited him at the hospital and sent him cards.

That night, Rea took the Taliaferros and a group that included one of the doctors who had assisted with Adam's surgery and McCulley to dinner at the Buckeye Hall of Fame Cafe. The popular restaurant covers 50,000 square feet and houses one of the Heisman Trophies that Archie

Griffin, the only two-time winner of the award, captured in the mid-seventies. Adam, who was disappointed that he didn't remember Griffin visiting him during his stay at the Ohio State University Medical Center, had been quite thrilled when he talked to the legendary running back earlier in the day.

During dinner, the Taliaferros got to know a little more about Rea. He grew up in dusty west Texas and came from a family of modest means. His father had never finished high school and his mother had to drop out of college when a cotton crop went bad. For as long as he could remember, Rea had wanted to become a doctor. His parents always encouraged him to pursue that dream, and the Taliaferros were sure glad he did.

Andre told Rea about visiting Curtis Williams, the University of Washington player who had been paralyzed at the end of October. Rea's mind flashed back to January 1; when TV cameras showed Williams watching from a wheelchair in a box seat at the Rose Bowl, Rea had thought about Adam. It reminded him of how close Adam had come to spending the rest of his life in a wheelchair.

Why was Adam walking again while Williams faced life as a quadriplegic? Rea said "the point of impact," when each player made his life-altering tackle, was the spilt-second determining factor. Fate, Rea said, had been kinder to Adam because his injury occurred much lower on the spinal column than Williams' did. How much movement a person regains, Rea said, is dictated by the severity of the explosion that essentially happens in the spinal column. Mere inches at that "point of impact" may have been all that separated the drastically different fates of Adam and Curtis.

"I'm sure that kid got just as good of care and I guarantee you that kid from Washington wanted to walk just as bad as Adam did," Rea said. "I think that's why, for us, Adam is so special. It reminds us of why we do this and it reminds us how glorious it can be, but it's also something we don't have much control over. Just like the kid at Washington, that's what happens with the majority of people."

Rea was ecstatic that it didn't happen to Adam, and not because it enhanced his already considerable reputation. He took such a liking to Adam over dinner that he felt it was like talking to his own son. Rea, in fact, had a hard time picturing Adam as a football player because he was so nice and humble.

Getting to know Adam did allay a concern Rea often has when a young person sustains a spinal-cord injury. Since most have an air of invincibility, they have trouble coping with a serious spinal-cord injury, especially if it has robbed them of their ability to run, drive a car, or, as in Adam's case, play football. "Because they're so body oriented they can't move away from that and that's not everybody, but it's a concern you have about some of them," Rea said. "Adam, you feel like he has a real chance to continue and contribute even without being able to be a cornerback from Penn State. There's much more than just a cornerback from Penn State there."

Adam and his family returned to their hotel room late that night just in time to see highlights of Adam revisiting the hospital on national TV. "It was weird," Adam said. "I never thought I'd be on TV for this. After games, we'd run back to the dorms to see if we made the ESPN highlights. I'd rather be there for something I did on the field."

He paused and flashed a wide smile. "But it was still cool to be on."

* * * * *

The next morning, Adam literally got an up-close look at his injury.

Dr. Jeff Laubenthal, who rode in the ambulance with Adam to Ohio State University Medical Center, took the family to a nearby Denny's restaurant for breakfast. As part of the one-year fellowship he was serving at Ohio State, Laubenthal, who aspired to work in sports medicine, had done an extensive research project based on Adam's case.

When Laubenthal and the Taliaferros returned to the hotel he asked them if they wanted to see Adam's MRI, X rays, and CAT scan. They were curious, so Laubenthal fetched the 4' x 6' poster with the three tests on it from his car.

Laubenthal's explanation of the tests didn't just fascinate Adam; it also impressed upon him how serious his injury had been. The MRI showed broken vertebrae pieces, excessive swelling in the spinal cord, and blood on top of it. "When I look at the pictures," Laubenthal said to Adam, "there's no way how I can see that you can walk."

"Man," Adam said, "I didn't know how bad or close it was."

Laubenthal had followed Adam's progress through newspaper and TV reports and periodic phone conversations with Andre. He would call Rea every time there was a new development. "I would say, 'Did you see that he moved his toe?!' or 'Did you see that he moved his leg?!' And being a little naive because I don't deal with spinal injuries every day, I was very excited."

Rea tempered that enthusiasm. "Jeff, don't get excited, he still has a lot to do," Rea would say. "Don't go throwing parties yet."

A deeply religious man, Laubenthal believed that a higher power and the timely response of the medical personnel at Ohio State played a major role in Adam proving doctors, and ultimately the ominous MRI, wrong. Nobody was happier than Laubenthal that he and the others at Ohio State University Medical Center were able to do just what Rea had cautioned against: throw a party for Adam.

"The last time I saw him, he had tubes in every orifice and was on a ventilator," Laubenthal said. "And to see him standing up now and talking with his brother, it's everything you look for as a doc. I'm 30 and plan to be a doctor for 25 or 30 more years, and I know I'll never see anything more inspiring than this."

* * * * *

That afternoon the Taliaferros and Joe Sarra met former Ohio State Coach John Cooper for lunch. Cooper, always somewhat of an embattled figure in Columbus, was fired following his 13th season at the helm. His dismissal came in January following a disappointing 8–4 season. There were a number of factors that led to Cooper's demise, but none loomed larger than the 2–10–1 career record he compiled against hated Michigan. The high point of the 2000 season, which started with five straight wins, may have been Ohio State's 45–6 pasting of Penn State, although even that day had been sullied in the eyes of some when Ohio State threw a fourth-down pass (shortly after Adam was taken off the field on a stretcher) and then tacked on a late touchdown.

Cooper still insisted he had done nothing wrong, and he cited a long-standing friendship with Paterno as evidence that he did not try to run up the score. It has been suggested that the late touchdown was in retaliation for Penn State's 63–14 spanking of Ohio State in 1994. "I've probably had as good a relationship with Joe as any coach I've ever competed against," Cooper said. "Certainly it would never be my intent to embarrass him, although they did beat us very badly in State College. People suggested we take a knee, but if we had taken a knee we wouldn't have run out the clock."

Paterno, sick with worry over Adam, almost certainly would have run out the clock had Penn State got the ball back, which is why that argument wouldn't even have been considered by angry Nittany Lions fans.

Had Cooper known how serious Adam's injury would turn out to be, he said he might not have allowed third-string quarterback Scott McMullen to put the ball in the air in those final two minutes. "It never crossed my mind that it was that severe," Cooper said. "Personally, I thought they'd take him to a hospital and he would be OK. I've never tried to deliberately embarrass any coach or player since I've been in the coaching profession. I certainly have a clear conscience."

The athletic director who fired Cooper firmly backed his claim. "I don't think he was trying to send any kind of a message or trying to demean Penn State or Adam in any way," Andy Geiger said. "I understand emotion and people misunderstanding but John Cooper would not deliberately embarrass anybody or do what he was accused of doing."

When asked about the pass and the late touchdown, Paterno said, "I don't want to get into that. That's got nothing to do with Adam."

Jordan Caruso, the Penn State offensive tackle, proved to be a little chattier on the subject, especially after he was informed that Cooper didn't realize the severity of Adam's injury. "That's what his excuse was?" Caruso said, "I don't believe that for a second. That was Coach Cooper putting it in Coach Paterno's face. That's what it seemed like to us. There was a lot of resentment but at the same time, Ohio State treated Adam great at the hospital."

That treatment is why Andre became upset when he was asked about the pass at a news conference following Adam's spinal-fusion surgery. Andre thought Cooper's sincerity showed again when he met them in Columbus. "I thought it was very nice for him to come back," Andre said, "and he didn't have anything to gain. It wasn't with TV cameras or anything. We had a chance to sit down and chat about a lot of things."

After lunch with Cooper, the Taliaferros still had a few hours before their flight, so McCulley drove them to a nearby mall. She stayed with Andre, Addie, and Joe Sarra while Adam and Alex went off on their own. Just as when they had been at Denny's earlier that day, people kept coming up to Adam and congratulating him. A Penn State player being celebrated in Columbus? Somewhere, even Woody Hayes would have been smiling at that.

The only thing the Taliaferros didn't do during their two-day trip was meet with Jerry Westbrooks, the running back who had been on the receiving end of the tackle that ended Adam's career. Westbrooks was out of town getting ready for the NFL draft. He didn't get selected in the draft, which took place a couple of weeks later, but Westbrooks did sign a free-agent contract with the Jacksonville Jaguars. That at least gave him a chance to fulfill his football dreams, which were never realized at Ohio State. He has said that he plans to get in contact with the Taliaferros one day, just to let them know how much he has been thinking about them.

McCulley, who put the Taliaferros back on a plane that night, perhaps best framed the significance of the two-day visit for both the Taliaferros and the people who have been inspired by what they have overcome. "You got the feeling that they had come full circle," McCulley said. "I wonder if Adam realizes what an inspiration he has been to even the people out here who have been a part of this. People need to see that. People need to hope."

* * * * *

A couple of hours after Friday turned into Saturday, Adam and Sharif Chambliss, a Nittany Lions basketball player he had befriended the previous fall, stood in line at the McDonald's in downtown State College. Partygoers and students who had a case of the late-night munchies filled the place. It seemed like old times.

Adam had returned to Penn State earlier that day, about two weeks after his triumphant return to Ohio State. He and his parents were among the tens of thousands of people who descended on Happy Valley for the weekend of the Blue-White game, the intrasquad scrimmage that marks the conclusion of spring practice. The Taliaferros had been at that game the previous April, when Adam got the VIP treatment that is accorded to recruits. A year later, he was a bona fide celebrity.

He got a poignant reminder of that in McDonald's. As he waited to place his order, a large hand gripped his head as if it was a basketball and slowly turned Adam around. When Adam saw who the hand belonged to, his eyes widened and a smile parted his face. LaVar Arrington pulled him close for a hug. Arrington, a two-time All-American linebacker and No. 2 overall pick of the Washington Redskins in the 2000 NFL draft, had called Adam a couple of times during his stay at Magee.

As they talked, Arrington showed just how touched he was by Adam's recovery. He took a small key from the necklace that hung on his thick-as-thighs neck and showed it to Adam. Arrington wore the key in honor of his father, who had lost a leg in Vietnam. His father, Arrington said, was his idol and his inspiration. He handed the key to Adam. "I want you to keep this because you went through a lot," Arrington said. "I always want you to remember this."

That may have been the most memorable moment of a weekend that gave Adam a sneak preview of what his life would be like in the fall.

His return to the football team became official Friday afternoon when he forgot to take out his earrings before attending a team meeting. Joe Paterno made, ahem, an editorial comment about the earrings. He didn't make Adam take them out, but the message didn't escape Adam. "When I get back up there," Adam said, "they'll be gone."

After the meeting, Adam accompanied his teammates to Beaver Stadium, which was in the midst of an ambitious expansion project. The University was adding club seats and private boxes to the facility, which is already the third-largest on-campus stadium in the country. Since there were no working elevators, players had to climb the stairs to check out the new, and pricey, seats. The exercise was noticeably taxing for Adam, and as the players were getting ready to walk back down the stairs, Gus Felder, a 6'5", 320-pound offensive tackle, told Adam to hop on his back. Adam happily obliged. Who needed elevators, anyway?

Arrington wasn't the only person Adam had been happy to see during the late-night excursion to McDonald's. He also bumped into his old roommate, J. D. Benson. Benson had withdrawn from school after just a semester, and Adam was worried because nobody he talked to had seen or heard from Benson in months. Adam and J.D. had become pretty good friends, and Benson visited him at Magee. As they chatted at McDonald's, Adam was glad to hear Benson talking about going back to school and playing at a smaller college.

The next day, Adam watched the Blue-White game from the sidelines. The game is mostly for younger players to get experience and for die-hard fans to get a peek at the team, as well as to polish their tailgating skills. The atmosphere is so relaxed that Joe Paterno, who is usually a stickler for order, retires to the radio booth and offers commentary alongside Penn State's regular announcers. The Nittany Lions assistants coach the game. By the second half, the sidelines usually prove to be much more interesting to watch than the game because there are always a handful of former players there.

Arrington, O. J. McDuffie, and Ki-Jana Carter were among the erstwhile All-Americans who had returned for the game. Brandon Short, the All-American linebacker who had been No. 43 before Adam, was also there. He eyed the "43" medallion that Adam was wearing and told him he was going to take it. They both laughed.

Fans were just as excited to see Adam on the sidelines as they were the teams' past heroes. During the players' autograph session that always precedes the game, Adam's line was the longest. There was even some pushing and shoving, another unmistakable sign of Adam's fame.

More pushing and shoving came right before the game when a handful of students, including a former football player, ran onto the field and refused to leave. They were protesting the racial climate at Penn State in the aftermath of a death threat received by a black student leader; the group was taken away in handcuffs. Adam's story seemed to be a perfect antidote to the escalating racial tension at Penn State. People from all backgrounds and races had pulled together to support Adam. In the end, the scrimmage didn't provide nearly as much compelling action as the pregame protest had.

Adam watched the game with Eric McCoo and Gerald Smith, neither of whom were playing, and laughed every time defensive coordinator Tom Bradley barked, "Taliaferro, get in there!" Being a spectator wasn't nearly as hard as Adam had thought it would be. He actually enjoyed himself. "I thought going up and watching the game I would be like, 'Man, I want to be out there so bad.' That's kind of secondary now," Adam said. "I'm just so happy to be walking."

After the game, Adam, wide receiver Tony Johnson, and Larry Evans, one of Adam's friends from back home, walked around downtown State College. As they made their way down College Avenue, well-wishers continually stopped Adam to congratulate him. "That's cool," Adam later said of the attention. "People care and want to know what's going on with me. They'll eventually get used to having me back there."

The sight of Adam caused one vehicle to pull over and park along the sidewalk. Hopping out of a sport-utility vehicle were McDuffie and Carter, the charismatic and crowd-pleasing players who had starred at Penn State in the early nineties. They spent the next half an hour chatting with Adam. They invited Adam's group to dinner that night. Adam and the others eagerly accepted.

They went to Damon's, a sports bar and restaurant about a mile outside of State College. Adam, content to listen to McDuffie and Carter talk about the NFL, was thrilled that he shared a bond with them as former Penn State football players. "I had never met O.J. or Ki-Jana Carter before," Adam said. "It seemed like they really cared."

Adam and his friends spent the rest of the night at McCoo's apartment. He didn't see his parents much that weekend, but Andre and Addie didn't mind a bit. They knew how much he missed school and the friends he had made at Penn State. Seeing him happy made them happy.

There had been one development during Blue-White weekend that caused Adam to ponder what his injury had cost him. On the day of the Blue-White game, Bhawoh Jue got picked in the third round of the NFL draft by the Green Bay Packers. Before his career-ending injury, Adam had been heir to Jue's right cornerback position, and he couldn't help but wonder a little about what might have been.

However, as often happened when those thoughts crept into Adam's mind, a dose of perspective that acted like cold water splashed on the face wasn't far behind. Shortly after Blue-White weekend, Adam visited Thomas Jefferson University Hospital in Philadelphia, where he had spent nine days before going to Magee, and realized just how lucky he was. "Seeing the condition some of those people are in," Adam said, "it's like, 'Man, I can't even think about playing football.'"

* * * * *

Near the end of February, Adam got behind the wheel of the car for the first time since his injury. What should have been an exhilarating feeling turned out to be an uncomfortable one. Adam didn't trust his reflexes. More than a month later, at the prodding of his mother, Adam finally started driving again. "It felt great," he said. Nothing, in fact, better symbolized his recovery of the freedom that had been snatched from him in a split second at Ohio Stadium.

Not long after that significant development, Andre followed through on a promise he made while Adam was in high school. If Adam earned a scholarship to college, Andre had told him, he would buy him a car. Since freshmen football players at Penn State are not allowed to have cars, Andre had told Adam that they would get him one after his freshman year.

They shopped around and Adam picked out a champagne-colored Pathfinder. He and his parents made the two-hour trip to Baltimore to pick it up and Adam, with Addie riding shotgun, followed Andre's black Taurus back to Voorhees. It was good practice for Adam. In a few short weeks, he would drive his new sport-utility vehicle back to Penn State.

The week before Adam returned to school on May 12 turned out to be a hectic one. There was a going-away party for him at the Voorhees health center where he had undergone swimming therapy for several weeks. He also attended a fund-raiser for the Adam Taliaferro Foundation at a Cherry Hill, New Jersey, restaurant early in the week. Two days later he took the train with his father and Joe Sarra to New York City. There he spoke at a fund-raiser for a group trying to find a cure for paralysis. Whenever the three of them were on the teeming New York City sidewalks, Sarra made sure no one bumped into Adam. Adam could only laugh and wonder just how protective Sarra would be when he got back to Penn State.

On Adam's final day at home he and Andre attended a party sponsored by Magee. Adam would always feel an allegiance to Magee. He had spent six months there, including three months as an outpatient. When his treatments at Magee ended on March 30, Dr. William Staas said he had regained 90 percent of his function and was working toward 100 percent. At the party Adam signed autographs and was a featured guest along with Philadelphia sporting legends Bernie Parent and Billy Cunningham.

The next morning, Adam turned in his celebrity status for what he really wanted: to become a college student once again.

His parents followed him up to Penn State and helped him get situated in the on-campus apartment he would share with football players Gerald Smith, Tony Johnson, and Jesse Neumeyer. Adam was slated to take one class, a freshman English course, over a six-week session, but he would be plenty busy with rehabilitation and various speaking engagements.

Andre and Addie took Adam to dinner that night and then said their good-byes, since they would be leaving State College first thing in the morning. Adam hugged Addie after she said, "Give me some love." He and Andre, in a typical father/son farewell, shook hands. That was as sure a sign as any to Andre that things were back to normal. "Some day," Andre said, "we'll hug."

The next morning the Taliaferros met Sarra for breakfast. "Let's call Adam," Sarra said. But remembering the loud music they had heard when they talked to Adam at around 11:00 the previous night, the Taliaferros decided they'd better let Adam sleep. He reached them on their cell phone as they were driving back to Voorhees. He called to wish Addie a happy Mother's Day. She had never had a happier one.

As much as Addie struggled when Adam first left home for Penn State, she didn't experience the profound sadness this time around. She knew Adam had to get back to his life, even if that life was 200 miles away. "Sure I miss him," she said, "but I'm so happy for Adam. And he knows we're only a phone call away."

That phone call came the day after the Taliaferros returned to a house that felt empty, yet at the same time felt so right. Addie had been thinking about Adam when he called her at the preschool where she teaches. The last time he had called her there from Penn State, he had told her to watch the TV closely the next day, that he was going to play a lot at Ohio State.

One play had changed everything for Adam, Addie, and Andre. Since then, they had been to hell and back. On this day, Adam assured Addie that he was OK and told her not to worry, that his life was getting back to normal.

They had made it.

Epilogue

Adam, wearing a black pullover shirt and matching pants, leaned on the podium and addressed a crowd of 450 at a Cherry Hill, New Jersey, hotel ballroom in mid-June. This was *The Philadelphia Inquirer*'s high school sports banquet for the 2000–2001 year. The previous June, Adam had been sitting in the audience as one of the honorees, the South Jersey football player of the year.

Now he was on the dais as the featured speaker. After the emcee gave Adam a lengthy, heartfelt introduction, the crowd awarded him a tearful standing ovation as he walked to the podium. Even Andre and Addie were standing.

"Live every day to the fullest," Adam told the young athletes, along with their coaches and parents, "because you never know what is going to happen tomorrow." Adam captivated the listeners with his soft-spoken, understated delivery. He spoke for three or four minutes.

Then it was Andre's turn to address the audience. "Always put the word *scholar* before athlete," he said. "That's what we always emphasized with

Adam. Even if he made it to the pros, the average career usually doesn't last more than four years. That's why you have to put scholar first, so you're prepared for the rest of your life."

Adam would be prepared, Andre said. And it was easy to believe him. As Adam signed autographs, posed for photos, and chatted with the young athletes and their families after the banquet, you got the feeling Andre was right: Adam would make it. Whether as a sports announcer—a career he is considering—as a coach, or in some non-sports-related field (Jerry Segal has promised him a spot in his firm if he becomes a lawyer), there is something about Adam's magnetic makeup that suggests he will be a success.

"You're an inspiration," said Gerri Marsden as she sat in her wheelchair—she has been paralyzed for 10 years—and clutched Adam's hand after the awards banquet. "I can't tell you how much you mean to me." Marsden's daughter, Sandy, a standout softball player who takes care of her mother and younger sister, had been named South Jersey's most courageous high school athlete.

Adam asked Marsden, whose 45-year-old husband died of cancer during 2000, about her medical battle. Coincidentally, she had also spent a lot of time doing rehabilitation work at Magee, and the two of them compared their therapies.

Adam was genuinely surprised by—and appreciative of—the attention the Marsdens were giving him. In his mind, Gerri and Sandy were the heroes. "*Your* family," Adam told Gerri Marsden, "is an inspiration to me."

* * * * *

Adam took one course when he returned to school in May, and Joe Sarra—whom Joe Paterno called a "hero" for the role he played in Adam's recovery—checked in with him almost every day during the first week. Shortly thereafter, Sarra's calls became much less frequent. "I guess he's letting me go off on my own," Adam said. By the end of June, in the second semester of the summer, Adam was taking a public speaking course (the irony, of course, was that in the previous nine months, he had been speaking publicly to folks around the world via TV interviews) and sociology. In the fall he planned to take at least three courses en route to working his way back into being a full-time college student. He wasn't having any problems walking around campus; he was lifting weights and still undergoing electro-stimulation therapy on his right hand with Penn State trainer George Salvaterra.

Most important, he was glad to be "back with the guys."

Adam came home occasionally during the summer. He returned for South Jersey's all-star football game, which was renamed the Adam Taliaferro All-Star Classic. Proceeds from the game benefit any athlete—whether from South Jersey or another part of the country—who suffers a spinal-cord injury. (In a related matter, by late June, $292,000 had been raised by the Adam Taliaferro Fund, which was established by Penn State to assist with any of Adam's medical expenses that were not covered by insurance.)

Adam also spent some time with his brother, Alex, who was working out and getting ready to play freshman football at Adam's alma mater, Eastern High. Alex's decision to play football frays Addie's nerves, but she and Andre have agreed that they won't hold him back. Alex, an aspiring wide receiver, said the scariest part about playing football isn't getting hit by a beefy linebacker; it is trying to live up to his brother's name.

As for Adam's personal life, his relationship with Jen had cooled. The couple broke up in April, ending a 20-month romance—the longest Adam had ever dated anyone. They still talked on the phone almost every night, but they were no longer committed to each other. Jen "was great during the whole time" he had been hospitalized, Adam said. "But once I got out of the hospital, she wasn't too happy when I hung out with my friends. She got angry and thought I spent too much time with my friends, and I thought I owe them, too. I guess we didn't see eye to eye."

Yes, a typical problem for a 19-year-old. It was a problem, but it didn't affect Adam as much as it might some others after a breakup. Adam had always been a laid-back sort, but his injury—and his subsequent recovery—have made him even more unassuming. Difficult situations now seem much more tolerable. "Before, there were certain things that I would stress out about," Adam said. "People would make me angry sometimes." Now it seems as if nothing—not even a breakup with his girlfriend—can ever stress him out. Not after what he has endured. "I'm just thankful for what I have, because it could have been a whole lot worse," he said of his broken neck. "I don't worry about things now because it's just not worth it."

Jen said she and Adam were taking some time apart "because things are different now. We're both different people. Our lives are completely different and we have to adjust." At around the same time she came home from Rutgers for the summer, Adam was headed to Penn State. "We went from being in high school together to this incident, and now we have to figure out if this is going to work," she said. "It's really difficult. I'm home for the summer and he's back at school. It's frustrating."

No matter what happens, Adam and Jen will always have a soft spot in their hearts for each other, will always remember their months together as a special time in their lives.

* * * * *

The word *miracle* is thrown around too loosely in today's society, most agree. Was Adam's recovery a miracle—considering that several doctors didn't think he would walk after examining him and his bleak MRI? Was it a miracle that he beat odds that one doctor estimated at 1-in-100 to walk again?

"This wasn't what I'd call a papal miracle," said Dr. William Staas, Magee's president and medical director and a man who believed Adam would walk from the first day he examined him. "It was a miracle that everything that should have happened *did* happen in a timely fashion and nobody screwed up. From the time he was injured, the people on the field handled him properly; they didn't make him worse. They got him on a spinal board; they immobilized his neck with a collar. They gave him intravenous steroids in the emergency room. . . . He had the appropriate surgery. Everything went smoothly and, as I said, that's kind of a modern miracle. And if we were to compare it to if he had the same injury 25 or 30 years ago, he probably would have been made worse because we didn't know how to move people safely at that time."

Marygrace Mangine said "miracle" is the only way to describe Adam's recovery. "I wish everyone who came in here could get this result—as far as a return of function," said Mangine, the Magee occupational therapist. "I see him as a miracle and he makes me say, 'Damn, why can't it happen to everybody?' I'd like to say it was my treatment . . . but it was his body."

Dr. Jeff Laubenthal, who assisted Adam during the ambulance ride from Ohio Stadium to the hospital on that chilling autumn day, says there is no logical reason as to why Adam is able to walk. "For me as a Christian individual, I think a lot has to do with the fact we got lucky, and God was on our side," he said. "I can't explain things like that. As a physician, I don't have a problem turning things over and explaining it that way."

Wayne Sebastianelli, the Penn State doctor, also speaks about a higher power when he talks about Adam's recovery. "So many factors worked Adam's way," Sebastianelli said. "Only one Being knows which factor was most important, and I guess we'll know when we get up there. The bottom line is, the cord was not cut. That left the door open . . . and then everything else had an influence on the preservation of tissue and nerve distribution in the spinal cord."

"He had every reason not to walk," Andre said. "It's angels. I'm not a Holy Roller. I don't go to church every week. I didn't pray every day and night before this happened, but I pray every day and night now."

Addie said the experience tested her faith. "I said to the Lord up above, 'Here's a kid who has never done anything [wrong] and his whole life was sports. Now he doesn't have it anymore. How could you do that to my child?' I've had Andre to kind of help guide me through that. Then you have those fools out in the street doing everything wrong and they just go on with life—and you have somebody that's good get knocked down. It's tough and some days it's hard for me to accept, but I deal with it because things happen for a reason. Adam will find his niche. I believe that in my heart because he is that type of person. Something good is going to happen to Adam out of this. I truly believe it. Maybe football was taken away from him, but more doors will open for him now."

"Adam will touch more lives now than he ever could have touched while playing football," said former Philadelphia Eagles defensive back Ray Ellis while visiting Adam when he was at Magee.

Dr. Staas said people gravitate toward Adam because he's a winner. He still examines Adam every few months, and during a recent visit he told him he has a duty to those who are paralyzed. "You've got a lot of responsibility. You represent hope for people with spinal-cord injuries," he told him. "Make sure you respect it."

"I will," Adam said.

"Be sensitive to that issue," Staas said as Adam's eyes widened. "And don't necessarily take the approach, 'I made it and so can you.'" That's the approach that Jerry Segal took with Adam, and it worked. Dr. Staas, however, wanted Adam to take a softer stance, to tell patients, "'I've made it, you have an opportunity to perhaps make it.' Everybody doesn't have the same injury or the same body. They may not make it to the same quality, but for most people with an incomplete injury, there's hope."

Perhaps hope is the greatest thing Adam had going for him. The hope and belief that he would walk again. His parents deliberately kept a little secret from him: they never told Adam that some doctors didn't expect him to ever get out of a wheelchair. "I didn't know I wasn't supposed to walk. I always thought I would," Adam said. "If I knew, it definitely would have made it tougher. I wouldn't have given up, but it would have been a shock."

Addie and Andre never considered telling Adam about the doctors' dark projections: that they didn't think he would walk again. "When you get that news, I think sometimes you may want to give up," Addie said. "You know the old saying, 'Sometimes, bad news is better left untold.' You don't need that in your mind. You don't need that messing with you."

Believing may have been Adam's first step toward healing.

* * * * *

The alarm clock went off in Adam's campus apartment, which he shares with three Penn State football players. It was 7:00 A.M. Time to get up, munch on a Nutri-Grain bar, and start another day of rehab; another day of weight lifting and exercise therapy, another day of classes at Penn State, another day of enjoying college life. "I thank God every morning that I can get up and walk," Adam said. "I don't take it for granted anymore."

Nine months earlier, lying prone on the wet Ohio Stadium field, he had told himself the same thing that he did on this sunny, lazy June morning: get up. His body wouldn't cooperate on that gloomy, damp day. Now he rolled over, turned off the alarm, and pushed himself into a sitting position.

Getting up never felt so good.

About the Authors

Sam Carchidi has been covering high school, collegiate, and professional sports since 1975. He has been a staff writer and South Jersey sports columnist at *The Philadelphia Inquirer* since 1984. Carchidi became hooked on sports at a young age—despite suffering through the Philadelphia Phillies' infamous late-season collapse in 1964. He has written for several national publications, including *Baseball America,* Athlon Sports, and *The Scouting Report,* and he was one of *The Philadelphia Inquirer* writers who contributed to the book *Worst to First: The Story of the 1993 Phillies*. He resides in Wenonah, New Jersey, with his wife, JoAnn, and their children SaraAnn, 14, and Sammy, 11.

Scott Brown is a sports writer for *Florida Today*. He has written two previous books, *Lion Kings,* the story of Penn State's 1994 offense, and *King of the Mount: The Jim Phelan Story*.